DAMMED

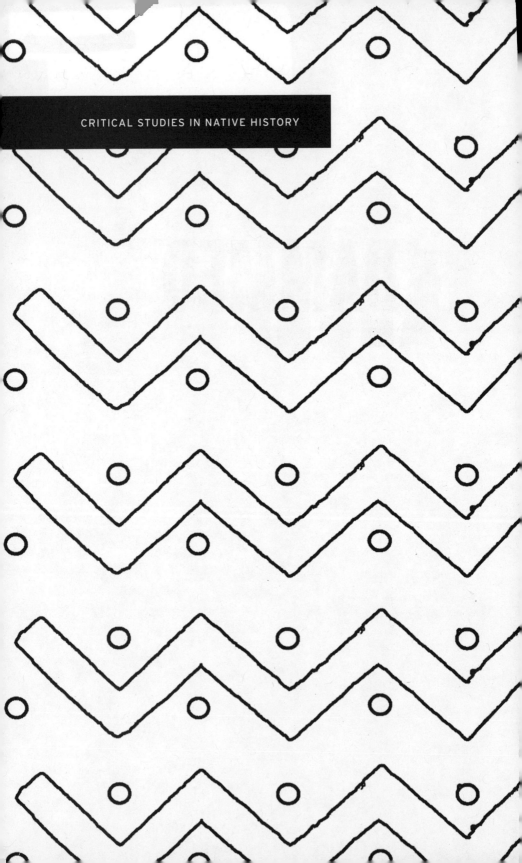

CRITICAL STUDIES IN NATIVE HISTORY

The Politics of Loss and Survival in Anishinaabe Territory

DAMMED

BRITTANY LUBY

UNIVERSITY OF MANITOBA PRESS

Dammed: The Politics of Loss and Survival in Anishinaabe Territory
© Brittany Luby 2020

24 23 22 21 20   1 2 3 4 5

University of Manitoba Press
Winnipeg, Manitoba, Canada
Treaty 1 Territory
uofmpress.ca

Cataloguing data available from Library and Archives Canada
Critical Studies in Native History, ISSN 1925-5888 ; 21
ISBN 978-0-88755-874-0 (PAPER)
ISBN 978-0-88755-876-4 (PDF)
ISBN 978-0-88755-875-7 (EPUB)
ISBN 978-0-88755-915-0 (BOUND)

Cover image by Arlea Ashcroft
Cover and interior design by Jess Koroscil

Printed in Canada

This book has been published with the help of a grant from the
Federation for the Humanities and Social Sciences, through the Awards
to Scholarly Publications Program, using funds provided by the
Social Sciences and Humanities Research Council of Canada.

The University of Manitoba Press acknowledges the financial support for
its publication program provided by the Government of Canada through
the Canada Book Fund, the Canada Council for the Arts, the Manitoba
Department of Sport, Culture, and Heritage, the Manitoba Arts Council,
and the Manitoba Book Publishing Tax Credit.

Funded by the Government of Canada | Canadä

To my ancestors who lived and died by the Winnipeg River—
Your stories flow through me, and without them this work
would not have been possible.

To the many children yet to be born along its banks—
May you sing of the future that your ancestors envisioned.

CONTENTS

LIST OF ILLUSTRATIONS

A MESSAGE FROM CHIEF LORRAINE COBINESS

Dalles 38C Indian Reserve (now known as Niisaachewan Anishinaabe Nation) has a unique history. It is caught between two dams on the Winnipeg River: it is downstream of the Norman Dam and upstream of the Whitedog Falls Generating Station.[1]

The Winnipeg River goes up. The Winnipeg River goes down. Band members do not know when water levels will change (or by how much). The Lake of the Woods Control Board and Ontario Power Generation rarely inform band members of scheduled changes.

Elders from Dalles have shared their stories with me. Some people drowned. Many people lost their livelihoods. As Anishinaabe people, our ability to hunt and fish, to pick *manomin* (wild rice), to live off the land—our ability to be self-sufficient—was taken away by the dams. Families broke up and left Dalles because of "managed flooding" in the 1960s and 1970s.

I can see the lingering damage of dam development on some families from Dalles. Relationships between relatives can be strained because the dams forced them apart for years. Today, when relatives share the same physical space, they sometimes seem to be disconnected.

What bothers me as Chief is the unfairness of it all. When flooding happens to other regions, such as a municipality, or to other people, such as farmers, compensation is received almost immediately. It might take a few months. It might take a year.

But Canada requires the Anishinabeg to use a separate system to see any type of flood relief. The Indian Act—still active today—says that status Indians are different, that reserve lands are different. It takes years to negotiate settlements with Canada for the flooding of reserve lands. As Anishinaabe people, we have to fight colonialism and paternalism.

Our community is going to start demanding active consultation with the Lake of the Woods Control Board and Ontario Power Generation. We want to negotiate flooding that respects our growing season, our spawning season, and our economy. We want a future that includes rice and sturgeon.

We need the support of other Canadians if we are to face the future with hope.

We have a lot of work to do as Canadian and Anishinaabe adults. We are role models for the youth. We must teach our children how past decisions shape people's lives and possibilities today. This book is a start.

I am optimistic that our children will work to make this country better together. When we teach history, we build common ground for the process of reconciliation. Again, this book will be a part of that process.

Ultimately, we have the same hearts and bleed the same blood. We need to acknowledge the human part of everybody's existence. At the most basic level, members of Niisaachewan Anishinaabe Nation just want to negotiate water management, human to human, in order to take care of ourselves and protect our way of life.

Chief Lorraine Cobiness, Niisaachewan Anishinaabe Nation
Transcribed and compiled by Emma Stelter, University of Guelph
April 2017

DAMMED

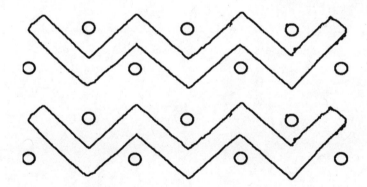

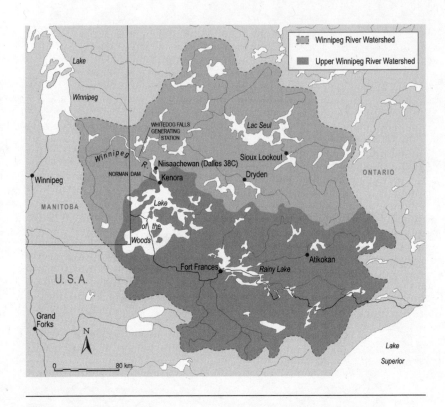

Figure 1. Map of the Winnipeg River watershed in the North American context.

LOOKING OUT FROM ANISHINAABE TERRITORY

When I close my eyes, I can still see the place of my birth: Lake of the Woods. This place is located about 180 kilometres east of the longitudinal centre of what is now known as Canada. It straddles three colonial borders, laying claim to parts of Ontario, Manitoba, and Minnesota. Kenora, my natal home, is at the north shore of Lake of the Woods. It is known for its jagged granite shoreline. It is known for islands of varying size, memorialized in verse as "jade-like gems."[1] "Jade" is a testament to the jack pine, birch, and poplar that somehow thrive on these rocky outcroppings. Kenora is most famous for its waterways: Lake of the Woods drains into the Winnipeg River and flows north toward Lake Winnipeg, Nelson River, and eventually Hudson Bay. Water is the lifeblood of Kenora's economy. It is by water that my ancestors, the Anishinabeg, inhabited this place.[2]

Controversy dominates the story of our origins. Place names suggest that the Anishinabeg originated here—or at least seventy kilometres northwest at Manitou Ahbee (Where the Creator Sits). It is likely that Gitchie Manitou (the Great Creator) envisaged humans there.[3] First Man, perhaps travelling by foot, made his way to Lake of the Woods, where he learned to fish, to trap, and to harvest *manomin* (wild rice). Archaeological evidence suggests that Indigenous Peoples have occupied Lake of the Woods since approximately 8,500–7,000 BCE, having followed the retreat of the Wisconsin glacier.[4]

Alternative accounts suggest that the Anishinabeg migrated to north-western Ontario from "somewhere along the shores of the Great Salt Water [Atlantic Ocean] in the East" around 800 ACE.[5] Edward Benton-Banai, an Anishinaabe cultural educator, suggests that my ancestors moved in search of manomin.[6] Manomin is a complex carbohydrate that flourished locally before the postwar boom in dam construction. The Kenora Centennial Committee also suggests that the Anishinabeg migrated to Lake of the Woods, but unlike Benton-Banai the committee does not date this migration. It suggests that the Anishinabeg moved to Lake of the Woods "as the white man displaced the Indians in the East." The committee further argues that the Anishinabeg displaced other Indigenous groups, becoming the primary occupants of Lake of the Woods by 1800.[7] Other authors suggest that the Haudenosaunee Confederacy pushed the Anishinabeg northward during the Beaver Wars. The Anishinabeg, in turn, violently displaced the Nehiyawak (Cree) and warred with the Dakota (Sioux) for occupancy of Lake of the Woods.[8]

However my ancestors arrived—whether by divine intervention, by foot as the glaciers retreated, or by canoe in search of aquatic plants or new land—what is certain is that Lake of the Woods and its outflow channels provided sustenance from time immemorial. Each of these otherwise conflicting origin stories reveals that the Anishinabeg lived by and relied on the water. By the 1820s, my paternal ancestors—associated with what is now known as Dalles 38C Indian Reserve—occupied a territory that extended roughly from Rough Rock Lake (near present-day Minaki, Ontario) in the north to Muskeg Bay (near present-day Warroad, Minnesota) in the south. James Redsky notes that "some Indians reported there would be other Ojibways who lived in the area as far south as Kasakas-kaw-chimakak (Leech Lake, Minnesota) and as far west . . . eventually as the Saskatchewan River." It is unclear during which years the Ojibway (who form part of the Anishinaabe Nation) occupied this terri-tory. We do know, however, that the Anishinabeg migrated between the north shore of Lake of the Woods and what would become Warroad, Minnesota, in the early 1800s since Redsky notes that Mis-quona-queb, an Anishinaabe leader, lived "at the entrance of the Winnipeg River" for a time and married a woman from Warroad.[9]

In this book, I explore the effects of hydroelectric development within this area of the Winnipeg River watershed from Rough Rock Lake to Muskeg Bay. By sharing an Anishinaabe perspective on hydroelectric development, *Dammed* challenges popular accounts of Canadian life after 1945. Canadians are often taught that the federal government took an increasing interest in economic development and social welfare in the postwar era, improving the working and living standards of many. This book is a stark reminder that the benefits of large-scale infrastructure projects and their environmental impacts were (and are) divided inequitably in Canada. The dividing line was (and is) highly racialized.

Long before dams were built along its shores, Lake of the Woods, "with its thousands of miles of irregular shoreline, provide[d] ideal spawning ground for the propagation of all sorts of fish."[10] For generations, these fish nourished my family. For example, I was told stories about Chief Kawitaskung (my paternal great-great-great-great grandfather, c. 1820–1914), who netted whitefish in the fall, consumed walleye during the cold of winter, and ate northern pike during the spring. We believe that pike tastes the best when the water is cold and its flesh is firm. During the summer, traders' accounts suggest, Kawitaskung might have feasted on sturgeon.[11] His wife, Jane Lindsay (birthdate unknown–c. 1916), taught Ogimaamaashiik (my paternal great-great-grandmother, 1885–1974) how to prepare these fish. Ogimaamaashiik roasted egg sacs from sturgeon like sausages and simmered whitefish bouillon.

Times changed. Ogimaamaashiik became known as Matilda Martin. But fish remained an essential component of our family diet. By the time of my father's birth in 1958, fishing provided Anishinaabe families with opportunities to work for pay in the tourist industry. My dad, Allan Luby (Ogemah), led American tourists to prime fishing locations on the Winnipeg River in exchange for spending money. Later, wearing goggles, he plumbed the depths of the river, searching for lost fishing tackle to incorporate into his own collection while continuing to fish for home consumption. Although fish provided sustenance for generations of Anishinaabe families, including my own, physicians working in and around Kenora had recommended that Anishinaabe families not consume fish caught on the Winnipeg River years before my birth (1984).[12] Hydroelectric damming between 1898 and 1958 likely contributed to the increased mercury content of family meals.

Anishinaabe families relied on more than fish. "Sheltered bays yielded thousands of acres of wild rice,"[13] a sacred gift from the Creator to the Anishinabeg. Anishinaabe families defined their territorial boundaries, in part, by manomin growth. Where there was manomin, there were Anishinabeg to harvest it.[14] This was true for many generations. Ogimaamaashiik believed that manomin provided her people with enough energy to carry out their day-to-day activities. Manomin fuelled trappers—such as her grandfather Kawitaskung—as they hunted for food and furs. She taught her daughter Hazel Martin-McKeever (b. 1927) that manomin was the most effective cure for constipation. Martin-McKeever knew to "put the wild rice, herbs, and lots of water in the big kettle and let it boil and simmer for a long time." She knew to strain the mixture and drink the remaining fluid. Experience revealed that water begat water.[15]

Family records of what the Anishinabeg ate and how they healed reveal that Lake of the Woods and the Winnipeg River were at the heart of Anishinaabe household economies. Unfortunately, during my father's growing-up years, manomin cropping on the Winnipeg River collapsed. Elders from Dalles 38C Indian Reserve maintain that the Norman Dam and the Whitedog Falls Generating Station caused water fluctuations that drowned hectare upon hectare of manomin. Today I purchase manomin in small quantities from the grocery store. And I know that Shoal Lake Wild Rice, packaged on Lake of the Woods, includes grains imported from distant lakes.[16]

The collapse of household economies experienced by the Anishinabeg is part of the story of twentieth-century colonization and industrialization in Canada. Natural resources in the Winnipeg River drainage basin drew settlers. Non-Indigenous newcomers moved easily inland along waterways "sheltered by high bluffs and tall forests."[17] Trappers and fur traders came first. Shortly after Kawitaskung was born, around 1820, the Hudson's Bay Company (HBC) established a post on Old Fort Island on the Winnipeg River.[18] But the Anishinabeg and the company did not compete for water resources—there were more than enough resources to share. Loggers and gold miners followed. Unlike the trappers and the traders, these newcomers drew water from Lake of the Woods for industrial use.

The sharing of water resources with the Anishinabeg was soon to change. John Kelly of Treaty 3 territory posits that resource sharing decreased sharply in the 1870s. To explain the inequitable division of resources, Kelly employs an analogy of a white man and an Indigenous man sitting on a log. The white man

Figure 2. HBC post at Rat Portage (Kenora, Ontario), 1857.
Figure 3. Keewatin Lumbering and Manufacturing Company mill, 1884.

requests "a little place on the log so that he might rest from his awful journey." So "the Indian willingly shared a piece of his log with the White Man. But the White Man felt like stretching himself and asked for a little more room. The Indian let him have a little more of his log." The Indigenous man continued to share his resources "like a decent host." As their relationship developed, "the Indian [became] cold and hungry and [was] barely holding on to the end of the log." The white man, in contrast, took control over their shared resources. By the 1870s, the white man had pushed the Indigenous man off the log, suggesting "that the Indian could sit on a stump further in the bush."[19]

This analogy resonates strongly on Lake of the Woods: in 1879, John Mather oversaw the construction of the sawmill for the Keewatin Lumbering and Manufacturing Company (KLM), establishing the first sawmill on the north shore. By 1890, seven large sawmills were operating near Kenora.[20] Lumbering became the primary industry for settler-colonists on Lake of the Woods. To fuel additional development, lumber barons such as Mather sought water power. Between 1893 and 1895, the Keewatin Power Company installed the Norman Dam at the western outlet of Lake of the Woods. According to some estimates, the dam raised the level of the lake by 0.9 metre to 1.8 metres.[21] When Mather dammed the western outlet, he blocked an artery in the Winnipeg River drainage basin. Flow patterns changed. And, when they changed, Anishinaabe labour practices and household economies—based on and around Lake of the Woods and the Winnipeg River—also changed.

Dammed tells the story of how Anishinaabe families adapted to industrial water fluctuations and their cascading effects, from the signing of Treaty 3 in 1873 to the 1970s, a difficult decade in Anishinaabe history. It tells of how the Anishinabeg, having forged a land-sharing agreement with the Crown, continued to use Lake of the Woods and the Winnipeg River as in years past—to fish, to harvest manomin, and to travel.

The ability of the Anishinabeg to live by treaty was complicated by settler conflict and collusion. In the early 1880s, settler access to resource-rich lands in Treaty 3 territory increased skirmishes between Canada and Ontario, drawing international attention to the profit potential of the region. In 1883, both Ontario and Manitoba staked the north shore of Lake of the Woods: "Ontario had claimed that its western boundary was a line drawn through Northwest [A]ngle of Lake of the Woods. . . . Manitoba had claimed as part of its territory part of the District of Thunder Bay." Canada supported Manitoba's claim in the hope of profiting from resources within its provincial borders. Canada controlled Crown lands in Manitoba, a power that it could not exert in Ontario. Colonial conflicts over timber, land, and minerals led to court. In 1884, the Judicial Committee of the Privy Council affirmed Ontario's boundary line.[22] Nonetheless, resource competition continued into the early twentieth century. Canada and Ontario feared that Anishinaabe water use could jeopardize the economic development of "the interior" and negotiated resource allocations to protect industrial interests.

When the provincial government reimagined reserve boundaries in 1915 to reduce "Indian" control over waterways, the Anishinabeg were excluded from any role in decision making. They responded with acts of passive resistance: families continued to conduct water ceremonies that asserted their custodial relationship with Lake of the Woods and the Winnipeg River. Things almost turned in their favour in the 1890s when industrialists developed the Norman Dam on the north shore of Lake of the Woods, prompting an international outcry: American residents living along the south shore of the lake claimed that the dam flooded acres of arable land. When the International Joint Commission on the Lake of the Woods Reference was formed in 1912 to conduct a cost-benefit analysis of the Norman Dam, however, the commission discouraged direct Anishinaabe participation and did not appear to consider Anishinaabe descriptions of environmental change originating in Canada.

In response, many Anishinaabe river users resorted to adaptation. Denied a public voice, they increased their engagement with settler-colonists—whether by selling traditional foods for cash, buying non-perishable goods, or banking—to ensure continuous occupation of treaty lands. During the interwar and Second World War years, they had to adapt to the building of the Norman Powerhouse at the western outlet of Lake of the Woods and a resurgence of pulp-and-paper industries to support the war effort. Following the war, they had to deal with a new threat as policy makers looked for more sources of electricity to fuel industrial expansion and viewed Lake of the Woods with interest. Here was water that could be turned into electricity. Between 1950 and 1958, the Hydro-Electric Power Commission of Ontario (HEPCO) constructed the sixty-eight-megawatt Whitedog Falls Generating Station.

HEPCO physically transformed the Winnipeg River to ensure provincial growth, and it used communication strategies to claim and remake the riverine environment, strategies that further undermined Anishinaabe autonomy and resulted in the inequitable distribution of benefits. Indeed, HEPCO developed preferential compensation programs that guaranteed the economic recovery of non-Indigenous users of the river. At the local level, Anishinaabe labourers took up jobs with HEPCO felling trees, driving trucks, or installing transmission lines. Partly because of their manual labour, HEPCO began operating the Whitedog Falls Generating Station at full capacity in June 1958.[23]

Dalles 38C Indian Reserve was now located among three hydroelectric generating stations. Those who worked for HEPCO hoped for job security. However, when HEPCO began to dismantle its labour camps near Whitedog Falls, their vision of continuous employment faded. They could also see that the Winnipeg River had changed. The reserve sat on the upstream (reservoir) side of the Whitedog Falls Generating Station, meaning that regulated water levels exceeded natural limits on an almost permanent basis. With dam operators keeping the water level at Minaki around 316 metres above sea level (Figure 4), it is reasonable to assume that the water level near the Dalles would have increased by a similar amount.[24] The reserve also sat on the downstream side of the Norman Dam and the Kenora Powerhouse, making it prone to rapid fluctuations in water levels which Elders have referred to as "flash flooding."

In June 1958, the long-term consequences of these riverine changes were unknown, but they became clear during the decades that followed. The Anishinabeg witnessed the collapse of the fishing economy on the Winnipeg River: rising water levels in the river increased levels of food and economic insecurity at Dalles 38C Indian Reserve. Food insecurity linked to mercury contamination upset Anishinaabe household economies, leading many Anishinaabe families to rely on federal services to ensure their survival. Anishinaabe mothers in particular struggled and developed new strategies to provide for their infants. The 1970s are generally remembered as a "dark time" in the community—families went hungry, and bank accounts sat empty.

By recounting these events and developments from an Anishinaabe perspective, *Dammed* disrupts popular narratives of Canada as an affluent society after 1945. Until recently, most studies on postwar Canada have attempted to explain the rise of economic modernization, infrastructure capacity building, and, most importantly, growth economics in the context of the atrocities of the Second World War.[25] They explore whether state funding was altruistically or politically motivated: that is, whether politicians funded change for the "common good" or the good of their respective parties.[26] Missing is a sense of how wealth distribution was shaped by perceptions of race.[27] Indeed, historical studies of Canada after 1945 have tended not to be

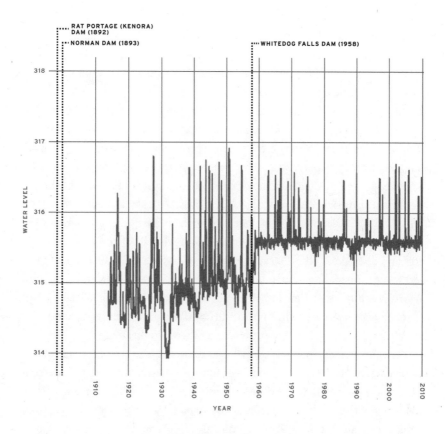

Figure 4. Water level of the Winnipeg River at Minaki between 1913 and 2016.

NOTE: In the words of Samantha Mehltretter, "This figure shows the change in water level at Minaki, less than 15 km downstream of Dalles 38C, after construction of Whitedog Falls Generating Station (located 20 km downstream of Minaki). Historically the water level was regularly below 316 m, and could be as low as 314 m (relative to the Geodetic Survey of Canada Datum [local 1923 adj.]); however, after Whitedog Falls G.S. was installed the water level at Minaki has been held at a minimum of approximately 316 m. While the Minaki gauge does not extend back to pre-Norman dam, the dates of construction of the Norman dam and the Kenora Powerhouse were included in the figure to demonstrate that these structures likely also influenced water level patterns along the Winnipeg River. The Minaki gauge (Gauge 05PE009) was used due to its proximity to Dalles 38C, which only has water level data records between 1992 and 2009." The water-level data presented in this figure was extracted from the Environment and Climate Change Canada Historical Hydrometric Data website (https://wateroffice.ec.gc.ca/mainmenu/historical_data_index_e.html) by Samantha Mehltretter on 8 March 2018.

closely connected to historical studies of Indigenous Peoples, nor have they been driven by a focus on First Nations territories and economies.[28]

Consider that affluence is presented as a nearly universal phenomenon. For example, J.M. Bumsted selected the title "Prospering Together, 1945–1960" for his discussion of the postwar era in his textbook *A History of the Canadian Peoples*.[29] A sense of progression, an economic fluorescence, is coded into his word choice. More importantly, prosperity is shared; Canadians, Bumsted suggested, are "prospering together." Textbooks are designed to relay standard knowledge, and through his book we can see that historians overwhelmingly agree that affluence positively affected the lives of most Canadians after 1945. This finding was explicitly supported by Michael Bliss, who summarized the period as follows: "The decades after 1945 were the age of peace and prosperity" and distinguished by "steadily rising levels of wealth" and "levels of mass affluence unprecedented in human history."[30] J.L. Granatstein and Desmond Morton echoed this view in "The War Changed Everything": "After 1945, Canada was a land of both opportunity and security. Steady growth in . . . purchasing power seemed to promise that there would always be more."[31]

This historical consensus was based on assessments of Canada's statistical majority. In 1950, individuals of European descent formed 95 percent of Canada's population.[32] Affluence was most evenly shared among this 95 percent, but this wealth was accumulated, in part, by extracting resources from Indigenous lands, a fact still not adequately represented in the historical literature on Canada's "prosperous era." Of the forty-two pages dedicated to the postwar period in *A History of the Canadian Peoples*, Bumsted devoted only half a page (or 1.2 percent) to the topic of "Aboriginals."[33] Given that in 1950 only 1.2 percent of Canada's population was classified as "status Indian," this might seem to reflect demographic realities; however, column-counting does not tell the whole story. Bumsted's treatment of affluence was not environmentally representative. The cost of affluence was disproportionately borne in Canada: although status Indians accounted for only 1.2 percent of the population, most environmental damage occurred on their lands. According to Métis intellectual Chelsea Vowel, "the violence that national myths commit is to delegitimize the very real pain that is the legacy of abuse and oppression."[34] This book makes clear that Indigenous Peoples did not form part of Canada's affluent society after 1945. Instead, it demonstrates how federal and provincial actors removed resources from Indigenous communities and reduced the income-generating potential of Indigenous families specifically to benefit

Anglo-settlers generally. Postwar Canada was not an affluent society; it was (and it remains) a colonial one.

Anishinaabe families developed multiple responses—*adaptation, coopera-tion,* and *passive resistance*—to survive federal and provincial encroachment on their lands and to maintain treaty territories. Adaptation refers to family strate-gies developed in response to environmental changes that allowed Anishinaabe men, women, and children to subsist on and off reserve. Cooperation is marked by Anishinaabe attempts to work with newcomers, despite compet-ing economic goals, to ensure the socio-economic stability of Anishinaabe communities. Passive resistance, in contrast, refers to non-violent expres-sions of discontent against federal and provincial legislation. These forms of resistance occurred within Anishinaabe communities; they were not public acts such as marches, sit-ins, or occupations. They were not organized across groups but within households and, at times, band offices. For this reason, they have been overlooked by historians who rely on the civil rights movement as a model for cultural recovery and radical change. By uncovering individual or family acts of resistance, I build on the work of Taiaiake Alfred and others who have shown that Indigenous Peoples across what is now known as Canada engaged in "a consistent struggle to revitalize various Indigenous cultural and political institutions in the hope of restoring the integrity of national commu-nities."[35] As Leanne Betasamosake Simpson has asserted, "presence is our weapon."[36] Alfred and Simpson maintain that Indigenous opposition to colo-nization has been continuous. This book offers proof of this claim.

In researching *Dammed,* I found evidence of resistance in the form of oral testimony from family-elected narrators, or Elders, who relayed family histo-ries of hydroelectric dam flooding to me, local historian Cuyler Cotton, and translator Barry Henry (see "A Note on Sources" at the back of the book). Members of Dalles 38C Indian Reserve nominated the following Elders to participate in my study: Alice Kelly (1946–2019); Roberta Jameson (birth-date unknown); Archie Wagamese (b. 1944); David Wagamese (b. 1948); Moses Henry (1941–2015); Joe Nabish (1933–2019); Marjorie Nabish (1932–2015); and Larry Kabestra (b. 1948). Additional interviewees were identified off reserve using the snowball technique.

Despite many hours spent conversing with Elders, I have limited the amount of their testimony quoted in these pages. This decision reflects community fears that Canada and Ontario could appropriate Elders' knowl-edge, using it against the Anishinabeg during negotiations about land (mis)use or in court. Anishinaabe Elders recognize—as anti-oppressive researchers Karen Potts and Leslie Brown have theorized—that "knowledge can be oppressive in how it is . . . utilized."[37] Band members at Dalles 38C Indian Reserve fear that government researchers lack the environmental knowledge to contextualize Elder testimony. Researchers employed by Canada and Ontario might not have lived along the Winnipeg River. As a result, they might be unable to envision the river system and thus to enliven Elder testimony. For Elders at this reserve, territorial presence is a prerequisite for knowledge. Without developing an Anishinaabe framework for analysis, government researchers risk misreading interviews with Elders.

My analysis is grounded in personal experience. I grew up in Treaty 3 territory but left as a teenager to earn a postsecondary education. Returning to the land was an important part of my research process. To make sense of environmental change and my relation to it, I travelled from Kenora to Dalles 38C Indian Reserve in all four seasons. I saw erosion downstream of the Norman Dam, a physical scar on the landscape caused by the release of water from Lake of the Woods. I saw manomin drown and counted geese in fewer numbers than the Elders remembered. I learned from these interactions with the land.

Anishinaabe teachings reveal that non-human beings are capable of imparting knowledge.[38] Receiving gifts or learning from plant and animal teachers requires relationship building, which depends on careful attention over time, a process that I call presence-ing.[39] Some Indigenous researchers have compared Anishinaabe education to an "apprenticeship (with human and non-human beings)."[40] Interactions with both human beings and the physical environment are considered enriching.[41] Presence-ing, for me, reinforced the interconnectedness of all living things. For instance, as the manomin fields and number of geese dwindled, family members, with fewer carbohydrates and less protein available to them, left Dalles 38C Indian Reserve.

My personal narrative was essential to constructing a culturally relevant and appropriate telling of environmental and social changes in northwestern Ontario. Simpson has called on intellectuals "who exist in the world as an embodiment of contemporary expressions of our ancient stories and traditions" to tell their own stories.[42] Linda T. Smith has similarly called on Indigenous scholars to use research to demonstrate and validate Indigenous methodologies. She encourages us to immerse ourselves in community, to honour Indigenous voices in our research, and, by so doing, to build resistance to dominant discourses.[43] If we, as scholars, honour Anishinaabe voices, then we acknowledge that experience informs understanding.

Whereas many formally trained academics seek *objectivity* in their work, I adhere to a worldview that makes it implausible. Cultural educator Basil Johnston explains that "to know" is a rough translation of the Anishinaabemowin word *w'kikaendaun*, but that is inaccurate; "to know" suggests that it is possible to have a clear and complete idea of something. Where I come from, it is understood that, in the words of Johnston, "knowledge may not be exact." Instead, a person who claims to "know" something "is saying that the notion, image, idea, act that that person has in mind corresponds to and is similar to what he or she has already seen, heard, touched, tasted or smelled."[44] The research findings that I present here—what I "know" about water development—are based on my experiences in Kenora and my interactions with Elders at Dalles 38C Indian Reserve.

I also adhere to an Anishinaabe understanding of *w'daeb-awae*. Johnston explains that w'daeb-awae, an approximate translation of the word *truth*, means that "a speaker casts his words and his voice as far as his perception and his vocabulary will enable him or her."[45] In this book, I present "crossing points" instead of "truths." Our stories—my personal narrative, my family history, and Elders' testimonies—are corroborated with archival sources from the Lake of the Woods Museum, the Kenora Public Library (particularly its holdings of local periodicals like the *Kenora Miner and News*), the Fort Frances Museum and Cultural Centre, the Archives of Ontario, the Ontario Power Generation Archives, and Library and Archives Canada.

If we, as readers and as writers, adopt the same geopolitical lens as Canadian and American source producers, then it is easy to overlook the causes and consequences of environmental changes and Indigenous understandings of them. However, when we engage in what Daniel K. Richter refers to as "visual reorientation," then a different perspective emerges.[46] For HEPCO employees, for example, Toronto was the "centre." The commission's headquarters, after all, were located in southern Ontario. From their perspective, the Whitedog Falls Generating Station appeared to be peripheral. Being on the land and working with Elders helped me to counter Canadian constructions of space and history. From the Anishinaabe perspective, Lake of the Woods was a bustling centre, whereas Toronto was peripheral. Kenora was isolated from other Anglo-Canadian centres, but it was (and is) an Anishinaabe homeland, with Lake of the Woods serving as a political centre. To the west of Lake of the Woods is Manito Ahbee. It has been revered by Indigenous Peoples across North America as a sacred space. Lake of the Woods and the Winnipeg River have facilitated travel to a spiritual centre. For Anishinaabe families, the north shore has not been peripheral but a hotbed of economic, political, and spiritual activity. It is a space where women and men have fished, raised their children, and worked for pay.

Looking out from Anishinaabe territory, I did not see isolated resources being extracted for central consumption. Instead, I saw an Anishinaabe centre being disrupted to serve a competing settlement. The history shared within these pages reflects the voices of survivors, people who traversed reserve boundaries to harvest and to feast and who experienced the compound damages of treaty mismanagement and exclusion from decision making. They, like other Indigenous communities, experienced decreased opportunities on reserve while many Canadians prospered. I am writing today because my ancestors—like many other families from Treaty 3 territory—responded creatively to environmental change. I am writing to commemorate their strength.

CHAPTER 1

BY WATER WE INHABIT THIS PLACE

Imagine that it is 1915.

"Tom, tom," Chief Powassan's drum sings. Taut deer sinew reverberates, reminding listeners of the Anishinabeg's relationship with four-legged beings. The wooden base holds firm, a testament to the strength of plant beings, who have sustained the Anishinabeg for generations. As Powassan plays, sound carries through water in the drum's base and across the bay. Colonial borders cannot sever such bonds. In the upper Winnipeg River drainage basin, drumming silences scratches made on paper by provincial and federal administrators—trying, so desperately, to divorce Powassan and others from their relations and the water. It quells the grumbling of administrators trying to confine the Anishinabeg to reserves.[1]

Many newcomers do not understand Powassan's song. Water sounds like money to them. In Powassan's time, newcomers were lured to Kenora by the promise of steady employment. Circulars suggested that Canada could rely on products manufactured on the north shore of Lake of the Woods.[2] The promise of work changed the demography of Treaty 3 territory. The population of the Canadian North was only about 60,000 in the 1870s, when the treaty was signed. British men tended to pass through Kenora, then known as Rat Portage, collecting furs from the local H B C trading post before paddling southeast toward Fort Frances. Such movements protected, albeit unintentionally, Anishinaabe water interests since few newcomers claimed proprietary interests in Treaty 3 territory. Then, in 1876, Frank Gardner, the first permanent white settler, established himself near Kenora. Others followed. By 1901, the Canadian North housed over 100,000 souls.[3]

Newcomers felt reassured by Mother Nature, who seemed to guarantee Kenora's industrial future. Here lay a body of fresh water said to stretch over nearly 4,500 square kilometres. And, as far as they were concerned, there was naught to compromise development. In 1915, the Legislative Assembly of Ontario had revoked An Act for the Settlement of Questions between the Governments of Canada and Ontario Respecting Indian Lands, which had given the Anishinabeg control over waterways running through or around their reserves.[4] It was replaced by An Act to Confirm the Title for the Government of Canada to Certain Lands and Indian Lands, a piece of provincial legislation deeming that waterways "shall not ... form part of such reserve[s]."[5]

Although Ontario had no constitutional authority over reserves, Canada did little to challenge its redefinition of Indigenous lands. Then, in 1924, Superintendent General of Indian Affairs Charles Stewart signed off on the Indian Lands Act, affirming Ontario's interest in Indigenous waterways and committing Canada to consulting with Ontario about water leases and sales on reserves. This meant that between 1873 and 1924 the Anishinabeg went from negotiating treaties that guaranteed fishing rights and protected their socio-economic interests in water to being excluded from government negotiations about water use in treaty territory. When Ontario redefined water as a public utility in 1905, Anishinaabe control over water resources was challenged by provincial administrators.

In Treaty 3 territory, both newcomers and the Anishinabeg recognized that water was power, but Chief Powassan knew that the two groups saw water differently. Newcomers sought to harness water for hydroelectricity, whereas the Anishinabeg worked to uphold Treaty 3 and protect the environmental relationships that it guaranteed.

Forever the Use of Their Fisheries

Approximately 3,000 Anishinabeg lived at Lake of the Woods when Crown officials penetrated their territory in the mid-nineteenth century.[6] Their subsistence economy consisted primarily of hunting, trapping, fishing, and harvesting.[7] Written evidence of large fish populations in Anishinaabe territories west of Lake Huron extends back to 1660, when trader Pierre-Esprit Radisson compared Lake Superior to a "terrestriall [sic] paradise." The region was resource rich. Radisson identified bear, beaver, and enough "assickmack" or whitefish to "make good cheare."[8] Other historians have used Radisson's travelogue to provide evidence of large-scale sturgeon fisheries in Anishinaabe territories, locating Radisson's claim to have seen more than 1,000 sturgeon being dried on the south shore of Lake Superior.[9] At the end of the eighteenth century, fur traders noted that the Anishinabeg were difficult trading partners, "content to live upon sturgeon and other native foods rather than engage in trade."[10] An unidentified observer, writing after 1857, associated Anishinaabe refusal to trade consistently with the Hudson's Bay Company with an "abundance of sturgeon." Indeed, large-scale fisheries and a steady supply of food led newcomers to criticize the Anishinabeg as "independent" and "sometimes even a little saucy" during cross-cultural encounters.[11]

Non-written sources such as totemic symbols suggest that fishing has been important to the Anishinabeg since time immemorial. Totemic symbols function as genealogical chains that link bands together.[12] In *Ojibway Heritage*, for instance, cultural educator Basil Johnston identifies five fish clans,[13] and Anishinaabe families continue to define themselves (and their relations) by clan. For example, Elder Alice Kelly of Dalles 38C Indian Reserve identified as a Sturgeon in 2012.[14]

In the past, as in the present, Anishinaabe men and women tried to emulate the character of their totemic animals. Catfish symbolize breadth and scope (likely intellectual), pike represent swiftness and elegance, sucker symbolize calmness and grace, sturgeon evoke depth and strength, and whitefish symbolize abundance.[15] Totems inform human behaviour. In 2012, Kelly acted like a sturgeon when she shared her community's struggle to access potable water at the Native American and Indigenous Studies Association conference in Ledyard, Connecticut. She had the emotional strength to communicate Dalles 38C's intergenerational pain to a public audience.[16] In the late 1800s, much like today, Anishinaabe men and women incorporated their clan fish into how they understood their world.

The existence and significance of fish clans reflect the social as well as the economic importance of fishing in the Winnipeg River drainage basin. Through totemic symbols, fishing was part of daily life. Fish provided social markers, behavioural guides, and food.

Totemic symbols indicate a relationship with water resources that extends beyond the element. Treaty 3 Elder Alex Skead explained that "there is a word older than manomin (wild rice) and that is *manitou gitigenan*, the 'Great Spirit's Garden.'"[17] As Treaty and Aboriginal Rights Research Director Andy Sky suggests, the concept of manitou gitigenan necessitates an under-standing of land and water resources as living gifts from the Creator, and, as with a garden, tending this gift requires ecological knowledge.[18] Elders from Dalles 38C Indian Reserve emphasize three teachings in the main-tenance of relations with other-than-human beings: (1) do not infringe on the well-being of other-than-human beings more than is necessary to sustain yourself, your family, and your community; (2) offer ritual tobacco in honour of what has been taken from the land and the river; and, (3) make seasonal offerings in gratitude to all Creation.[19] Maintaining the Creator's gifts requires recognition of the land as a shared resource: Anishinaabe resource managers offered thanks to all creatures who shared the Great Spirit's Garden. Literature warns the Anishinabeg against overconsumption and neglect. Indigenous cautionary tales, as noted by Potawatomi scien-tist Robin Wall Kimmerer, feature "legions of offended plants and animals and rivers [who] rise up against the ones who neglected gratitude."[20] Chiefs and leaders entered treaty negotiations with the clear goal of maintaining access to manitou gitigenan. Land and water resources were not to be ceded; instead, the Anishinabeg sought to accommodate newcomers while uphold-ing their sacred duty to manage resources.

Anishinaabe treaty demands illustrate the extraordinary value that the Anishinabeg placed on water for fishing in the Winnipeg River drain-age basin and a clear sense of what they thought future relationships with newcomers should look like. During the treaty negotiations in 1869, which ultimately failed, Anishinaabe negotiators presented thirteen conditions under which they would consent to treaty. Condition thirteen reads thus: "Every married woman gets fishing terine [*sic*] and cord line to make four nets every year."[21] The condition was designed to ensure that waters could continue to be fished according to long-standing practice, by seines and by women.[22] By demanding that Anishinaabe women receive fishing gear,

Figure 5. Anishinaabe water offering, c. 1890.
Figure 6. Anishinaabe women drying fish, 1912.

negotiators were working toward retaining their fishing rights. They wanted tools to continue Anishinaabe patterns of water use.

Access to water and fishing rights was so important to the Anishinabeg that they refused to sign a treaty until their demands were satisfied. In 1872, Commissioners Wemyss M. Simpson, Simon J. Dawson, and Robert Pither remarked that Anishinaabe leaders were making "extravagant demands" of the Crown.[23] Colonial records reveal, however, that Anishinaabe Chiefs and leaders had regularly demanded compensation from newcomers for territorial access: they had exacted presents from HBC traders and federal surveyors for passage *through* their land. There is no evidence to suggest that Anishinaabe Chiefs negotiated a payment schedule that would allow newcomers to access the territory continuously. Indeed, in 1857, geographer John Palliser indicated that his promise to move out of Anishinaabe territory influenced his "friendly parley" with a Chief at Fort Frances.[24]

Anishinaabe Chiefs and leaders later granted surveyor Simon J. Dawson "full permission to explore the country." Confusion about Anishinaabe demands might have arisen from Dawson's report in 1859, which suggested that "payments should be made in the shape of yearly presents of such articles as would be useful to them."[25] In recommending payment-in-kind, Dawson gave the Crown the power to manipulate access fees: goods were not specified, and the value of gifts could vary on an annual basis. Given this tradition of gift giving for territorial access, Anishinaabe Chiefs and leaders appeared to strike a hard bargain in the 1870s. However, new demands from the Anishinabeg were in fact in response to new requests from federal agents who wanted to settle people in, not pass through, Anishinaabe land. The Anishinabeg wanted to define and to receive fair compensation for continued access to their territory.

Chiefs and leaders set terms on which they would build a more permanent relationship. These terms were not left to the discretion of the Crown (and hence could prove to be more costly). In July 1872, frustrated Commissioners Simpson, Dawson, and Robert Pither reported to Secretary of State for the Provinces Joseph Howe that, because of their concerns about water rights, "Indians could not be induced to go into the discussion."[26] From the Anishinaabe perspective, fishing rights were no extravagance. Anishinaabe negotiators had expressed concern that "settlers would interfere with the fisheries, from which they [had] derive[d] their chief means of sustenance" since the 1860s.[27] Elaborating on Anishinaabe refusals to enter treaty, Dawson noted that fishing rights were "strongly insisted upon and had great weight with the Indians."[28] Chiefs and leaders refused to sign a treaty that required the surrender of their fisheries or challenged their relationship with water regardless of the draw on federal coffers.

Treaty 3, finally concluded in 1873, granted the Anishinabeg the protection that they sought. Commissioner Dawson recalled that Crown representatives promised that the Anishinabeg "would forever have the use of their fisheries."[29] Commissioners well understood that without such a guarantee no agreement would have been reached. In saying this, Dawson asserted that the Anishinabeg retained usage rights over local fisheries; fishing territories were explicitly identified as *theirs*. There is no indication that fisheries were to be located on reserve land; rather, the Anishinabeg appear to have protected fishing territories regardless of location. Indeed, Treaty 3, as published by the government of Canada, expressly provides for the right of the Anishinabeg to "pursue their avocations of hunting and fishing throughout the tract surrendered."[30]

In addition to unaffected water use, Paypom Treaty guarantees the Anishinabeg "fifteen hundred dollars every year in twine" for the making of nets. Paypom Treaty, as set down by Joseph Nolin, is considered a written Indigenous document. Nolin was a Red River Métis hired by Lake of the Woods District Chiefs to record the 1873 negotiations. The treaty consists of notes from his personal diary and has long been absent from historical analyses of treaty making in Canada. One possible explanation of its absence from the literature is that Paypom Treaty was not made available for public viewing until the 1990s. Around 1906, Treaty 3 signatory Chief Powassan of Shoal Lake First Nation entrusted the treaty to Carl Linde, "a photographer and a friend to the Indian People."[31] Some years later Elder Paypom, of Shoal Lake First Nation, purchased the document from Linde to protect Anishinaabe treaty records from settler ownership and control. The treaty was subsequently treated like *wiigwaasabakoon* (birch bark scroll), a sacred object. Elder Paypom oversaw ceremonial viewings of the document. Public access to Paypom Treaty was thus limited until his death in 1990, whereupon his successor donated the text to Grand Council Treaty 3. Paypom Treaty has been readily available for analysis only since then.

Both Anishinaabe and dominion sources demonstrate that hard, realistic bargaining by the Anishinabeg took place. The Anishinaabe position was designed to guarantee the material and cultural survival of the people. Once

Treaty 3 was signed, the Department of Indian Affairs and the Department of the Interior surveyed Anishinaabe territories and assigned reserves. The locations of reserves recognized Anishinaabe water use. In a memorandum for the Department of the Interior in Ottawa dated 24 June 1874, Minister David Laird determined that reserves "should be confined generally to localities heretofore cultivated by the Indians and occupied by them as camping and fishing grounds."[32] Early officials attempted to keep treaty. In an unsigned letter dated 1886 to George Foster, the minister of mines and fisheries, former Treaty Commissioner Simon J. Dawson was said to oppose non-Indigenous fishing on Lake of the Woods. The author supported Dawson's position, arguing that "the Indians of this country are a fish-eating people; they live almost entirely on that food."[33] By 17 December 1890, Dawson had garnered the support of Superintendent General of Indian Affairs Edgar Dewdney, who determined that fisheries on Lake of the Woods "should be reserved for the common use of the Indians of Treaty 3, as from this Lake they have always been in the habit of deriving their principal sustenance."[34]

The dominion recognized Anishinaabe water use and protected the fisheries accordingly. This protection culminated with An Act for the Settlement of Questions between the Governments of Canada and Ontario Respecting Indian Lands (1891), which confirmed Anishinaabe proprietary rights over water running through or around reserve lands. The 1891 act held that "the waters within the lands laid out or to be laid out as Indian reserves in said territory . . . shall be deemed to form part of such reserve."[35] By confirming Anishinaabe ownership of waterbeds adjacent to reserve lands in the 1894 joint agreement, the governments of Canada and Ontario protected ancestral fishing grounds and thus upheld the treaty right to fish.[36]

Federal recognition and protection of water rights were manifested in surveys and maps. For example, in British Columbia, the Department of Indian Affairs consciously located First Nations communities near water to reduce settler conflict over arable lands and the cost of guardianship (First Nations were guaranteed independent access to stable food supplies).[37] Dominion officials similarly approved reserves to provide water access in northern Ontario.

Some of the earliest reserve maps (produced by federal surveyors) in the Winnipeg River drainage basin clearly extend reserve boundaries across adjacent waterways. Consider A.W. Ponton's 1890 survey of Dalles 38C

Indian Reserve. Ponton allotted Chief Kawitaskung and his band the waters below the northernmost rapids to the "high rocky country," distinguished by its "timberwood with jack pine." Approximately one year later Ponton's map was approved by J. Nelson, the federal agent "in charge [of] I.R. surveys."[38] Elder testimony suggests that the allotted stretch of water included long-established fishing grounds.[39] That local Anishinabeg relied on riverbeds and built communities along the shore was common knowledge among newcomers and recognized by the Department of Indian Affairs in the immediate aftermath of the treaty.

Although the government recognized First Nations water rights, the Anishinabeg realized that newcomers understood water differently. In these early days of government agreement to protect fishing and water rights, the seeds of encroachment were sown: Treaty 3 guaranteed non-Indigenous peoples access to resources. The Anishinabeg recognized that newcomers used water for dams, canals, and other public works. Recognizing that resource access could lead to misuse, they took steps to ensure that they would be compensated if newcomers broke treaty and infringed on Anishinaabe water rights.

During the treaty negotiations in 1873, Chief Powassan, from Lake of the Woods, demanded that Commissioner Dawson "look to where the waters separate," rhetorically using water as a symbol of difference. He then reminded Dawson that "the trees you have taken . . . are the property of those you see before you."[40] Powassan recognized that Anishinaabe and non-Indigenous lifestyles and resource uses differed; it was essential to establish a relationship based on mutual respect—where separation demanded negotiation or compensation. On 1 October 1875, Lake of the Woods District Chiefs signed for waterfront reserves. The Chiefs agreed to the following clause: "It is also understood that the Government shall have the right to construct canal locks or other public works . . . should they so desire. In such case, the Indians to be duly notified and if the Fisheries should be destroyed thereby the Indians to be fairly dealt with in consequence."[41] The Anishinabeg thus guarded against having their interests damaged by future public works. If they lost some of their water resources, then they would receive new fiscal resources in exchange.

Figure 7. Reserves in Treaty 3 territory.

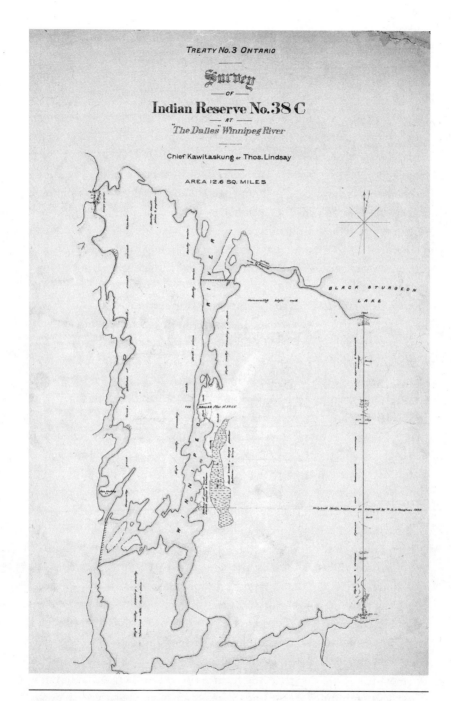

Figure 8. A.W. Ponton's 1890 survey of Dalles 38C Indian Reserve. A boundary line is visible between "I" and "V" in "RIVER." A second boundary line connects the northwestern tip of the peninsula to the southernmost tip of the island (bottom left). These lines bound waters running between the mainland reserve and the reserve island to Dalles 38C.

Water for Power and Prosperity

But what of Ontario? The government of Ontario saw water as a riparian right. In 1859, *Chasemore v Richards* determined riparian rights in Ontario, assigning "the right to the enjoyment of a natural stream of water on the surface, *ex jure naturae*, [to] the proprietor of adjoining lands, as a natural incident to the right to the soil itself."[42] Landowners were entitled to use adjacent waters as they wanted, without needing special permission. Dominion maps—like Ponton's 1890 survey of Dalles 38C Indian Reserve—extended similar rights to the Anishinabeg.

Before 1900, Ontario envisaged water as the key to provincial growth and prosperity because water attracted settlers and industry. In an attempt to draw settlers to the Winnipeg River drainage basin, for example, the province exclaimed that "the Wabigoon River [a tributary of the English River] flows north and west, a broad navigable stream with abundant water-power at intervals" that a hard-working man could use to his profit.[43] The settler could benefit from domestic consumption, irrigation, or power from water wheels. Ontario's promotional literature linked a seemingly inexhaustible water supply to visions of individual success. Promoters reminded settlers that there was "no water rate to meet" at Lake of the Woods and that "good spring water" abounded there. They pronounced that "there is no good reason a thrifty man cannot make a living here."[44] Ontario valued water instrumentally to lure settlers to the northwest. Provincial definitions of water as a resource over which no usage rights were recognized (until claimed by the adjacent property owner) mirrored this value system.

Provincial officials also visualized local hydroelectric generation as a "symbol of anxiously awaited industrialism."[45] Government pamphlets actively encouraged its local industrial use. Targeting prospective investors, literature on the Rat Portage and Rainy River District claimed that "the chief resources of the country lie in the rich quality and large extent of mineral deposits."[46] Ontario touted mining operations in gold, silver, iron, mica, asbestos, talc, and quartz as prime candidates for hydroelectric development. It was believed that "possibilities . . . are only beginning to be made known" and that "the future will witness here the upbuilding of extensive mining."[47] According to the province, future success in northwestern Ontario also depended on the establishment of the lumber industry. Ontario promised that "the various streams are richly lined with timber of the finest quality in great quantities."[48] All that the northwest needed was private investment. Provincial emphasis on water as a riparian right amounted to a de facto protection of Indigenous rights. Because Ontario's promotional campaign met with little success and few settlers moved into Treaty 3 territory, the Anishinabeg maintained control over waterways on reserve lands.

There was also little threat from hydroelectric development at the turn of the twentieth century. First, few people lived in and around Kenora, whose population hovered around 1,800 in 1891 and peaked near 6,000 in 1911, so power demands remained low.[49] Second, Anishinaabe inhabitants enjoyed provincial protection of their water rights because of technological limitations. As one historian noted, "without the turbine, generator, and high-voltage transmission line, Ontario's splendid hydraulic resources would continue to pour almost unused." The water wheel was not an efficient power converter; its use was limited to a few strategic and highly localized sites.[50] Although water wheels could produce power at an industrial scale, development was highly unfeasible on isolated rapids in the Winnipeg River drainage basin because finished products could not be easily transferred to markets. North Americans made little advance in long-distance energy transmission until November 1896, when a generating station in Niagara Falls successfully powered the city of Buffalo over a thirty-two-kilometre-long transmission circuit, the longest circuit for commercial purposes up to that time.[51]

After the successful transmission from Niagara Falls to Buffalo, Ontario business and municipal elites reconceptualized water as a solution to the province's energy (i.e., coal) shortage.[52] Early-twentieth-century announcements made by the province emphasized that water was available to determined settlers and industrialists, often in response to public pressure for the government of Ontario to fund hydroelectric initiatives. Beginning in 1902, manufacturers and municipal leaders from Waterloo County hounded Premier William Ross to deprivatize water. They argued that Ontario had been largely dependent on Great Britain and the United States because it lacked coal. It relied on international imports to produce energy in the steam era. Hydroelectric power combined with Ontario's abundant water resources promised economic independence. The Berlin Board of Trade claimed that hydroelectric development was akin to national defence; deprivatization would benefit all Canadians.[53] Conservatives supported such views and pressured the Laurier government to prevent all exports to New York and to devote energy resources to Ontario.[54]

Yet Premier Ross struggled to imagine hydroelectric power as a public good.[55] In the spring of 1903, he announced that "we are willing to allow municipalities, Toronto, and the rest, to develop energy there and they will not be curtailed. But Ontario must not get into debt because of it."[56] Ontario did not consider hydroelectric generation a profitable enterprise and supported privatization for fear that provincial investment would benefit few residents. Ross emphasized that the government of Ontario would not fund projects unless they were for the "substantial benefit of all."[57] He maintained that provincial coffers could not be drained to benefit manufacturers alone. At the time, Ontario understood water, or hydraulic potential, as a private or municipal concern, and its attitude reflected a standard stance on fiscal prudence and technological limitations. Large projects would incur debts at a time when Ontario had yet to establish a substantial tax base. From the moment of this announcement, however, Ross faced opposition from organized municipalities and manufacturers. Interest in Ontario's waterways burgeoned as acceptance of individual ownership and use declined.

The year 1905 was a pivotal moment in water's transition from private interest to public utility. The Conservatives, known to support public power initiatives, were voted into office.[58] Following his election, Premier James Pliny Whitney redefined water as a provincial resource: "I say on behalf of the government that the water powers all over the country shall not in future be made the sport and prey of capitalists and shall not be treated as anything else but a valuable asset of the people of Ontario, whose trustees the government of this people are."[59] Water could no longer be claimed by individual property owners; it was now a provincial asset that could be regulated for electricity production. Water needed to be protected and controlled by Ontario for the benefit of Ontario residents generally.[60]

The Legislative Assembly of Ontario created the Hydro-Electric Power Commission of Ontario, an administrative body, through An Act to Provide for the Transmission of Electric Power to the Municipalities (1906). The 1906 act allowed HEPCO "to distribute electric power to the municipalities, but also to regulate private utilities."[61] The following year it was repealed and recast as The Power Commission Act (1907). The 1907 act established a "wholesaler" and "retailer" system between the commission and the municipalities, making electricity available at favourable contracted rates.[62] Some

Ontarians initially protested against the commission, resulting in "long and delicate negotiations with farmers along the route [of a transmission line from Niagara]."[63] In 1910, Adam Beck, chairman of the commission, worked to gain the support of farmers in Ontario. He required a public relations campaign to quell dissent among agrarians who feared losing valuable land to serve manufacturers' interests. Ontario thus normalized understandings of water as a hydroelectric resource and, perhaps more importantly, a provincial resource through law and education.

It was only when the province adopted a policy denying private ownership of the waterbed that Ontario sought to redefine Anishinaabe water rights. Anishinaabe reserves at Lake of the Woods were set along the shoreline.[64] Prior to 1906, water rights on reserve lands could be derived from two sources: Treaty 3 and riparian rights. In accordance with Treaty 3, the 1891 act and the 1894 joint agreement extended reserve boundaries from shoreline to shoreline, or headland to headland, greatly increasing territories designated exclusively for Indigenous use. The Indian Act guaranteed riparian rights to waterways running through reserve lands to the band since land was held in trust by the Crown rather than individual members.[65] Furthermore, the Indian Act expressly sets land apart for the "use or benefit" of the bands.[66] This is not to suggest that the Indian Act purposefully guaranteed riparian rights; indeed, the act was touted as a tool of directed civilization. "Beneficial entitlement," as understood by the Department of Indian Affairs, referred to the adoption of settler agricultural norms, not Anishinaabe territorial use.[67] Nevertheless, legal apparatuses that guaranteed "beneficial entitlement" for First Nations to, or use of, reserve lands directly challenged the government of Ontario's hydroelectric development goals; rapids that needed to generate electricity for "the people of Ontario" fell within Anishinaabe territories.

Eroding Water Rights and Anishinaabe Resistance

In recognition of the obstacle posed by Anishinaabe water rights, the attorney general of Ontario hoped to amass information regarding "the character of each reserve as to which water powers existed."[68] Waterways in northwestern Ontario now mattered to provincial politicians and policy makers, and the attorney general needed to define newly acquired access. As early as March 1906, Edmund Leslie Newcombe, the deputy minister of justice, determined that no known reason existed "why the title to a reserve may not be subject to a right on [the] part of the province."[69] Newcombe believed that Ontario could take water for its own use regardless of reserve boundaries. His interpretation hinged on shared constitutional powers over water between the federal government and provincial governments. Even though reserve lands were federal creations under Section 91 (24) of the Constitution Act, 1867, Ontario had the primary responsibility for making water use and allocation decisions.

By the 1910s, concerns about Anishinaabe control of water resources ran through the correspondence between government officials at the provincial and federal levels. As Deputy Minister of Lands, Forests, and Mines Aubrey White wrote to Deputy Superintendent General of Indian Affairs Duncan Campbell Scott, "I find there are rivers of considerable size running through them and it surely never was intended that lands under a river should belong to the Indians."[70] Scott proposed the repeal of the 1894 joint agreement as a solution to Ontario's water access problems. Scott wrote that, "if the reserves are confirmed as surveyed, we would [be] require[d] to repeal the statute of 1894 and substitute therefor [sic] an enactment which would cover the settlement of the reserve question." Settlement involved "say[ing] nothing about waters or fisheries."[71] By removing the headland-to-headland clause, Ontario could access Anishinaabe water resources since its repeal would effectively limit reserves to lands. To manage the burden of loss, Scott proposed that White restrict Anishinaabe water power to no more than 500 horsepower. Scott appears to have sought some form of financial compensation from larger projects for his wards, suggesting that "a percentage of the gross earnings of water powers when developed" be provided to the First Nations.[72] Despite this limited attempt to secure a revenue stream for his wards, Scott placed Anishinaabe interests after provincial goals to open Treaty 3 territory to newcomers.

Three months after the issue was initially raised by Ontario, the Department of Lands and Forests and the Department of Indian Affairs were ready to discuss a draft of the proposed repeal. In March 1915, Scott submitted his comments to White for consideration. Scott highlighted basic typographical errors in the proposed repeal (e.g., replace "1884" with "1894"). He also demanded that islands remain part of existing reserves: "I wish to make clear . . . that we shall get the islands which are shown on the plans as part of the reserves."[73] Although it is impossible to confirm

Figure 9. A water-based community, c. 1900.

without a copy of White's draft, Scott might have attempted again to secure a revenue stream for his wards: "I trust that you [White] will make it 50% as I suggested."[74] Did Scott envision equal profit-sharing between developers and First Nations? Did he hope to mitigate the very loss that he facilitated? Whatever his intention, Ontario did not incorporate his recommendations in 1915. The dominion was consulted about the form of the 1915 act (and federal officials helped to erode Anishinaabe water rights); however, Ontario discarded the limited protections sought by the Department of Indian Affairs.

In April 1915, the government of Ontario infringed on the federal government's jurisdiction and claimed to repeal Indian water rights granted by the 1891 act and affirmed by the 1894 joint agreement. An Act to Confirm the Title of the Government of Canada to Certain Lands and Indian Lands, passed in 1915, was almost identical to the 1891 act, except for the following provision: waterways "shall not be deemed to form any part of such reserve."[75] Once passed, the 1915 act challenged Indian water rights derived from Treaty 3—a challenge that shaped provincial maps. Unlike Ponton's 1890 survey of Dalles 38C Indian Reserve, cartographic depictions of the reserve after 1915 curbed Anishinaabe jurisdiction at the shoreline. Despite limited provincial authority over reserve lands, the government of Ontario suppressed Anishinaabe interests and asserted its rights over Anishinaabe territories.

The province might also have been emboldened by the outcome of *Keewatin Power Company and Hudson's Bay Company v The Town of Kenora* (1906), in which property lines for waterfront properties were debated. Justice Anglin ruled in favour of Kenora, determining that "a Crown grant of lands bordering navigable rivers conferred ownership only to the water's edge." The Ontario legislature affirmed Anglin's decision in 1911, overriding the Court of Appeal's 1908 decision that property owners indeed had claims to navigable riverbeds.[76] Ontario mistakenly believed—given protracted negotiations—that the dominion would pass legislation agreeing to exclude First Nations from access to water courses, thus validating Ontario's repeal and aligning laws. The dominion neither challenged nor validated Ontario's repeal for approximately ten years.

In March 1924, Canada and Ontario agreed to "settle all outstanding questions relating to Indian Reserves in the Province of Ontario."[77] Superintendent General of Indian Affairs Charles Stewart (Canada),

Minister of Lands and Forests James Lyons (Ontario), and Minister of Mines Charles McCrea (Ontario) formed a memorandum of agreement to divide land, mineral, and water resources between the governments. Its authors paid scant attention to water resources and focused primarily on the disposition of mineral rights on reserve lands. Clause 8 of 10, however, reveals Ontario's continued interest in industrially viable rapids. It reads thus: "No water power included in any Indian Reserve, which in its natural condition at the average low stage of water has a greater capacity than 500 horse-power, shall be disposed of by the Dominion of Canada except with the consent of the Government of the Province of Ontario."[78]

Duncan Campbell Scott's handiwork is visible in the text: territory is defined by its electrical potential. Canada, particularly the Department of Indian Affairs, could manage waterways with limited industrial potential without provincial interference. Indigenous title was compromised by the permission clause: Canada had to request permission to sell or lease waterways. Ontario would grant or withhold consent. Clause 8 also demanded "the division of the purchase money, rental or other consideration given therefor [sic]." And so, according to the settler state, the Anishinabeg did not have an exclusive right to industrially viable waterways or revenue generated therefrom. Ontario claimed the legal authority to influence Anishinaabe water use and to profit from waterways formerly reserved for the "use or benefit" of bands.

HEPCO proceeded to develop over 186,000 horsepower after 1924, to the detriment of Indigenous communities in Treaty 3 territory, but the Anishinabeg rejected provincial (re)definitions of their reserve lands. They continued to host ceremonies to connect with waters running "between the projecting headlands of any lake or sheets of water not wholly surrounded by an Indian Reserve" years after An Act to Confirm the Title of the Government of Canada to Certain Lands and Indian Lands was passed. Consider, for example, the continued use of the *mitigwakik*, a ceremonial instrument also known as the water drum, as an act of resistance. The mitigwakik is handcrafted exclusively by members of the Grand Medicine Society.[79] Standing from forty to fifty centimetres high, its frame is made of basswood or cedar. A pine insert, sealed with pitch, forms the drum base. Tanned deer hide is used to create a drumhead.[80] The mitigwakik earned its English name, however, for the water that partially fills its frame. Upon completion, the mitigwakik is "audible at great distances" when played.[81]

Given its birth at the hands of a medicine man, the sounding of the mitig-wakik "informed one instantly that a medicine ceremony was in session."[82]

Through these ceremonies, Anishinaabe participants asserted a continued relationship with water and all Creation. Derrick Bresette, an Anishinaabe drummer with Morningstar River Singers in Toronto, suggests that the shape of the drum symbolizes the shape of the Earth. The circular shape of the mitigwakik prompts Anishinaabe viewers to reflect on their relationship with Creation. As Bresette explains, "when the singers are sounding the drum and the dancers are coming around that drum," they think "about those things that Mother Earth provides for us."[83] The mitig-wakik functions as an inherently political technology.[84] For the mitigwakik to sound, a recognized spiritual authority must stand behind the drum. Audibility depends on the operation of a social system that competes with Western (Christian) worldviews, particularly hierarchies of nature.

The unity between the Anishinabeg and Creation is further symbol-ized by the material construction of the mitigwakik. These drums are built entirely of local natural resources. They sound when members of the plant world (basswood, cedar, and pine), the animal world (deer), the water world (H_2O), and the human world (drummer) work in unison. According to Paul Nadjiwan, an Anishinaabe drummer from Manitoulin Island, the drum is used "to communicate with the powers of relationship."[85] Relationships reinforced through ceremonial play counter Western understandings of the natural world.

Cherokee author Thomas King argues that Christian origin stories, particularly the fall of Adam and Eve in Genesis, encouraged Westerners to position themselves in competition with nature. He explains that "the post-garden world we inherit is decidedly material in nature, a world at war—God vs. the Devil, humans vs. the elements."[86] Members of the Ontario legislature had likely been socialized to believe that water—as an element—could be separated from the Anishinabeg, that boundary lines could be drawn between the reserve and the river, that the 1924 act could be written and approved by provincial officials.

In contrast, members of the Grand Medicine Society rejected Western divisions of the natural world when they drummed; they sounded their sacred bonds to the waters flowing through the Winnipeg River drainage basin. Anishinaabe poet Al Hunter of Manitou Rapids, Ontario, explains: "The earth is water. We are water."[87] Sometimes compared with blood in

Anishinaabe writings, water could not be pulled from Anishinaabe bodies or communities.[88] The politicized message of the drum was (and is) that the Anishinabeg are interconnected with the Winnipeg River drainage basin; it encouraged a mental map that conflicted with Western (re)definitions of Anishinaabe space.

Perhaps unsurprisingly, Anishinaabe healers used the drum actively to reinforce their connections to waterways prior to 1915, and evidence of the mitigwakik often survives in written records in the form of complaints. Settler-colonists living in Kenora (and likely Anishinaabe converts to Christianity) considered drum use a form of noise pollution. In July 1893, a colonist observed that Anishinaabe families had gathered "on the outskirts of town [Rat Portage]" to collect their treaty money. It was on this "vacant common" that Anishinaabe men, women, and children engaged in cere-monies "incomprehensible to the white onlooker."[89] Approximately one year later a colonist bemoaned Anishinaabe drumming that "rent the air asunder" as sound travelled "down the [Winnipeg] [R]iver" toward town.[90]

Neither record directly identifies the mitigwakik or the water drum. However, complaints of sounds audible at great distances reflect anthro-pological descriptions of the water drum.[91] The Anishinabeg played an "enormous variety" of membranophones (drums); alternative instruments would have been available for local use.[92] Rat Portage and "down the river," though vague, are also suggestive territorial markers. During the 1890s, Chief Kawitaskung oversaw both Rat Portage Indian Reserve and Dalles 38C Indian Reserve.[93] Despite his Christian conversion, he lived on a "medi-cine reserve."[94] Dalles 38C (and off-reserve territories claimed by band members) remained hotbeds of activity for the Grand Medicine Society. It is likely that the Anishinabeg met on these lands to drum.

Summertime complaints further imply mitigwakik use. Distinctions between membranophones determined who played them, where they were played, and when they were played. Grand Medicine Society ceremonies, which might require mitigwakik use, frequently occurred during the summer months as kin groups throughout the Winnipeg River drainage basin left their familial traplines and hunting grounds to meet at shared harvesting sites (e.g., blueberry and manomin grounds). Ceremonial activities included "puberty rights, marriages, dances, [and] religious performance[s]." These activities peaked from June to August—at the same time that Kenora resi-dents complained about Anishinaabe drumming.[95]

Written records of mitigwakik use decline in the early 1900s, likely in response to amendments in 1895 to the Indian Act. Federal modifications to Section 114 criminalized all dances and ceremonies that involved giving away goods (e.g., clothing, food, and tobacco) or money. Section 114 also "proclaimed it an indictable offence for 'Indians' or 'other persons' to engage in, or assist in celebrating, or encourage anyone else to celebrate" banned Indigenous dances and ceremonies.[96] Participants would be charged with a minimum two-month sentence. Federal authorities, however, could impose a sentence up to six months.[97] Bans appear to have been motivated by federal anxieties about Indigenous territorial use. One Indian Agent claimed that dancing "unsettled" Indigenous participants.[98] Dancing was feared to upset reserve boundaries. In 1905, R.S. McKenzie, the Indian Agent in Kenora, recommended removing Powassan's chieftainship as a penalty for "urging the Indians to hold these Feasts and dances" in and around Shoal Lake Indian Reserve. McKenzie further suggested that Powassan be "sent to jail for a time at hard labour"—all in an attempt to establish "lines" of acceptable conduct.[99] By July 1911, at least one Chief had been incarcerated for ceremonial dancing in territory covered by Treaty 3.[100]

Yet imprisonment did not seem to dissuade the Anishinabeg from affirming their unique relationship with all Creation. In 1921, Duncan Campbell Scott hinted that dances upset federal map-making initiatives and attempts to solidify reserve boundaries. In a circular to Indian Agents at Kenora and Fort Frances, Scott wrote that "you should . . . prevent them from leaving their reserves for the purposes of attending fairs, exhibitions, etc." He further advised that "you should suppress any dances which . . . unsettle them from serious work."[101] Federal agents imprisoned ceremonial participants in an attempt to solidify reserve boundaries and to ensure the settlement of reserve lands. Had federal tactics succeeded, one could argue that local Anishinabeg accepted (however unwittingly) Western (re)definitions of Anishinaabe space—but mitigwakik use continued "way out on the lake."[102]

The Anishinabeg maintained competing definitions of space—particularly their interconnectedness with water—by holding ceremonies on Lake of the Woods and the Winnipeg River. Although ceremonial sites on or near reserve lands fell into disuse after 1895, cultural practice flourished away from the watchful eye of the Indian Agent after 1915. Hazel Martin-McKeever (b. 1928), for example, remembers that "there were a lot of pow-wows in the distant islands." She was born to a Christian family, and her mother, Matilda Martin (Ogimaamaashiik), never allowed her to attend them: "It was a no-no." Although Hazel never witnessed mitigwakik use, she "hear[d] the drums at night." Her family feared that drum use was "evil."[103] Medicine songs, it was (and is still) believed, connected local Anishinabeg to the spirit world. And this connection to all Creation, strong in Anishinaabe territory at large, blurred the lines between humankind and water, between reserve lands and waters. Ongoing ceremonial practice suggests that the Anishinabeg did not believe that the 1915 act or the 1924 act disconnected them from their water resources.

Relocation, as a strategy for cultural survival, is encoded in local oral testimony. Lake of the Woods is believed to have been created by a water spirit, a *Manitou*. This Manitou so loved its creation that it transformed into a rock, an unmovable island. But it also sought to protect the Indigenous inhabitants of Lake of the Woods. Manitou said, "I'll make a maze of this lake . . . to confound those who might try to drive my people from it."[104] The islands guaranteed Indigenous inhabitants protection from harm. Ceremonial practice "way out on the lake" not only reaffirmed Anishinaabe relationships with water but was also a strategy derived from an alliance between the Indigenous occupants of Lake of the Woods and the spirit world. Provincial laws, federal laws, and surveyor's boundaries were not heeded on Lake of the Woods after 1915 or 1924. Instead, local Anishinabeg continually reinforced their connection to water through song. They did not abide by provincial reimaginings of Indigenous lands. They lived their lives in defiance of them.

CHAPTER 2

RISING RIVER, RECEDING ACCESS

Ogimaamaashiik answered to Matilda Martin now. After John Kipling Sr., her first husband, died, she married a "white man" named Edward Martin. They trapped north of Dalles 38C Indian Reserve for a few years after wedding. She cannot remember exactly when they moved to town; it was sometime around 1915.

In town, Matilda lives in a small house with a summer kitchen overlooking Rideout Bay. She likes to watch her relatives come and go from her window. Her proximity to the Winnipeg River means that band members visit often. Sometimes they bring fish. Other times they bring manomin. Gifts offered to Matilda in exchange for her advice, her translation services, or her telephone depend on the season and flow patterns—manomin does not grow in February or in deep water. If not for her seven children, the house might have felt lonely during winter months. Flow patterns determined more than gifts; they determined whether band members could visit at all. The Norman Dam made stretches of the ice road between town and reserve unsafe. People would have to be overconfident or desperate to risk a visit—at least if they planned to ride into town entirely by sled.[1]

Between 1887 and 1893, settler-colonists constructed dams to modify the flow from Lake of the Woods into the Winnipeg River. The Rollerway Dam came first. It raised the low level of the lake by 0.91 metre. It would be replaced by the Norman Dam only six years later.[2] Artificial water fluctuations on Lake of the Woods were dramatic, varying from "0.9 feet [0.3 metre] in 1899 to as much as 6.3 feet [2.0 metres] in 1913."[3] Although an unexpected release of water could make boat travel unsafe near the Norman Dam, changing water patterns seriously limited Anishinaabe mobility during the winter months. Removing stop logs could break up ice roads downstream. By making ice roads unreliable, these dams made it difficult for Anishinaabe families to maintain their livelihood year-round: traplines became inaccessible to some; others feared travelling to town to trade.

The Anishinabeg were not alone in their suffering. Minnesotans complained that the Norman Dam jeopardized their earning potential by inundating their fields. According to one account, irate Minnesotans responded by attempting to blow up the Norman Dam with dynamite.[4] The International Joint Commission (IJC) intervened by holding an inquiry into Lake of the Woods water levels. Its goal was to maintain peace between Canada and the United States and to determine the costs and benefits of water regulation on Lake of the Woods. Unfortunately, the commission ignored what was happening to Anishinaabe communities downstream of the Norman Dam.[5] The commission's failure to consult Anishinaabe families about their experiences of environmental change made adaptation necessary. Families responded creatively to settler-colonial activity, preserving the Anishinaabe Nation along a changed system until settler-colonists remodelled the river in the 1950s.[6]

Changing Water Patterns and Unstable Ice Roads

Land and water influenced the livelihood of Anishinaabe families who lived along the Winnipeg River; hydroelectric development at the western outlet of Lake of the Woods affected the stability (and hence reliability) of Anishinaabe ice roads along the river. The Anishinabeg had been creating and maintaining ice roads along central corridors for winter travel for generations. Offering a present-day perspective on the practice, former Chief of Dalles 38C Indian Reserve Allan Luby (Ogemah) suggests that ice roads were critical to regional Anishinaabe transportation at the turn of the twentieth century. Transportation across frozen rivers and lakes made geographic sense: "There

Figure 10. The Norman Dam before 1926.

were no hills. It was very easy to get from point A to point B," which makes sense because Lake of the Woods is in the Precambrian Shield, famed for granite outcroppings, muskeg, and difficult overland travel. Luby noted that "all the main communities were always on the water." Travel across frozen waterways thus offered the shortest, most direct route to family or trade. Intergenerational transportation routes followed "straight lines."[7]

Band members of Dalles 38C relied heavily on ice roads for travel between reserve and town. Elder Matilda Martin (Ogimaamaashiik) said that "we used that road all winter [c. 1885–1908]. All the Indian families did. There were fifteen families there one time in that reserve. They used the same road."[8] Martin did not refer to an alternative winter route. Like members of some of the other families, she travelled the ice road on foot. According to her memoirs, it facilitated an exchange of Anishinaabe furs and handicrafts for store merchandise. Beginning in 1902, she became solely responsible within her family for walking to town to secure pantry fare. On a regular trip, she collected "a quarter bag of flour, ten pounds of sugar, some tea, and a few other necessities." To secure capital for her purchases, she would leave her toboggan behind the HBC store and sell moccasins near the front of the store.[9]

The exchange that Martin described was a standard occurrence. The *Rat Portage Miner and Semi-Weekly News* reported that "the Indian" generally used the ice road to "[bring] in his furs and [take] out flour."[10] The press made specific references to in-town exchanges with local Anishinabeg when specialty trades occurred. For example, when Mr. Hook secured three highly valuable silver fox skins, the *Rat Portage Miner and Semi-Weekly News* reported that "the Indian . . . came up from Whitedog [Wabaseemoong]" to trade.[11]

Ice roads also improved Anishinaabe access to Western medical care. In 1893, Dr. Thomas Hanson, an employee of the Department of Indian Affairs, travelled from Kenora to Dalles 38C "very quickly by dog train" to examine band members.[12] Hanson's use of the ice road for medical visits received more frequent media attention than Anishinaabe travel. That year local newspapers reported again that Hanson had "made a trip down to the Dalles 38C by dog train" to help treat the grippe.[13] His use of the ice road remained a popular news item in 1906, when he travelled down the Winnipeg River to investigate "a little sickness," likely at Dalles 38C. Within a week of his visit, Martin used the ice road to bring her husband's body to town for burial. John Kipling Sr. had succumbed to his illness.[14]

Ice roads provided essential service routes for up to five months of the year. Knowledge keepers maintain that ice on Lake of the Woods can come in as early as November. Spring breakup generally occurred between 29 April and 5 May, though a variance of four to six weeks was common.[15] In other words, as the temperature dipped below zero degrees Celsius, ice roads improved access to Western medical practitioners and their reme- dies during an era when the Department of Indian Affairs did not provide reserves such as Dalles 38C with full-time medical care. Nor did the feder- ally funded schoolhouse include a nursing station. John Kipling Sr., a lay missionary from Selkirk, Manitoba, was its only full-time employee.[16] Of course, Anishinaabe medicines continued to be widely and effectively used. As recently as 2012, Elder Alice Kelly taught Anishinaabe youth that Dalles 38C was a medicine reserve.[17]

To facilitate ice travel, the Anishinabeg kept large populations of sled dogs. They provided the muscle needed to pull the sleds across the ice. When the Marquis of Lorne travelled through Lake of the Woods in 1881, his chronicler, W.H. Williams, disparaged the camp conditions of the Anishinabeg living near Rat Portage. Williams was particularly disturbed by the number of unpenned dogs allowed to roam the summer settlement. He wrote, sarcastically, that "the very extensive canine population sent out a strong delegation to take up their quarters among the Indians."[18] He insulted local Anishinabeg by classing Anishinaabe families with their dogs. Williams suggested that they socialized and shared accommodations—a union that interfered with Lorne's official progress across the North-West Territories toward the Rocky Mountains. But the insult offers important insight into Anishinaabe water use. Local Anishinabeg considered sled dogs sufficiently valuable to relocate them during the summer months. Although Williams saw the dogs as unmanaged and unrestrained—he suggested that they were masters unto themselves, capable of organizing their own "delega- tion"—they were, in fact, being kept and cared for by the families to whom they belonged. Dogs had enough value to be provided with regular super- vision and care.

Families managed large dog populations because alternative methods of transit (aside from foot travel) were difficult to access in the early 1900s. In Riding Mountain, Manitoba, west of Dalles 38C, some families replaced dogs after horses were introduced, presumably by settler-colonists in the 1870s. According to Marilyn Peckett, the Anishinabeg occupied Riding

Mountain since the early nineteenth century, though evidence of earlier Indigenous occupation exists. She suggests that settler-colonial presence increased in the 1870s, shortly after Manitoba was surveyed.[19] Although horses might have been traded before this time, settler-colonists brought domesticated work animals such as horses with them into Riding Mountain in greater numbers. Peckett does not provide a date for the arrival of horses (or their point of origin), but it seems likely that Anishinaabe use of horses increased with their availability. Wagon travel eventually became the most popular form of transit and the dog sled fell into disuse.[20] No such change occurred at Dalles 38C. Matilda Martin (Ogimaamaashiik) maintained that "not many Indians will keep a horse, you know."[21] She recalled only one man with a horse during her time on the reserve, between 1885 and 1908. Given that no earthen road connected Dalles 38C to town until the 1980s, there was no practical incentive to replace dogs with horses. Water travel remained the best transit option in the often rocky and sometimes boggy Precambrian Shield.

Accessing train services could be both dangerous and impractical. During the Treaty 3 negotiations, Anishinaabe leaders attempted to secure free and unlimited travel on the Canadian Pacific Railway (CPR) in exchange for shared access to their territories. Lieutenant-Governor Alexander Morris denied their request, indicating that he represented the queen, not the company.[22] Train stations were eventually built around, rather than on, the reserve. Chief Kawitaskung (Thomas Lindsay), escorted to Winnipeg by the Indian Agent at Kenora, relied on the ice road to access more "modern" transit services. He was taken by dog sled to the agent's house in town.[23] In 1910, the Grand Trunk Pacific Railway built a station at Winnipeg River Crossing (now known as Minaki). The Canadian National Railway (CNR) assumed control over Winnipeg River Crossing in 1922. However, the CNR did not stop in Kenora, making it impractical for day-to-day use. Whereas locomotives connected important cities in Manitoba and the northwest, reserves remained off the tracks. Ice roads retained their importance as thoroughfares for Anishinaabe families, especially since CPR access often required a trip to Kenora and the CNR travelled around Kenora.

Difficult access does not mean that the Anishinabeg in Treaty 3 territory did not use train services. Evidence suggests that Anishinaabe blueberry pickers made use of the CPR and CNR during the summer months. Grant Bogart, a former CPR employee, remembered that around 1914 "it [the train from Kenora to Scovil Lake] was all crammed full of berry-pickers.... More Indians than white people."[24] Elders Ella Dawn and Walter Redsky of Shoal Lake First Nation used the Greater Winnipeg Water District Railway and the CNR to access blueberry patches at Ena Lake and Armstrong Lake, respectively.[25]

Given the importance of ice roads to winter travel, the standards for their care were high. Residents of the Kenora District expected that ice roads would be "bushed out as soon as the first solid ice appeared," a likely reference to the practice of staking bushes at wide intervals along the transit route.[26] These bushes pointed out the safest paths along or across the ice during periods of low visibility such as blizzards. When asked to describe how Anishinaabe families selected road markers, Allan Luby (Ogemah) explained that "anything green will do" because travellers needed to be able to distinguish road markers from a winter landscape of whites and greys. Modern practice suggests that Anishinaabe families used jack pine to bush out transit routes. In December 2018, for example, ice roads southeast of the Norman Dam (remember that the current flows the strongest in a north-westerly direction) were bushed out using jack pine. This tree grows in thin soil over the granite of the Precambrian Shield, making it one of the most common pine species in the area. It also retains its needle-like leaves beyond one growing season.[27]

The technology of making ice roads appears to have originated in both Anishinaabe and non-Indigenous communities. The Office of the Minister of Agriculture further outlined effective maintenance activities for ice roads in the nineteenth century. To eliminate drift heaps, George H. Henshaw recommended that Canadian communities "encourage the growth of a close belt of trees along the sides of the road, or [undertake] the more difficult task of planting hedges and keeping them in order."[28] Hedges functioned as windbreaks. Henshaw further recommended the maintenance (or planting) of coniferous trees because the leaf loss of deciduous trees would reduce the effectiveness of any improvement. The written record does not indicate whether Anishinaabe families encouraged the growth of coniferous trees along the ice road.[29] Henshaw further recommended "breaking the road" or running a sled across fresh snow to flatten the route.

Regular Anishinaabe use of ice routes would create comparable improve-ments to the road. Along Lake of the Woods, "winter trails" (so named by the *Rat Portage Miner and Semi-Weekly News*) were maintained by the Crown

Figure 11. Photograph of an active ice road in Kenora, 2012.

timber agent until winter 1905. Residents appear to have adopted Crown timber standards as their own. They bemoaned the loss of federal funding in 1905 and the transfer of responsibilities for road care from the Crown to lumbermen. Labourers now had to "mark out their own roads on the lake."[30] Similar complaints were not voiced about ice road conditions along the Winnipeg River—along routes both actively claimed and used by the Anishinabeg from Dalles 38C, Whitedog, and Grassy Narrows reserves. Did Anishinaabe families continue the practice of bushing out or breaking the road through their lands? Kenora residents said little about ice roads on the Winnipeg River. Their silence suggests that Anishinaabe territories remained well maintained by an alternative source.

Hydroelectric development at the western outlet of Lake of the Woods affected the stability of these ice roads. Intergenerational knowledge that had allowed Anishinaabe families to travel safely along the ice was compromised by industrial operations. Currents increased randomly and artificially when stop logs were removed to produce power.[31] Which sections of the river froze (and to what extent) now depended more on electrical demands than on nature's course. Drastic environmental change, particularly in freezing patterns, was captured in local prose. Prior to the establishment of the Rat Portage Dam in 1892, a Rat Portage resident claimed that Hebe's Falls froze during the winter months: "The walls of the narrow gorge through which pass the seething, foaming waters of the Winnipeg or 'River of Rapids' were of ice, carved into facades of columns and fluted stalactites.... Below, where all was dark shade, a partially formed ice bridge appeared."[32] Ice below the falls was "dark" and presumably unstable.

As a general rule, dark ice is low density and therefore unable to support additional weight. Given natural flow patterns, it is possible that ice was being eroded from the bottom up. Yet the outlet appeared to be immobile. Natural flow allowed freezing. Stability increased as one moved north of the outlet.[33] Matilda Martin (Ogimaamaashiik), for example, walked across the ice north of Miller's Rapids—just a short distance from the western outlet. In 1924, the *Kenora Miner and News* substantiated poetic renderings by reporting that Kenora Bay, near the outlet of Lake of the Woods, had frozen over by November in 1876.[34] Before dam development, the north shore of Lake of the Woods and large sections of the Winnipeg River froze during winter months.

Printed warnings about ice stability do not seem to have appeared in Rat Portage until the construction of the Norman Dam in 1893. Following dam development, local journalists advised skaters to avoid shortcuts from Rat Portage to Norman, a neighbouring community, across the bay. An anonymous journalist at the *Rat Portage Weekly Record* explained that the current was "apt to wear away the ice from below and spots may become so thin as to be dangerous" that year.[35] Changing water flow, caused by dam operations, meant that former ice routes became unreliable.

What was happening to the ice? As the Norman Dam drew water from the reservoir, ice on the south or Kenora Bay side of the dam fractured along the shore. Eventually, fractured ice would drop. If ice reformed along Kenora Bay, then it froze in a bowl shape. Fissures created structural weaknesses that even the harshest winters could not overcome. Downstream of the dam— where ice connected reserves such as Dalles 38C, Whitedog, and Grassy Narrows to town—the ice weakened in response to changing levels. Water released by the Norman Dam into the Winnipeg River lifted ice from the shore, and ice downstream of the dam broke up. A frozen river could quickly become open water. Should levels stabilize, a thin layer of ice might form over open water. New ice would be more unreliable and, in many cases, too thin for safe travel.

Industrial operations thus compromised the stability of Anishinaabe transit routes. Pine markers could no longer guarantee safe passage along the Winnipeg River toward the western outlet of Lake of the Woods. Poor ice conditions could landlock Anishinaabe families for extended periods during the winter months. Prior to the Rollerway and Norman Dams, Anishinaabe families limited winter travel during winter freeze-up and spring thaw. As Allan Luby (Ogemah) explained, "you'd set up camp, and you'd wait" for the water to transform.[36] Anishinaabe families exchanged stories, some entertaining and others encoded with socio-cultural directives, during these transitional periods. Occasional isolation from family and trade was short-lived. After a few weeks of deep cold, short trips became possible. Within a month, families could cover greater distances by foot or sled. After 1887, however, the transitional period never clearly ended. Knowledge keepers lost the ability to gauge ice thickness and strength north of the western outlet. Elder testimony suggests that Anishinaabe men from Dalles 38C limited winter treks toward Rat Portage because of perceived travel risks. Urgencies—such as food shortages—led Anishinaabe men toward the western outlet. Elder Jacob Lindsay suggested that by the 1940s "there were fewer and fewer people. Most of them drowned."[37]

It is difficult to enumerate the cost of damages that the Province of Ontario and dam operators, working in tandem, caused to Anishinaabe ice roads. How do we evaluate the loss of potential trade? Reduced medical access? How can we calculate family loss?

The International Joint Commission

These questions were of little concern to the International Joint Commission when it inquired into water levels between 1912 and 1917. The concept of a commission dated back to the Boundary Water Treaty of 1909, an agreement between the Dominion of Canada and the United States intended to "prevent disputes regarding the use of boundary waters."[38] Both governments envisaged the commission as an organization capable of moderating international conflict over shared natural resources. Specifically, the commission was "to settle all questions which are now pending between the United States and the Dominion of Canada, involving the rights, obligations, or interests of either in relation to the other."[39] The original script of the treaty excluded First Nations whose boundaries overlapped the forty-ninth parallel. Only the interests of Canada and the United States—both with historical ties to British colonialism—were protected by the treaty. Each treaty partner had a historical legacy of eliminating Indigenous access to natural resources (e.g., land) to encourage the settlement of predominantly Anglo-Protestant settlers. It seemed to be unlikely that the treaty would protect competing Anishinaabe claims to international waterways.

Indeed, the successful operation of the International Joint Commission depended, in part, on perceived mutual interest between Western nations. Transboundary cooperation ensured that both the Dominion of Canada and the United States could achieve their goals of territorial and industrial expansion. Attempts at transboundary cooperation were not unique to 1909. The Reciprocity Treaty of 1854 had eliminated protective colonial tariffs to allow for freer trade across borders. Reciprocity brought prosperity to "Canadian" producers until it was abrogated by the United States in 1865. Despite its abrogation, the Reciprocity Treaty of 1854 revealed that international cooperation could facilitate joint economic growth.[40]

Yet the commission did not take shape on Lake of the Woods until the 1910s. American complaints about industrial flooding predated the Boundary Waters Treaty. Minnesotans mailed a series of affidavits to the American government to draw attention to the artificial flooding of the south shore in 1907.[41] Limited action was taken by the United States at this time—American officials wrongly assumed that high water levels fell within their natural limits.[42] It was not until 1912 that formal letters of reference were submitted by the governments of both the United States and the Dominion of Canada to call for a formal investigation of Lake of the Woods water levels. Both parties demanded that the commission determine whether artificial flow was desirable in Lake of the Woods. If so, then which artificial level would "secure the most advantageous use of the . . . waters"?[43]

In response to these demands, the first International Joint Commission— its parameters defined under Article IX of the Boundary Waters Treaty—was furnished in 1912. Washington and Ottawa sought out trusted federal agents to represent their respective national interests. Washington called on Obadiah Gardener to act as the commission's American chairman, who was then joined by James A. Tawney and R.B. Glenn. Ottawa asked Charles Alexander Magrath to be the Canadian chairman and appointed additional committee members Henry Absalom Powell and Pierre-Basile Mignault. Equal representation by the United States and the Dominion of Canada did not accurately reflect the geography of Lake of the Woods. Seventy percent of the drainage area fell within Canadian boundaries.[44] American and Canadian members, however, hoped to share in the economic advantages of hydroelectric development along the north shore. In their final report, Commissioners Gardener, Tawney, Glenn, Magrath, Powell, and Mignault advocated that any judgement ought to depend on "not only all practicable uses to which these waters can be put on their own watershed [e.g., agriculture, fishing, and transportation], but also all beneficial uses which the energy developed thereon may serve in the adjacent territory."[45] Implicit was the belief that hydroelectric power stations could serve both nations regardless of their exact boundary locations.

Canadian industrial interests—those in favour of the Norman Dam— might have coalesced against other "practicable uses," such as Anishinaabe transportation. Although the dominion representatives came from different parts of Canada, they shared the belief that technological innovation such as power generation or rail transportation could strengthen the dominion—its territorial grasp and its economic potential. Consider that Chairman Charles Alexander Magrath was recruited from his home in Lethbridge, Alberta. Magrath had firmly established himself as an advocate of capitalist development, becoming Lethbridge's first President of the Board of Trade in 1899. Magrath's interest in energy-related industries is evidenced by his employment with the North Western Coal and Navigation Company as well as his position as Fuel Controller during the First World War.[46] Years after the Lake of the Woods question was settled, Magrath became Chairman of the Hydro-Electric Power Commission of Ontario—a position he held from 1925 to 1931.[47] His life history reveals a keen desire to fuel national growth with coal and, later, water—an ideological position that made him a likely advocate for artificial regulation of Lake of the Woods by the Norman Dam.

Ottawa partnered Magrath with Henry Absalom Powell. He was a Conservative Member of Parliament from New Brunswick from 1895 to 1900. In 1896, he sat on the Standing Committee of Agriculture and Colonization in the House of Commons. His position might have predisposed him toward the Keewatin Lumbering and Manufacturing Company—which stood to benefit from potential power production at the Norman Dam—as milling operations had significantly increased the population of northwestern Ontario.[48] Powell also served on the Select Standing Committee on Railways, Canals, and Telegraph Lines. Once again his occupation suggests a personal commitment to national growth, be it economic or demographic. Curtailing the operation of the Norman Dam might have reduced shipments along the rail line between Thunder Bay and Winnipeg. The rail industry, for which Powell advocated, depended in part on the processing of raw materials on the north shore of Lake of the Woods. It seems to be unlikely that he would assume a contrary position as an active member of the commission.

Pierre-Basile Mignault appears as an outlier on the commission. He was a lawyer based in Montreal. What connected Mignault to Powell and Magrath was the geographic distance and physical disconnect between Lake of the Woods and his home. Ottawa called Magrath to the commission from Alberta and Powell from New Brunswick. The dominion's decision-making body therefore had no clear ties to Lake of the Woods residents or geography. Yet distance is not necessarily akin to neutrality. Two of these federally appointed representatives displayed a strong interest in Canadian industries, and decisions made by these three men depended largely on evidence submitted during public hearings. From the outset, Magrath, Powell, and Mignault lacked sufficient familiarity with the Winnipeg River drainage basin to anticipate Anishinaabe territorial, predominantly extra-market, use. Damages recorded in the *Final Report of the International Joint Commission on the Lake of the Woods Reference* reflect the commissioners' geographic and pro-industry biases. That Ottawa would furnish the commission with pro-industrialists reflects larger trends in Canada's resource sector. Good politics was good business, and Ontario, in part, was a "client of the business community."[49] International decisions were made with little attention to how the Anishinabeg inhabited Treaty 3 territory.

Anishinaabe Exclusion

In fact, Canada and the United States had written Anishinaabe participants out of the International Joint Commission by employing the language of nationhood and citizenship during its formation. The commission originated, after all, from an international agreement designed to protect the interests of Canadian and American citizens who shared waters. The public appears to have adopted federal terms—or frameworks—in its evaluation of the commission's proceedings. Consider that the editorial team of the *American Journal of International Law* identified the commission as a symbol of "comity between nations."[50] Years later Manton M. Wyvell argued that both parties hoped to curb "strong feelings and even hatreds" by creating the "machinery of peace" between equal adversaries: Canada and the United States.[51] Canadian law had long (re)defined Anishinaabe interests as subject to, rather than independent of, the dominion. As historian John Milloy explains, "the Canadian federal government took extensive control of reserves and tribal nations [through the 1876 version of the Indian Act]. Traditional Indian government was dismissed and replaced by Indian-agent-controlled models of white government."[52]

This (re)definition of Anishinaabe nationhood is critical to understanding Indigenous exclusion from the commission. Although there was no explicit bar against Indigenous participation in the hearings, there was also no clause for Indigenous inclusion. As members of an unrecognized nation, on-reserve Anishinaabe men and women discovered that their interests were deemed secondary to those of the dominion. As members of an unrecognized nation, Anishinaabe men and women were to function as auxiliary—not foundational—members of national plans for economic growth.

During the hearings, federal organizations—considered representative of the public interest—submitted data to the commission. The Dominion Water Power Branch, the Department of Public Works of Canada, and the Department of Indian Affairs rendered "valuable services" to Magrath, Powell, and Mignault. Commissioners also thanked "individuals in both countries" for sharing their knowledge of the lake.[53]

Again there were implicit barriers to Anishinaabe inclusion. The commission relied on local sources of communication (e.g., the *Kenora Miner and News*) to recruit "any person" to submit information about lake levels.[54] It also called on "interested parties."[55] According to the Indian Act, however, the Anishinabeg, as "Indians," were wards of the state, which meant that they were treated as minors without the full privileges of citizenship.[56] The Department of Indian Affairs was to protect and to represent Indigenous interests; federal law technically disqualified the Anishinabeg from the commission's call.

Exclusion is not a necessary result of this legal reality, but it did not stimulate public demand for Anishinaabe participation. Indeed, Canadians following the *Kenora Miner and News* might have assumed wrongly that federal agents accurately represented Anishinaabe interests. In October 1915, the newspaper noted that G.G. McEwen of the Department of Indian Affairs in Ottawa and Constable Hans Hansen of Kenora had left town "to make an inspection and report on the lands owned by the Indian Department in this district." McEwen and Hansen were to estimate whether reserve lands "would be affected by any permanent change in levels of the Lake of the Woods."[57] There was no subsequent media report on their findings, but federal agents rarely prioritized Indigenous interests. Instead, the Department of Indian Affairs was linked to the ministries responsible for natural resources and western development.[58] The dominion government favoured industrial interventions that fuelled national economic growth and not Anishinaabe environmental uses that maintained an extra-market economy. It is unlikely that McEwen reported changes to ice roads since these roads were off reserve and thus outside his assignment.[59]

Not only were Anishinaabe participants excluded from the IJC hearings as wards of the state, but evidentiary norms further limited their ability to submit data. The commission based its decision on "extensive field surveys and the collection, analysis, and coordination of a vast amount of physical data." For example, the commission appointed Arthur V. White of Toronto and Adolph F. Meyer of Minneapolis as consulting engineers on the Lake of the Woods question.[60] White and Meyer produced an atlas. Sheet No. 4, which depicts Garden Island, Lake of the Woods, was part of a map collection showcasing "low lands bordering on the American and Canadian sides of the lake."[61] The map adhered to non-Indigenous cartographic traditions. The scale was clearly marked.

Anishinaabe maps, in contrast, unfolded like stories. They were not topographic representations of the Winnipeg River drainage basin. Instead, map-makers prioritized "the intersection of streams and the presence of lakes"—critical details for individuals travelling by canoe.[62] These visual cues did not require Anishinaabe maps to conform to non-Indigenous standards of scale. They conformed instead to the piece of paper on which they were drawn, and available materials dictated the scale of the map. Map-makers used long lines to represent hard paddling, and the difficulty of the route determined the distance between key points. Patterns of line use appear to have originated centuries earlier, as evidenced by pictorial writing (pictographs) in the Precambrian Shield. A pictograph from Annie Island, Lake of the Woods, for example, reveals that someone journeyed for approximately one month to reach the site, and the arduous journey was represented by one long, crooked line."[63]

Anishinaabe map users required local knowledge to trace and evaluate authorship. Map-makers might not have signed their maps by name, but authorship could be inferred from totemic symbols. Low population density also allowed readers to identify authorship by birth and marriage patterns (or totemic groupings) etched onto records of land use.[64] In contrast, the cartographers who produced Sheet No. 4 were clearly identified: "Adolph F. Meyer and Arthur V. White." They also made their credentials visible: "Consulting Engineers" is scrolled across the top of the map. Magrath, Powell, and Mignault could read and evaluate this submission. Given the cartographers' printed accreditation, the commissioners could assume that what was legible was also accurate.

An alternative mapping tradition meant that the Anishinabeg faced material barriers to participation in hearings. Federal representatives lacked the knowledge to read and evaluate Anishinaabe representations of space. Limited recognition of alternative forms of mapping are evident in the IJC claim that, "prior to the reference, the only surveys in the Lake of the Woods watershed were the ordinary public-land surveys, and they did not extend over the entire area."[65] The absence of evidence suggests that the disparity between Anishinaabe and non-Indigenous standards made it difficult to communicate spatial knowledge across cultures.

Non-Indigenous men occasionally filtered Anishinaabe knowledge for submission to the commission. Captain J.T. Hooper of Kenora, for example, attributed his ability to judge water fluctuations to local environmental knowledge and had developed his "standard" high-water mark through conversations with "the Indians." Indigenous informants told Hooper that Lake of the Woods reached "extreme high water" levels in 1876. Hooper referred to the "Indian" origin of this information in a letter to Arthur White.[66] He also suggested that representatives of the commission could assess the standard themselves by travelling along Lake of the Woods. Nature had recorded the high-water mark in the form of stained cliff faces along the lakeshore. Many of the 14,000 islands in Lake of the Woods, it seems, recorded the same details that local Anishinabeg had passed on orally.[67]

Alternatively, Hooper indicated that representatives of the commission could turn to HBC records: "The Indians *and* the Hudson's Bay Co. claimed it was higher [in 1876] than it had been for some years." Hooper himself "made a standard of low water" using HBC records.[68] Text could be and was privileged over alternative forms of evidence (material and oral) that would have facilitated Anishinaabe participation.[69] Hooper's submission reflected exclusionary evidentiary norms. And there is no known record of White corroborating multi-sensory evidence with textual records along the north shore or of recognizing Anishinaabe ways of knowing. Anishinaabe evidence of water fluctuations, if presented, was indirect on the Canadian side.

Not all witnesses included Anishinaabe knowledge in their testimonies, as did Hooper. White and Meyer deepened Anishinaabe exclusion by obscuring Anishinaabe patterns of land use from submitted maps. For example, they assessed soil grade by non-Indigenous standards. They did not account for distinct patterns of environmental use, specifically the adaptive planting and harvesting techniques that allowed Anishinaabe families to grow food in soil labelled unusable by federal agents. To ensure production in such harsh environs, Anishinaabe families planted seeds on islands or along the lakeshore, where the moderating effects of the water attenuated frost.[70]

Yet White and Meyer suggested that Garden Island had no agricultural value.[71] This finding conflicts with the place name—Garden Island—which emphasizes soil productivity. Seeds planted on Garden Island might have been more resistant than southern varieties. Corn planted in the north, for example, appeared to be "so stunted that [it is] more like [a shrub] than the plant which is common to more southerly latitudes."[72] Its strange shape is tied to genetic modifications. "Indian corn" planted and consumed by Anishinaabe families originated in southern Mexico. To allow the crop to grow, tribes to the north (including the Anishinabeg) had to develop frost-resistant strains through careful seed selection. No known attempt was made to understand Anishinaabe seed and garden management or to consider the science behind Anishinaabe harvests on seemingly unusable lands. No known attempt was made to reconcile place names (borne of Anishinaabe land use) with Western science.

An opportunity to assess potential damages to Anishinaabe territories thus went unnoticed. Expert findings favoured settler-colonists and their patterns of economic growth. Land along the north shore was believed to have little economic value in its "natural state." Lumber and flour mills, however, produced marked profits. With skewed data, the commission conducted a cost-benefit analysis of the Norman Dam. The commissioners ruled overwhelmingly in favour of Canadian operations and valued the continued development of the dam.

Anishinaabe Adaptations

Ultimately, the International Joint Commission recommended that an elevation of 1,061.25 feet (323.47 metres) above sea level be set as the maximum water level in Lake of the Woods.[73] Canadian industry benefited from this recommendation, gaining considerable flexibility in its operations. Consultation was required only if the lake rose to the maximum level. A new governing body, the Lake of the Woods Control Board, would determine how much water to "waste" or to "conserve" at either extreme. Fluctuations of up to five feet (over one and a half metres), however, were deemed acceptable by the commissioners.

It was not until the 1920s—years after the commission's findings had been submitted—that the media directly linked compromised ice travel to dam operations at the north shore. Damage to Anishinaabe transit routes only became visible once Canadian industry was protected. In December 1924, Mayor of Kenora John Brenchley issued a warning to residents through the *Kenora Miner and News*. The article acknowledged that, "prior to the enlarging of the east branch of the Winnipeg River, the current was not so strong towards the Tunnel Island shore." The article further identified that changing ice patterns could confuse regular ice travellers. The popular short-cut across Kenora Bay, from Tunnel Island to town, had posed "little danger" in years past. The reliability of ice travel across the bay had informed the "local habit of crossing the ice."[74]

Brenchley's public announcement was designed to revise local under-standings of Lake of the Woods and surrounding areas. The mayor stated that, "since the capacity of the power plant is more than three times what it was, more water of course goes through the east channel [and causes] a stronger current and thin ice."[75] Brenchley attributed changes in ice quality to the Kenora Powerhouse, a facility located on the east side of Tunnel Island constructed in 1892 and enlarged by Kenora in 1906.[76] He said nothing of the Norman Dam, located on the west side of Tunnel Island. Both systems draw water from Kenora Bay. Despite this oversight, it is clear that dam oper-ations jeopardized ice travel along the northern shores of Lake of the Woods.

By 1925, public announcements about shortcuts had hardened. The *Kenora Miner and News* published clear warnings about ice travel around Tunnel Island, not recommendations for alternative use: "The ice towards the Tunnel Island shore is never safe, at any period of the winter, because of the strong current which runs underneath [caused by releasing water into the Winnipeg River] to the eastern outlet of Lake of the Woods."[77] Dam oper-ations, as Mayor Brenchley's announcement revealed, had compromised the structural integrity of ice roads near town. The Kenora Powerhouse (and, though never explicitly identified, the Norman Dam) made the final leg of Anishinaabe travel from reserve to town dangerous. The dams not only compromised ice stability but also damaged Anishinaabe improve-ments to their roads. Pine markers might have sunk as rising water levels opened packed routes.

Dams caused more than environmental changes. By compromis-ing Anishinaabe ice roads, the Kenora and Norman Dams jeopardized Anishinaabe access to capital (through trade) and public services. There was no other direct route between Kenora and reserves such as Dalles 38C, Whitedog, and Grassy Narrows.[78]

Winter had always been difficult for Anishinaabe families. During the long, cold months, families faced the greatest risk of "rabbit starvation," an acute form of malnutrition caused by an overreliance on lean proteins.[79] These proteins needed to be coupled with carbohydrates (or fat) to stave off hunger. To help facilitate survival as resources dwindled during the winter months, Anishinaabe families broke into smaller groups. The modern era and machinery, symbolized by the Norman Dam, did little to ease the winter burden. In October 1922, Indian Agent Captain Frank Edwards reminded Kenora residents that local Anishinabeg were "almost destitute in the winter" and "suffer[ed] very greatly from the cold."[80] The first wave of hydroelectric development at Lake of the Woods exacerbated seasonal difficulties. From December to February, Anishinaabe families relied on trapping and big-game hunting. Unreliable ice, however, meant that traplines established before the dams were constructed might not have been safely accessible for the duration of the season. Male providers who relied on ice roads to reach their lands took substantial risks to check their traplines. Elder Alice Kelly recalled that male providers occasionally drowned on reserve.[81]

The *Kenora Miner and News* recorded drownings and near drownings in areas of the Winnipeg River drainage basin used by Anishinaabe families. For example, in December 1923, "a couple of people broke through, but fortunately they were able to get out" near Tunnel Island. In November 1925, a drowning occurred in the Winnipeg River near Minaki. The newspaper noted that "the drowned man broke through the thin ice while walking across the river, as the current is quite rapid in spots at that point."[82]

Those providers who did reach their traplines were more likely to face disappointment than did their predecessors. In the spring of 1925, the Norman Dam released large amounts of water, killing thousands of muskrats in Lake of the Woods. Indeed, low lake levels nearly "deplet[ed] the lake," causing "their houses [to freeze] up and thousands of rats were frozen to death along the shore and shallow inlets."[83] By May 1925, the *Kenora Miner and News* announced that the previous winter had wrought economic disaster: "Many of the Indians of the district are experiencing a period of hard times . . . as there has been very little doing in their line."[84] Although the correlation between water fluctuations and low muskrat populations was first discussed in the local newspaper in 1925, Anishinaabe families had likely experienced shortages since the 1890s.

Hungry families recognized the fragility of their harvesting economy in the face of environmental change—especially after fluctuations of up to 1.5 metres were recommended by the International Joint Commission. Economic adaptation resulted. The families knew that their interests had been—and would likely continue to be—underrepresented by federal agents. Flood damages likely influenced their decision to open personal savings accounts within five years of the commission's recommendations. In 1921, "Indians Starting Bank Accounts" headlined the *Kenora Miner and News*.[85] The article noted that "no less than forty-six [Indigenous people] have started savings bank accounts." Initial deposits, particularly investments made by individuals from Dalles 38C Indian Reserve, Rat Portage 38B Indian Reserve, and Big Island Indian Reserve came from on-reserve timber sales. These individuals decided to bank the twenty-five dollars per head that Indian Agent Captain Frank Edwards distributed for the loss of wood resources.

Early saving also followed a "prosperous blueberry year."[86] Elders Alice Kelly and Marjorie Nabish explained that blueberry crops were relatively protected from flood damages.[87] Early newspaper reports affirm their claims. In 1898, for example, shortly after Ontario paid the Keewatin Power Company to install stop logs at Norman Dam, the Rat Portage Railway Station managed to ship "from 4 to 10 tons of blueberries every day" out of the district.[88] Given that blueberry plants have a lifespan of twenty to fifty years, crops unaffected by lake fluctuations of roughly one metre would have been protected (albeit unintentionally) by the IJC recommendations. Blueberries thus became a reliable source of income in the face of environmental change. Matilda Martin (Ogimaamaashiik) remembered picking berries at Ena Lake (or nearby Corn Lake) for over forty years. Her first reference to berry-picking dates to around 1906, a time when her son, John Kipling Jr., was still in his *tikinagun* (cradleboard). Her last berry-picking season occurred in the 1950s. Martin reported that she "was getting old" and that her "feet were tired walkin[g] up the hill."[89] The same elevation that prevented Martin from picking in her seventies protected the crop from water fluctuations during her youth.

It is difficult to estimate how much profit families would accrue through berry sales. Few official records of berry sales exist because individuals who purchased harvested goods directly from status Indians without a permit risked persecution under the Indian Act.[90] In 1915, the *Kenora Miner and*

Figure 12. Anishinaabe group paddling to berry camp, c. 1920.

News estimated that berry transactions earned local Anishinabeg "thousands of dollars."[91] Ten years later it was anticipated that the blueberry business in Kenora would generate a net profit of $50,000 to $75,000.[92] Reflecting on her individual earnings, Martin claimed less than $200 for her baskets as an active picker in the 1920s.[93] However, the average annual wage in 1920 was approximately $125, and the average Canadian woman earned less than her male counterpart—approximately $75 per year. The average annual wage for Canadians at large decreased by 11 percent in 1930 and remained depressed until 1940.[94] Few families thrived on these annual wages as the cost of living outpaced average earnings across Canada. Compared with her non-Indigenous counterparts, Martin earned a sizable income as a married woman. Saving these cash earnings must be seen as an adaptive strategy as Anishinaabe families saw fit to "prepar[e] for the inevitable raining day."[95] Bank savings supplemented seasonal rounds.

Cash savings were an adaptation; they marked a cultural shift in temporal thinking.[96] Prior to the 1920s, environmental cues allowed the Anishinabeg to "keep time," to transition between economic activities. Heavy reliance on environmental cues meant that temporal orientation was local. The Anishinabeg reacted to present cues; they functioned in relation to the immediate future or the recent past.[97] They did not save or reserve time for daily tasks. Anthropologist Alfred Irving Hallowell claimed "their rhythm is elastic in the extreme and except when motivated by hunger or necessity they are dictated to a large degree by external circumstances."[98] The opening of bank accounts suggests that necessity motivated the Anishinabeg to think in relation to the distant future.

Yet there was no identifiable shift in labour. Trapping, hunting, and harvesting continued to have greater significance than wage employment. Although families sold their berries for money, survival did not yet demand seasonal employment in industries operated by settler-colonists.[99] Instead, families continued trying to eke out a living from the land. Banking activities reveal that local Anishinabeg were proactive; they moved "away from their general practice of spending their money as soon as it [was] received" and sought new strategies for survival.[100] Saving money allowed for the continued use of ancestral territories. It simultaneously marked the beginning of an in-between life for many Anishinabeg—life between water fluctuations of 1,056 and 1,061 feet (321.87 and 323.39 metres), between subsistence and cash economies, between town and reserve. Income produced during the berry harvest could be banked in town to shield Anishinaabe families from winter scarcity. Cash could be withdrawn, and flour, tea, and canned goods could be purchased in town. The risk of travelling along unstable ice roads to withdraw cash and to shop remained. Ironically, environmental change might have increased Anishinaabe use of savings accounts while increasing the risk of accessing them.

CHAPTER 3

POWER LOST AND POWER GAINED

In the 1960s, shortly after the Whitedog Falls Generating Station began operations, band members at Dalles 38C Indian Reserve struggled to make sense of manomin loss on the Winnipeg River. The crop had sustained their ancestors for generations. Manomin was so reliable that they had used it to mark time. The "wild rice picking moon," or *Manominikegiisis*, lasted from mid-August to mid-September, but very few people had managed to pick manomin after the start of the Whitedog Falls Generating Station.

Shortly after the Indian Agent collected the children for residential school, the Norman Dam opened its gates. Those left behind did not see the Hydro-Electric Power Commission of Ontario release water into the Winnipeg River from Lake of the Woods. They did see, however, a ripening crop sink beneath the waves. A few seasoned harvesters responded. They believed that Poplar Portage, an important field, could be saved by building an Anishinaabe dam. To stop the Winnipeg River from inundating their harvesting areas as settlers generated electricity, they piled rock upon rock where the river narrowed. They did not ask HEPCO for permission. How could they? Settler men who managed the river made little effort to communicate with the Anishinabeg.

Band members failed to regulate the flow of water in manomin fields with hand-piled rocks. No crop rebounded because of their efforts. But they left the rocks behind. They built a monument of the Anishinaabe effort to survive in a changed river system.

Among the non-Indigenous residents of Kenora, histories of hydroelectric development after the Second World War differ from Anishinaabe accounts. Whereas the Anishinabeg associated the postwar era with manomin loss and the further erosion of their ability to have a voice in decisions affecting natural resources, non-Indigenous residents viewed the arrival of dams and generating stations as long-overdue progress. From town, the establishment of the Whitedog Falls Generating Station appeared as the culmination of developments that had begun in the early decades of the twentieth century, when the recommendations of the International Joint Commission seemingly opened the area for "business." So-called progress had been put on hold during the Depression but gained momentum in the 1950s when HEPCO entered Anishinaabe territory.

HEPCO did so to find solutions to predicted energy shortages. In the Northwestern Division, power demand increased by 250 percent between 1945 and 1957.[1] HEPCO lacked the infrastructure to service Ontarians at this rate of growth. Since the province had already compromised Anishinaabe claims to water resources in the prewar era, HEPCO worked to eliminate non-Indigenous competition for water resources in northwestern Ontario in the 1950s. It did so by consulting with provincial decision makers rather than with mill operators, such as the Ontario-Minnesota Pulp and Paper Company, which began operations in the region in the early 1940s.

HEPCO's strategy was in keeping with the socio-political climate of the 1950s, an era when the Canadian government was "committed to unprecedented levels of state involvement in the economic order."[2] Canadians in the 1950s believed that states could curb economic recession, and they showed unprecedented support for federal programming. William Lyon Mackenzie King's Liberals responded to public demand by incentivizing economic growth with federal loans to small businesses and export credit insurance. They also sought to improve employment opportunities by extending support to unions.[3] In this climate, HEPCO could not ignore grievances from the mill: federal policy had primed it for expansion. If the mill perceived HEPCO as a threat to its operations, to the steady employment of hundreds of unionized men, then HEPCO—a publicly owned utility— likely would have been pressured to establish equilibrium.

In contrast, First Nations did not pose the same political threat as the mill, and little existed in law to pressure HEPCO to consult with band members. Instead, it appears that HEPCO worked through federal agents

to avoid discussing directly with First Nations the environmental consequences of hydroelectric development. Although a combination of federal
initiatives and provincial Crown corporation communication strategies cut
competitors out of decision making, concerned Anishinabeg never accepted,
and in fact rejected, government-led initiatives to redefine Anishinaabe
space for the benefit of HEPCO.

Hydroelectric Development and the Arrival of HEPCO

Industrialists were first attracted to the north shore of Lake of the Woods in
the 1910s and in 1920 the Province of Ontario granted Edward Wellington
Backus, an American financier, timber rights along the English River.[4] In addition to timber rights, Beniah Bowman, minister of lands and forests, granted Backus "a lease of the water power known as the White Dog Rapids on
the Winnipeg River" and "all water power privileges . . . which the Minister
. . . may deem expedient for the utilization of the waters . . . for power purposes."[5] Premier of Ontario Ernest Charles Drury, lambasted for facilitating
the lease, was soon enveloped in scandal.[6] Such terms could have enabled
Backus to develop a hydroelectric generating station on the Winnipeg River with limited public consultation. Instead of developing this site, Backus
purchased the Norman Dam from the Keewatin Power Company and constructed a power station at the western outlet of Lake of the Woods. He also
purchased the Kenora Powerhouse from the Town of Kenora. With provin-
cially sanctioned access to wood and water, Backus began construction of
a pulp-and-paper mill in 1922. Almost 2,000 able-bodied men poured into
Kenora seeking employment.[7]

But it was not to last. Provincial grants did not protect Backus from the
stock market crash of 1929, and his company fell into receivership in 1932.[8]
The Great Depression stymied industrial development. Mill operations
slowed as the demand for newsprint fell in the 1930s. Industrial demands
for electricity declined in turn. In his self-published memoir, *Oatmeal and
Eaton's Catalog*, Ken Collins of Dryden, Ontario, claimed that at his mill
"every square foot of space . . . became storage areas filled with unsold paper
products."[9] Mill operators could meet Kenora's energy demands with electricity generated by the Norman Dam and the Kenora Powerhouse alone.
Canadian energy demands did not increase dramatically for almost a decade.

Then, in 1939, the King Liberals determined that paper production was critical to Canada's war effort. The Ontario-Minnesota Pulp and Paper Company, "an outgrowth of the reorganization of [the] Minnesota and Ontario Paper Company," took over mill operations shortly thereafter.[10] Industry resumed. Technological innovations such as transistor radios and electric wringer washers stimulated new household energy demands, and high employment rates after the Second World War meant that more Canadians had the money to purchase and plug in these electric devices. Historian Doug Owram suggests that "unemployment remained well under 4 per cent through the postwar period." He claims that Canadians born between the "late war and about 1955 or 1956" were the "best-fed" and "best-educated" overall since they belonged to a period of sustained economic growth. Indeed, Owram argues that individuals born during this period expected their standard of living to improve.[11]

HEPCO came to fear power shortages northwest of Marathon and southeast of Kenora as consumer demand on the electrical grid increased. A solution existed in the "underdeveloped" water resources in the Winnipeg River drainage basin. Thomas Henry Hogg, chairman and chief engineer of HEPCO, envisaged major postwar expansion and planned to invest in new generating facilities. The company eyed the White Dog Rapids near the Whitedog Indian Reserve.

Prior to building the Whitedog Falls Generating Station, HEPCO identified competing river users and conducted considerable research on the Winnipeg River with three goals in mind: (1) to determine peak operating levels for a head pond, or reservoir, that would stretch from the Whitedog Falls Generating Station to the Norman Dam, (2) to estimate the damages that established river users might incur as HEPCO raised the Winnipeg River to peak operating levels, and (3) to identify who had a right to compensation for flood damages. The research revealed at least two competing interest groups: the Ontario-Minnesota Pulp and Paper Company and the Anishinabeg. HEPCO would not treat these competitors equally. Whereas it sought to pacify the mill, the largest employer in Kenora, through negotiations, it neglected Anishinaabe families to streamline dam construction and operation. Sam Horton, the former vice-president of Ontario Hydro, told former Chief Allan Luby (Ogemah) in 1992 that "we were too busy building a country to think about the Aboriginal people living on the land

[that] we would be affecting."[12] The treatment of competing interest groups by HEPCO would be determined, in part, by historical research.

The Most Deserving Recipient of Water Power Privileges

HEPCO organized an offensive to protect itself from industrialists who might launch competing, policy-oriented claims to the Winnipeg River. In the spring of 1955, E.T. Ireson of the Generation Department requested that W.S. Campbell, the assistant solicitor, "investigate [land] rights that may be affected" by the Whitedog Falls power site as well as "Crown Leases, Licences of Occupation, Timber and Pulpwood Licences, Mining Claims or Water Power Rights."[13] Research was the first step in identifying competitors.

In response to the request, Campbell launched a fact-finding mission, tracing Crown leases and patented lands. The first two pages of his memorandum appear to be a simple notification of lease and licence types in the immediate area. Indeed, the report is formatted as a numbered list. Point 6, however, breaks the mould: it is not a status notification but a nuanced interpretation of Backus's Whitedog Rapids lease of 1920. The lease—then over thirty years old—made the Ontario-Minnesota Pulp and Paper Company a competitor.

Aware of this threat, counsel drafted a legal argument in Point 6 for the nullification of Backus's lease. Campbell suggested that the water power lease had been tacked on to the Lake of the Woods and English River Pulpwood Limits: water rights were never, counsel implied, one of Backus's genuine interests. Campbell argued that "the White Dog Power Site becomes enormously tangled up with the much greater controversies over . . . timber limits." These conclusions were drawn without consulting the mill. A close reading suggests that "investigative" work was deeply intertwined with HEPCO's larger goal of establishing authority in the Winnipeg River drainage basin. Internal correspondence labelled the mill an "uninterested party."[14] Campbell's memorandum appears to have been circulated within the Generation Department, ensuring that HEPCO employees understood the Ontario-Minnesota Pulp and Paper Company as a mill with timber (not water) interests.

When this position was adopted, HEPCO had yet to receive approval for the Whitedog Falls Generating Station from the Department of Public Works. By presenting the mill as having secondary interest in Whitedog

Figure 13. Contemporary imagining of White Dog Falls, c. 1920 (based on a newspaper clipping dated 11 December 1920).

Rapids, HEPCO positioned itself as the most deserving recipient of "water power privileges." HEPCO claimed primary interest in the site. Employees were versed in counsel's language of primary and secondary interest. This hierarchy of rights was linked to public demand: province-wide consumption had increased from 4,000 kilowatts to 1,558,500 kilowatts between 1910 and 1939.[15]

HEPCO's hierarchy of interest was used to rationalize the redirection of rights-related questions away from the pulp and paper mill. Internal correspondence emphasized that Backus had failed to develop Whitedog Rapids during his leasehold. Counsel presented this failure as evidence of his supposedly limited interest in water. Although the agreement between Backus and Ontario did not specify an expiration date, Campbell argued that "Backus would have lost any rights in the power site through a possible default in carrying out his ... obligations." Campbell urged the Generation Department to confirm default through the Department of Lands and Forests. Campbell suggested that HEPCO had no legal or ethical responsibility to contact the Ontario-Minnesota Pulp and Paper Company: "It seems to me [counsel], it would be primarily the obligation of the Dept. of Lands and Forests to inform the Commission whether or not there still existed any commitments to the Backus interest with regard to this power site."[16]

Conveniently, Ontario as represented by Beniah Bowman, the minister of lands and forests, retained the right to nullify the 1920 agreement.[17] Ireson was instructed to contact the minister "and specifically ask for his assurance that there is no outstanding obligation to the Backus interests or any successors of them [e.g., the Ontario-Minnesota Pulp and Paper Company]." Although both HEPCO and the Department of Lands and Forests served provincial interests, Campbell emphasized that "the Government should give a ruling on this point rather than the Commission's Legal Department."[18]

Ontario revoked Backus's lease and gave HEPCO "water power privileges." With no further right to Whitedog Rapids, the mill could only demand compensation from HEPCO for flooding damages and capital losses. HEPCO ensured site access through legal, non-confrontational routes.

Research not only allowed HEPCO to identify competitors and to establish a hierarchy of interests at Whitedog Rapids but also normalized its claim. General descriptions of the Whitedog Falls Generating Station—circulated as early as 1955—included a brief history of dam development in the drainage basin, particularly at the northern outlets. This history encouraged readers to see water rights as fluid. It began with reference to the "natural discharge" of Lake of the Woods into Darlington and Rideout Bays on the lower Winnipeg River. Nature was the first to control water resources, but control changed hands in 1879 when John Mather, unnamed by HEPCO, developed water power for his sawmill. The anonymous corporate author emphasized that water flowed among users, from nature to Mather to Backus: "Various power plants were progressively built, abandoned and rebuilt by various agencies."[19] Change was presented as the only constant in the drainage basin. The anonymous author inserted HEPCO into this "progressive" pattern. The Ontario-Minnesota Pulp and Paper Company was also part of the progressive pattern, but its interests had faded. Backus had (likely) defaulted on his lease of Whitedog Rapids. The mill's hydro-electric grip on the north shore was presented as impermanent: "The two main presently operating plants . . . are now the property of the Ontario-Minnesota Pulp and Paper Company Limited."[20] The use of "presently" and "now" downplays the mill's right to water resources.

Secrecy and Misdirection

As presented by HEPCO, history dictated change. History was a tool through which to rationalize losses incurred by the Ontario-Minnesota Pulp and Paper Company: "progress" had long demanded that upstarts in the Winnipeg River drainage basin wrest water resources from established users. Water ought to flow from Backus. Such a rationale was critical to dam development: HEPCO predicted that the mill would suffer losses once the Whitedog Falls Generating Station began operations. As early as August 1955, N.E. Tregaskes, a generation engineer, demanded a supplementary study of "lands bordering the Winnipeg [R]iver upstream from Whitedog Island to Norman [D]am at Kenora." Research conducted by the legal department in 1954 had been limited to lands in the vicinity of Whitedog Island. Tregaskes assumed that raised tailwater would "reduce the head of the hydro plants at Kenora by one foot and the Commission will probably have to make compensation in some form for the power so lost."[21]

Tregaskes' use of the phrase "have to" is of particular interest. It suggests that HEPCO had an obligation to pay for environmental change.[22] Employees at HEPCO knew that it could not jeopardize mill operations. Damages could be rationalized—political threats could be neutralized—if the pulp and paper mill accepted HEPCO's compensatory scheme. "Energy returns" were presented as one possible form of compensation. Although the modifier "probably" suggests a top-down exchange of hydro services (i.e., energy in recognition of loss), the Tregaskes proposal reveals that HEPCO was swayed by industry. The mill, it seems, retained the right to question HEPCO's operations and had the political clout to demand change in its operations. Secrecy could help to manage industrial outcry before the Whitedog Falls Generating Station began operations.

When HEPCO began conversing with the Ontario-Minnesota Pulp and Paper Company, it withheld damage estimates. Internally, employees detailed how the reservoir for the Whitedog Falls Generating Station would reduce the power potential at the Norman Dam and the Kenora Powerhouse, two generating stations owned by the mill. By September 1955, internal reports confirmed the belief held by Tregaskes that operations at the station would raise tailwaters at the Norman Dam. Design plans indicated that water would back up through Dalles Channel—at Dalles 38C Indian Reserve—and into Darlington and Rideout Bays at the northern outlets of Lake of the Woods.[23]

The increase in water levels would affect the mill in several ways. Its hydroelectric generators depended on the kinetic energy of water dropped from Lake of the Woods into the Winnipeg River. A hydraulic turbine would convert the energy of flowing water into mechanical energy, which in turn would be converted into electricity by a hydroelectric generator.[24] The bigger the drop between Lake of the Woods and the Winnipeg River, the greater the amount of kinetic energy captured by the hydraulic turbine and thus the greater the amount of electricity converted by the hydroelectric generator. By raising tailwaters (or "reducing head") at the Norman Dam, HEPCO jeopardized the mill's ability to independently power pulp and paper production. In September 1955, hydro employees figured that the operation of the Whitedog Falls Generating Station would either stymie paper production or increase demands for energy purchases. HEPCO predicted a change in the division of power in the Winnipeg River drainage basin—just five years prior, HEPCO had purchased power from the mill to service Dryden.[25]

To reduce the impact of the Whitedog Falls Generating Station on mill operations, HEPCO employees imagined how they might provide equivalent energy returns to the mill. Commission Approval 7273 authorized the construction of the Whitedog Falls Generating Station and a circuit

Figure 14. Switchboard and equipment at the Kenora Powerhouse, 1923.

breaker at the Kenora Service Station to incorporate Whitedog Falls into the Northwestern Division. Plans also included "a three-breaker 115 kV station for the supply of the Ontario-Minnesota Paper Co."[26] Although the paper mill may have approved such plans as additional power would facilitate expansion, HEPCO does not appear to have notified mill operators of anticipated damages and the potential compensatory role of this construction.

When HEPCO entered negotiations with the mill in the spring of 1956, its employees did not clearly detail predicted changes to water levels at Rideout and Darlington Bays. Instead, records suggest that they negotiated additional power sales with mill officials. The mill agreed to purchase energy from HEPCO as early as 1958.[27] HEPCO connected the mill to its electric grid and expected energy sales. The mill, in contrast, agreed to purchase additional power to expand operations. Secrecy likely ensured that HEPCO had the mill's support for the Whitedog Falls Generating Station during the early stages of it's development.

HEPCO appears to have withheld information from the mill even after the service agreement was signed in 1956, perhaps because the mill was seen as a political threat. In January 1957, S. Crowley asked the Generation Department to predict "gain in power at Whitedog" and "loss in power at Kenora" at varying water levels. H.M. McFarlane responded. He began his calculations at 1,034 feet (315.16 metres) above sea level—the "natural" level of the Winnipeg River, the level at which the Norman Dam was designed to operate. McFarlane appears to have selected 1,038 feet (316.38 metres) above sea level for experimental purposes. HEPCO's licence of occupation, granted by the Department of Lands and Forests, assumed that Whitedog Falls Generating Station would maintain water around 1,036 feet (315.77 metres) above sea level (the "ordinary high-water mark") in the reservoir.[28] "Gain in power" implied a benefit for HEPCO and referred to improved functionality. "Loss of power" referred to reduced functionality in Kenora, which would have negatively affected power production by the Ontario-Minnesota Pulp and Paper Company (see Table 1).

The study presented the pulp and paper mill as an adversary, not as a business partner. McFarlane discovered that HEPCO would experience improved operational functionality if the mill experienced reduced operational functionality. This adversarial frame made open negotiation (or information sharing) a high-risk activity. HEPCO stood to lose electrical power if the mill pressured the Department of Lands and Forests to maintain clearance levels.

Table 1. Effects of Regulated Water Levels at Minaki on Regional Power Production.

ELEVATION AT MINAKI [FEET]	DISCHARGE (CFS) TOTAL RIVER	DISCHARGE (CFS) PLANT FLOW	GAIN AT WHITEDOG HEAD (FEET)	GAIN AT WHITEDOG HORSE-POWER	LOSS AT KENORA HEAD (FEET)	LOSS AT KENORA HORSE-POWER	NET GAIN IN HORSE-POWER
1,038	10,000	10,000	5.51	5,312	2.40	2,314	2,998
1,037	10,000	10,000	4.46	4,300	1.75	1,687	2,613
1,036	10,000	10,000	3.38	3,258	1.20	1,157	2,101
1,035	10,000	10,000	2.26	2,179	0.75	723	1,456
1,034	10,000	10,000	1.08	1,041	0.36	347	694

Source: "H.M. McFarlane, Memorandum: Whitedog Falls Generating Station: Effects of Regulated Water Levels at Minaki on Power Output at Whitedog Falls Generating Station and on Power Plants at Kenora, 5 March 1957," Whitedog Falls Generating Station, OPG, FP3–10901, Item [65].

McFarlane maintained that "natural" levels (1,034–1,036 feet or 315.16–315.77 metres above sea level) would result in "undesirably low forebay levels at the Whitedog Falls Generating Station."[29]

To ensure optimal functionality, HEPCO needed the Department of Lands and Forests to change clearance levels. It would be easiest to gain clearances from Ontario without competing industrial demands. McFarlane's study presented new clearance levels (1,037–1,038 feet or 316.08–316.38 metres above sea level) as an optimal solution for industry in general. Consider that McFarlane devoted a column to "net gain." At 1,036 feet (315.77 metres) above sea level, for example, generating stations at Kenora would lose 1,157 horsepower; however, the Northwestern Division would gain 2,101 horsepower. Using McFarlane's calculations, HEPCO argued that it could offset losses at Kenora. It would be easiest to argue for the "greater good" of the Winnipeg River drainage basin (think "net gains") if the greatest losers were silenced.

Compensation for Power Lost

In February 1958, the Whitedog Reservoir (or head pond) reached an operating elevation of 1,036–1,037 feet (315.77–316.08 metres) above sea level.[30] As Tregaskes and McFarlane predicted, hydroelectric generation at the Norman Dam and the Kenora Powerhouse declined. The pulp and paper mill tried to adapt to riverine change by increasing the amount of water drawn from Lake of the Woods. It operated at 100 percent turbine gate opening at Norman Dam.[31] However, a 1.24-foot (0.38-metre) reduction in head decreased the commercial efficiency of the powerhouse. Elevated tailwater levels meant that turbines collected insufficient kinetic energy to meet the mill's electrical needs. The mill then purchased additional electricity to supplement power produced by corporate dams. The initiative did not restore operational efficiency.

In 1960, the mill finally approached HEPCO to demand compensation for recurring losses. Despite predicting such losses, HEPCO responded with a call for research. It suggested that engineers had "computed increased tail water elevations" but that further work was necessary to "investigate the actual conditions . . . since the Whitedog headpond was raised to its operating levels."[32] The mill's claim for damages required substantiation.

Throughout the investigation, HEPCO downplayed the causal relation-ship between the Whitedog Reservoir and reduced functionality at the Norman Dam and Kenora Powerhouse. For example, McFarlane suggested that "water levels at the Lake of the Woods plants increased co-incidentally with the increase in Minaki elevations."[33] Language is a slippery thing. The use of "co-incidentally" implies an unexpected meeting of two entities (here the Whitedog Reservoir and the mill's hydroelectric generators). HEPCO wrote chance into its reports, weakening the connection between its oper-ations and the threat that they posed to cost-efficient paper production.

It was under the guise of happenstance that representatives from both companies agreed to meet in March 1960. J. Hamer, the area manager, consented to visit the mill site in Kenora and to tour the Norman Dam and Kenora Powerhouse with W. Leyder. Both Hamer and Leyder sought "a mutually acceptable method of providing replacement power."[34] Yet Hamer had positional advantage during these friendly discussions. HEPCO's use of redirection and secrecy in earlier communications presumably put mill employees (like Leyder) in a position of seeking remedies for incurred damages instead of preventing operational losses.

By June 1960, HEPCO and the pulp and paper mill were prepared to enter a remedial contract. Shortly after Hamer's site visit, the commission "conceded that the tailwater elevation" had been "raised to some extent" by the Whitedog Falls Generating Station. The parties agreed that "replace-ment power would be acceptable ... in lieu of lost head."[35] HEPCO engaged in preliminary engineering discussions with mill officials to "draft" a recom-mendation for replacement power.

Although the language of possibility (e.g., the words *could* and *may*) is laced throughout HEPCO's recommendation, the plan maximizes on the 1958 design for a 115 kilovolt circuit.[36] F.C. Lawson, the assistant director of operations, suggested that replacement power could be supplied to the mill through a tie line. HEPCO later deemed an extra tie line unnecessary: an existing breaker could carry the compensatory load.[37] By keeping the 1958 design (and McFarlane's earlier calculations) internal, HEPCO might have forced the mill into a dependent position but spun this dependency as a sign of cooperation. The commission framed dated designs as creative concessions to the outside world. It is unlikely that this was coincidental.

As early as 1957, McFarlane had submitted a cost-benefit analy-sis confirming that commercially feasible power production at Kenora would cost HEPCO approximately 2,000 horsepower at the Whitedog Falls Generating Station.[38] HEPCO, it appears, raised water levels knowing that remediation would be more lucrative than damage prevention. It is hardly surprising that the Generation Department "recommended that this Commission and the Companies enter into a formal contract to put this agreement [for transfer of replacement power] into effect."[39] HEPCO had been waiting for the opportune time to repurpose its 1958 design.

The pulp and paper mill negotiated with HEPCO from a weak position. Ontario had revoked the mill's right to generate power at Whitedog Rapids. The commission then raised tailwater levels on the Winnipeg River and reduced the amount of power generated at the Norman Dam. Yet federal policies guaranteed that the mill would have a position at the negotiating table. HEPCO could not jeopardize mill functionality when federal policy dictated business expansion and full employment.

In June 1960, the commission suggested that "since this company already continuously purchases from Ontario Hydro at Kenora an amount of power which is in excess of their own generating capacity there, the question of replacing peak power is . . . a minor consideration."[40] But to how much additional energy was the mill entitled? HEPCO distilled the Winnipeg River, a complex fluvial system, into discrete data points to formulate an answer. Theoretically, the energy produced is proportional to head. Whitedog Falls Generating Station impacts the energy output in Kenora by raising the tailwater elevation, which reduces head and, by extension, energy production.[41] HEPCO developed a ratio to infer the energy that *could* have been produced if Whitedog Falls Generating Station did not exist. HEPCO offered to transfer, free of charge, "lost energy"—energy that could not be produced due to environmental modifications—to the mill as a form of compensation.

A few months after HEPCO proposed the ratio to compensate for "lost energy," F.C. Lawson, the assistant director of operations, contacted solicitor Lorne McDonald to prepare a draft agreement for the pulp and paper mill. Lawson explained that "the purpose of the agreement is to provide that Hydro recompense the Ontario-Minnesota Company for the reduced generation at their Norman Dam and Kenora [P]owerhouse due to raised [tailwater] elevations." Although the mill had long purchased energy from HEPCO, the revised contract was to guarantee that "free power and energy [are] to be the means of recompense." Lawson suggested that "free energy" be determined monthly. More specifically, he recommended that losses at

Figure 15. Generators at the Backus-Brooks Powerhouse, c. 1925.

the mill "be calculated at the end of [each] month and provided free during the following month."[42]

This program for energy compensation guaranteed regular communication between HEPCO and the mill, a competing riverine user. Regular contact resulted in a mutually beneficial relationship between river users: both the mill and hydro could operate and generate income. Both industries operated for many years to come.

Circumnavigating the Anishinabeg

Unlike its evolving relationship with the pulp and paper mill, HRPCO invested little human capital in establishing regular communication with Anishinaabe river users. Indeed, there was little incentive to do so. Band members at Dalles 38C, One Man Lake, and Whitedog Indian Reserves were political non-entities: they were denied the right to vote until 1960. The Anishinabeg were also suppressed at the local level. They had limited control over governance on the reserve because the federal government determined how band meetings were conducted, who would preside over them, and what constituted a quorum. The Indian Agent could rule that a quorum consisted of himself and the Chief.[43]

Although First Nations now had the right to bring land claims against Canada, oral testimony suggests that the Indian Affairs Branch did not actively communicate this change to band members living in the Winnipeg River drainage basin. Furthermore, many Anishinaabe communities in the area lacked the money to hire legal aid.[44] Because little existed in law to pressure HEPCO into direct consultation with First Nations, it directed questions about reserve lands to Department of Citizenship and Immigration, Indian Affairs Branch.

The Ontario government's denial of First Nations rights to water running through reserves in 1915 and the International Joint Commission's failure to consult with the Anishinabeg two years later had normalized industrial incursions into Anishinaabe territories since the early 1900s.[45] In this context, HEPCO avoided having direct conversations with competing Anishinaabe river users and sought permission from the Indian Affairs Branch. HEPCO's records of written and verbal correspondence with Indian Agents create the impression that the commission fulfilled its obligation to negotiate access to reserve lands.

Consider how HEPCO used a band council resolution (BCR)—acquired from the Whitedog Indian Reserve in June 1956—to change reserve lands in ways that conflicted with Anishinaabe understandings of the agreement. The commission requested a meeting with the Indian Affairs Branch to seek permission to clear an access road 6 miles long by 100 feet wide (approximately 10 kilometres by 30 metres) through the reserve. HEPCO also asked for permission to modify the access road according to ground conditions through this BCR.[46] The commission appears to have extended permission to clear an access road through the Whitedog Indian Reserve to general clearing for the reservoir at both Whitedog and One Man Lake Indian Reserves.

Elder Charlie Fisher considered HEPCO's permissions flawed. He stated that ten families had occupied One Man Lake Indian Reserve in 1956. These families considered themselves independent from the Whitedog Indian Reserve, but they lacked an elected chief to represent their band interests in June 1956. Fisher implied that HEPCO would have needed an additional BCR from One Man Lake Indian Reserve to clear land for the reservoir. But HEPCO could not acquire a resolution under the Indian Act because the reserve did not have an elected council and thus could not achieve a council majority. However, Gordon Cooper, the Indian Agent who presided over the council meeting, was considered the final arbiter of reserve lands.[47] He appears to have fixed HEPCO's categorical problem by allowing Whitedog's band council to speak on behalf of One Man Lake.

Indeed, Cooper—responsible for "set[ting] down how band meetings are to be conducted [and] what notice shall be given"[48]—does not appear to have alerted the ten families living at One Man Lake to HEPCO's meeting call. Nor do records exist to suggest that HEPCO independently sought their attendance. Families from One Man Lake were unaware of the meeting scheduled by Indian Affairs and HEPCO. Representation appears to have been accidental. Fisher explained to attorney Andrew Chapeskie that "I just happen[ed] to be there. I didn't specifically [go] to hear.... I just happened to drop in there." The exclusion of Fisher from the negotiating table—and that of the community that he represented—aggravated social tensions between Whitedog and One Man Lake. Fisher accused Whitedog's Chief and councillors of becoming yes men: "We [band members of One Man Lake] had no dealing with anybody, other than the deal they made at Whitedog, that, to give 'em okays."[49]

However, Whitedog's Chief and council might have been un(der)-informed about the specific content of the resolution. Fisher claimed that Indian Affairs and HEPCO coordinated a single meeting with local Anishinabeg. Council believed that the commission wanted a road. It believed that a road "might help us [Whitedog band members] with our transportation to go and get our groceries in town."[50] It did not anticipate flood damages. HEPCO did not invest substantial energy in developing rapport with the Chief and council. Fisher suggested that this consultation meeting lasted approximately sixty to ninety minutes.[51] Given council's focus on access to town for groceries, it seems unlikely that anticipated environmental changes were explained in full.

Internally, HEPCO deemed prolonged conversations with local Anishinabeg unnecessary. As early as 1955, the Generation Department "[did] not anticipate any trouble in so far as Crown land [was] concerned" since the Department of Citizenship and Immigration, which held reserve lands in trust for the Indians, supported goals for provincial expansion.[52]

HEPCO relied on federal support to begin construction at the Whitedog and One Man Lake Indian Reserves without obtaining signatures from the Chief and council. This oversight went unnoticed until February 1967, when O.E. Johnston, a hydraulic development engineer, noted that "we do not believe any agreement was signed."[53] Despite engaging in the BCR process, HEPCO did not ensure its completion. The commission found an acceptable method to minimize direct engagement with competing Anishinaabe river users: that is, the Indian Agent, a functionary vested with "total authority over reserve land[s]" to ignore (or tacitly allow) development on those lands.[54]

HEPCO also relied on provincial agents to help manage conflicts over Anishinaabe territories. Trapping families understood that Treaty 3 had granted signatories and their descendants the right to continue harvesting activities on unoccupied Crown lands.[55] Families from Dalles 38C Indian Reserve made regular use of lands from the reserve to Rough Rock Lake. HEPCO required access to some of these lands to build a transmission line; however, it did not want to negotiate with trapping families. In September 1955, it applied for right-of-way along a 22.5-kilometre route from "a point on the Canadian National Railway" near Minaki to Whitedog Falls.[56] The Department of Lands and Forests responded with a licence of occupation. Granted in 1955, it included policing rights, a modification to the standard form, which required the approval of Clare E. Mapledorm, the minister of lands and forests. The modified licence allowed HEPCO to police "all unalienated Crown Lands lying within a strip of land 2 miles in width . . . extending from Minaki on the Canadian National [R]ailways to a point in the vicinity of . . . Rough Rock Lake."[57] "Unalienated" did not mean unoccupied.

When the Department of Lands and Forests granted policing power to HEPCO, it gave the commission the right to displace Anishinaabe families from lands protected by Treaty 3. Families living in accordance with Treaty 3 became "trespassers" on their ancestral lands. As early as 1 January 1956, HEPCO had legal authority to remove trespassers from the protected zone.[58] Removal allowed the commission to construct the Whitedog Falls Generating Station without engaging in meaningful conversations about Anishinaabe treaty rights or land use. HEPCO could curtail negotiations by legally removing Anishinaabe competitors from the permit zone.

The possibility of Anishinaabe exclusion from the licensed area is implicit in the commission's internal correspondence about how best to exercise its policing permit. HEPCO did not want to prevent Canadian and American cottagers from accessing their seasonal properties; indeed, the cottage industry generated substantial revenues in the area during the summer. But how could the commission limit Anishinaabe use of the Winnipeg River but continue to attract revenue-generating cottagers? HEPCO explained that "[the road] was never intended to exclude the owners or licensees from use as far as their property."[59] The key word here is *property*. Although there was no explicit racial bar, property owners were most often Anglo-Canadian or Anglo-American.

HEPCO categorized individuals without ownership papers—such as Anishinaabe trappers—as the "public," "squatters," or "undesirables."[60] O.E. Johnston recommended that "the public should not be allowed to use the road except by special permission."[61] The permission process made it difficult for Anishinaabe trappers to qualify for entry because it required all members of the public to have insurance. Under the Indian Act, individual band members could not own land on reserves. All property was held in trust by the Crown. Without property, individual band members struggled to register for home and contents insurance. Given that foot and boat travel were the most common from reserve to town, neighbouring communities, or harvesting areas, it is unlikely that the Anishinabeg held vehicle insurance.

Should an Anishinaabe person qualify for insurance, he or she would have struggled to harvest fur-bearing animals from ancestral grounds: Clause 6 of HEPCO's application form read "I undertake that I shall not transport . . . firearms . . . in my vehicle when using said road." More problematically, individuals might have been barred from walking their traplines. Clause 6 specified "nor shall I drive into any camp area but shall restrict my operations to the road system proper."[62] The permission process thus disincentivized Anishinaabe use of the policed zone. If a permit was granted, economic use would have been complicated.

In 1959, HEPCO revealed that policing rights had been secured "to keep unauthorized and undesirable persons away from the road and station during the period of construction."[63] Given the association of "desirable" with "property," the statement was heavily racialized. The commission acquired policing rights to keep "undesirable"—uninsured, unpropertied, likely Anishinabeg—"persons away from the road." Spatial barriers further reduced Anishinaabe opportunities for on-the-ground negotiations with HEPCO. It became difficult for the Anishinabeg, as "trespassers" who could be forcibly removed from off-reserve lands, to discuss land use.

Land access was critical to Anishinaabe negotiations with HEPCO because it allowed the Anishinabeg to engage in face-to-face conversations with commission employees. Elders described these encounters as critical to knowledge development in a legal environment that allowed HEPCO to bypass band members and communicate instead with the Department of Citizenship and Immigration, Indian Affairs Branch. Elder Jacob Lindsay of Dalles 38C, born in 1930, implied that developers rarely shared plans with band members. To elucidate his point, Lindsay selected the blasting of the Dalles Channel in the 1950s as an example. This environmental modification predated construction of the Whitedog Falls Generating Station by five years. Lindsay "just heard about it." He "was not aware of anything being promised or compensated."[64] Elder Willie Cobiness learned about blasting at Dalles 38C through a meeting at Rat Portage Indian Reserve. He claimed that "the Indians were told [about the blasting] by Frank Edwards, the Indian Agent who was in charge of everything." They appear to have been promised houses, "but nothing was ever given to the Indians." Cobiness believed that "the Indians were misled (giionimaawag Anishinabeg)" and that "it was all done for nothing.[65]

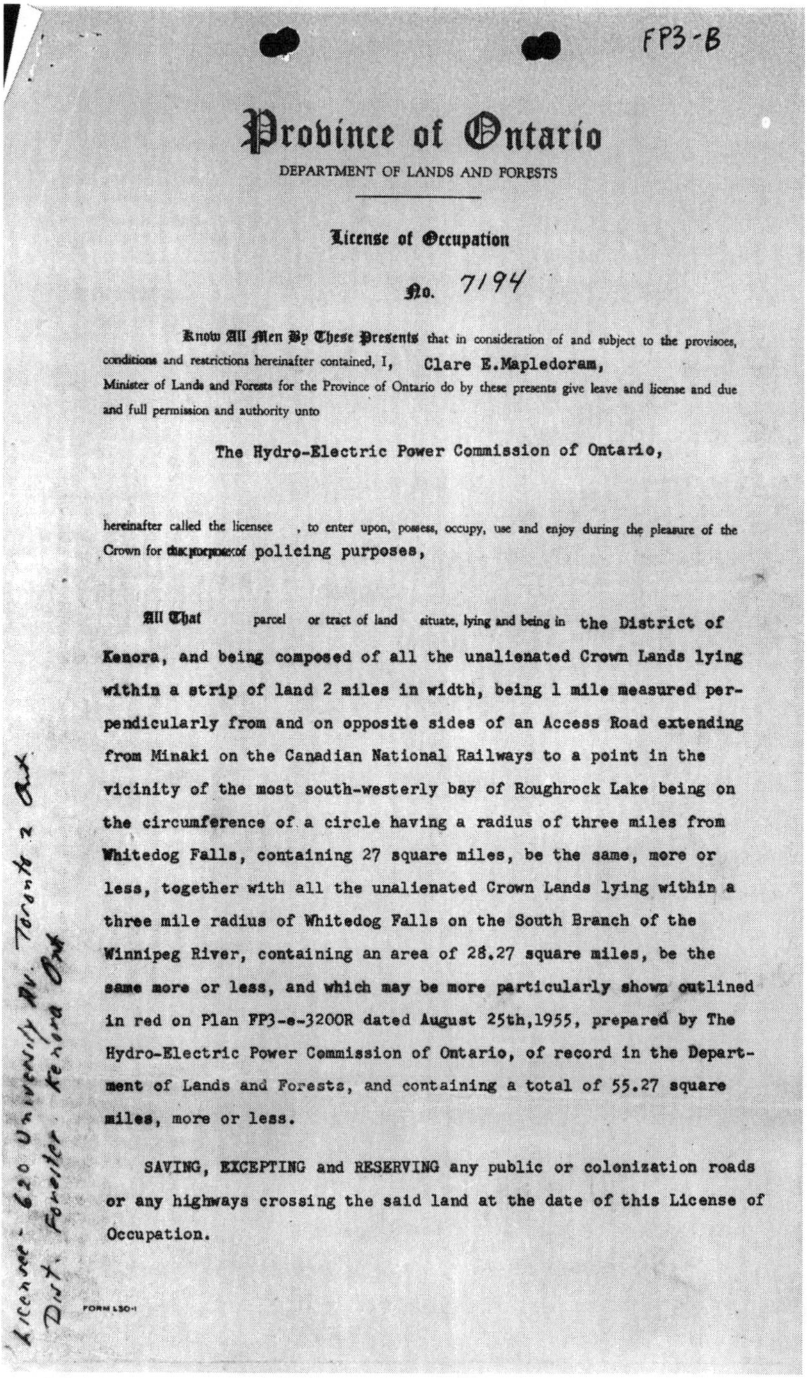

FP3-B

Province of Ontario

DEPARTMENT OF LANDS AND FORESTS

License of Occupation

No. 7194

Know All Men By These Presents that in consideration of and subject to the provisoes, conditions and restrictions hereinafter contained, I,   Clare E.Mapledoram, Minister of Lands and Forests for the Province of Ontario do by these presents give leave and license and due and full permission and authority unto

The Hydro-Electric Power Commission of Ontario,

hereinafter called the licensee   , to enter upon, possess, occupy, use and enjoy during the pleasure of the Crown for the purpose of policing purposes,

All That   parcel   or tract of land   situate, lying and being in   the District of Kenora, and being composed of all the unalienated Crown Lands lying within a strip of land 2 miles in width, being 1 mile measured perpendicularly from and on opposite sides of an Access Road extending from Minaki on the Canadian National Railways to a point in the vicinity of the most south-westerly bay of Roughrock Lake being on the circumference of a circle having a radius of three miles from Whitedog Falls, containing 27 square miles, be the same, more or less, together with all the unalienated Crown Lands lying within a three mile radius of Whitedog Falls on the South Branch of the Winnipeg River, containing an area of 28.27 square miles, be the same more or less, and which may be more particularly shown outlined in red on Plan FP3-e-3200R dated August 25th,1955, prepared by The Hydro-Electric Power Commission of Ontario, of record in the Department of Lands and Forests, and containing a total of 55.27 square miles, more or less.

SAVING, EXCEPTING and RESERVING any public or colonization roads or any highways crossing the said land at the date of this License of Occupation.

FORM LSO-1

Licensee - 620 University Av. Toronto 2 Ont
Dist. Forester Kenora Ont

Figure 16. Licence of occupation, 1956.

Elder Charlie Fisher learned that HEPCO would modify his community through informal discussions with company labourers: "They [hydro workers] didn't cut the trees down [at my father's place], they wanted to see how high the water was going to come up."[66] Fisher learned that hydro workers expected the water to rise by talking about which trees were to be cut and why. Anishinaabe men and women learned about construction details through face-to-face contact. Given limited outreach by white-collar staff, Anishinaabe men and women relayed their concerns to low-level employees during these conversations. On-the-ground communication between band members and labourers thus became the most accessible (and most frequent) regarding environmental modifications. Low literacy rates and educational barriers on reserves increased the importance of these face-to-face interactions with hydro labourers. Although these conversations were not necessarily effective, they are important because they happened, not because the Anishinabeg reached their objectives.

Indeed, unlike the Ontario-Minnesota Pulp and Paper Company, the Anishinabeg failed to establish a feedback loop with HEPCO. At times, hydro labourers (much like their superiors) refused to engage in meaningful dialogues with band members. Attorney Andrew Chapeskie asked Elder Charlie Fisher, "Did you have any conversation with the guys who were slashing around One Man Lake?" Fisher responded in the negative: "No, because they were always busy." Yet he pushed back when labourers tried to shut down conversation. Face-to-face contact allowed Fisher to challenge the perceived barrier of lack of interest. "We tried," he maintained.[67] Sustained attempts at communication occasionally resulted in altercations. For example, when HEPCO allocated funds to move families from One Man Lake to Whitedog to protect them from flooding, Fisher attempted to negotiate an alternative. He approached a hydro employee and proposed moving the former reserve to higher ground. The employee—who likely lacked the power to enact change—refused to hear Fisher's proposal. Conversation shut down when the employee asserted, "All you guys [Anishinabeg] just have to fuck off and that's it—no more."[68] During construction, then, physical proximity ensured that Anishinaabe families were heard—even if their utterances were rejected or ignored by HEPCO employees.

In June 1958, with the construction of the Whitedog Falls Generating Station complete, communication between the Anishinabeg and hydro labourers declined significantly. HEPCO developed a site management plan that reduced opportunities for dialogue with Anishinaabe competitors. Although the commission operated few remote-controlled dams in the 1950s, the Whitedog Falls station was designed to be "controlled from Kenora, with no resident attendants."[69] A 1956 filing memorandum revealed that the decision was a "great departure from normal operating procedure."[70] To facilitate the decision, the commission allocated money to maintain a "minimum costs jeep type road."[71] Fisher suggested that HEPCO also used such roads to transport materials from Kenora to dam sites.[72] After 1958, road maintenance allowed for twenty-four-hour access to the dam in emergency situations.

New operating procedures meant that HEPCO had only a transitory presence at the Whitedog Falls Generating Station. Headquarters recommended visits (for site checks), rather than a fully attended station, because it was difficult to secure "satisfactory personnel for the plant."[73] Once the dam was completed, the commission dismantled the work camp and evacuated employees who had shared ground with Anishinaabe families living along the Winnipeg River. Given that Whitedog and One Man Lake Indian Reserves were the largest population centres near the station, "satisfactory" implies non-Indigenous labourers. A refusal to hire Anishinaabe men or women reduced opportunities for sustained communication between band members and HEPCO.

Anishinaabe Responses

Unable to sustain face-to-face contact with HEPCO, Anishinaabe families living on Whitedog and One Man Lake Indian Reserves attempted to overcome environmental barriers to communication by filing a damage claim through the Indian Affairs Branch. The first recorded claim was submitted in 1959, just one year after HEPCO dismantled its construction camp and began remote operation.[74] In the submission, band members claimed over $260,000 in damages to their "wild rice, harvesting, fishing, [and] hunting" grounds.[75]

This shift from on-site verbal complaints to the submission of written complaints through an intermediary was an adaptive strategy. Many band members did not trust Indian Agents. Elder Charlie Fisher, for example, levelled insults at the Chief and council of Whitedog for participating in federally directed band meetings. Prior to 1959, band members were most likely to express their discontent on the ground and without supervision by

Indian Affairs. Increased reliance on Indian Affairs in 1959 was intended
to protect an otherwise diminishing homeland.

A few years later, in 1963, Anishinabeg continued to use intermediaries
to launch complaints against HEPCO. Intermediaries remained necessary
as the commission communicated with residents of Ontario through letters
and service announcements. Its standards of communication (particularly
written communication) put the Anishinabeg, who were not well served
by the education system, at a severe disadvantage. Captain Frank Edwards,
an Indian Agent at Kenora, bemoaned the quality of education provided to
Anishinaabe children as early as the 1920s. In 1926, Edwards challenged
the use of the word *training* as a descriptor for Indigenous education and
suggested that Anishinaabe children received, at best, "casual attention."[76]
A decade later, in 1938, he suggested that "academic training" was useless
in a society that refused to incorporate Indigenous graduates and suggested
that Indigenous youth "be given a School training that would enable them
to make a living and business out of natural resources."[77]

These casually attended youth were the fully grown band members
seeking recompense in 1963. Perhaps their Indian Agent, Eric Law, contacted
William Moore Benedickson, the Liberal MP for Rainy River, to follow up
on damage claims that year. Benedickson inquired about "a damage claim
by the Indians of Islington [Whitedog] Reserve No. 29 and One Man Lake
No. 29."[78] His query prompted a letter exchange among HEPCO's engineering, property, and legal divisions. Benedickson successfully breached the
communication barriers in the commission. His query resulted in a flurry
of activity, including a memorandum from the chairman of HEPCO. It did
not, however, produce the desired outcome: dialogue and recompense.

Instead, HEPCO used the written word to justify its actions on and off
reserve. First, the commission implicated Indian Affairs in any failure.
The deputy director of property argued that "negotiations were carried on
. . . to arrange proper compensation for rights." He further claimed that
"an agreement was reached with the Indians [in 1956] and approved by
the Department of Citizenship and Immigration."[79] HEPCO claimed to
have participated in the federal permission process and made it clear that
federal agents had sanctioned development on Indigenous lands. In 1956,
presumably, the commission had been unable to estimate the amount of land
required for an access road, the amount of fill needed for the rock dam, and
so on. HEPCO had promised, however, to settle with Whitedog and One

Man Lake Indian Reserves "when the surveys had been completed" and "proper compensation" calculated.[80]

In 1961, HEPCO appears unilaterally to have "compute[d] the amount of the damages" and sent a cheque of $20,310 to "the Indians through the Government at Ottawa."[81] The Indian Affairs Branch appears to have accepted a cheque valued at a twelfth of the damages estimated by band members themselves. Also, by accepting HEPCO's cheque, Indian Affairs suggested that "proper compensation" need not consider ricing or trapping. Throughout the commission's response, Indian Affairs was constructed as an informed partner. Earlier written documents—band council resolutions and cheques—were likely listed to end the discussion. Written evidence of Indian Affairs cooperation seems to have curtailed conversation about access (and subsequent damages) to reserve lands.

Second, HEPCO turned to provincial documents to further counter damage claims. Hydro employees—such as the deputy director of property—emphasized that fishing and ricing damages had occurred off reserve, "that is to say on Crown Lands under the jurisdiction of the Ontario Government."[82] The deputy director appears to have mimicked General Counsel Lorne McDonald's position on the 1959 claim: the commission is not liable for "losses off of the actual reserves." McDonald noted that the Department of Lands and Forests, a branch of the Ontario government, granted trapping and fishing licences to local Anishinabeg. Under Ontario's licensing system, "the law [is such that] Indians take conditions as they find them." McDonald emphasized that the Anishinabeg had "no proprietary interest" in their traplines or fishing grounds; Ontario strictly granted use.[83] Issued licences were invoked to argue that local Anishinabeg could launch "no claim in law against the Commission." Indian Affairs initially countered that Treaty 3 protected Anishinaabe "right[s] to pursue their avocations of hunting and fishing throughout the tract surrendered," thus entitling them to compensation.[84] According to the deputy director of property, however, Indian Affairs had issued no formal response to McDonald's opinion in 1961. Implicit here is the suggestion that Benedickson—pursuing an issue dropped in 1961—ought to interrogate the Department of Citizenship and Immigration. HEPCO had a document collection suggesting that negotiations had occurred to the satisfaction of the government of Canada. Anishinaabe damage claims, the commission argued, had no legal backing. Further dialogue was refused on these grounds.

Anishinaabe exclusion from meaningful conversations about hydro-electric development exacerbated poverty on reserves historically, but its effects are still felt today. Elder Terry Greene from Dalles 38C associates dam development with contemporary economic inequities: the downstream dam, the Whitedog Falls Generating Station, "makes money, but it destroys this. It destroys the land . . . our way of life . . . our way of living." Greene has not abandoned the fight of his people for recognition and recompense. To build a better future, he says, "we need to educate our youth to stand up for our rights. . . . Once non-Native people get a chunk of land, they think they own it forever and ever. The Creator doesn't look at it like that." Greene is waiting for a new generation of hydro developers to negotiate fair use under treaty rather than provincial and federal laws.[85] Anishinaabe youth are being prepared for a future that addresses historical wrongs through inclusion in decision making.

CHAPTER 4

LABOURING TO KEEP THE RESERVE ALIVE

When he was a young boy in the early 1950s, Elder Larry Kabestra over-heard conversations between his mother and father about life on the re-serve, murmurings of the economic challenges that his community faced. He heard that tourists liked "Indian" guides but that business owners did not want to hire them. He heard that game wardens made it difficult to feed the family because they did not recognize treaty law and demanded that Anishinaabe hunters apply for provincial licences. Larry heard his father, Robert, say that he believed that he could find other ways to earn some *zhooniyaa*. The Hydro-Electric Power Company of Ontario had recently moved equipment into the territory. They would surely need men to drive it. Larry beamed. He knew that his father could drive—a boat at least. Larry had seen him navigate the rapids near Dalles 38C Indian Reserve. He had seen his father manoeuvre around boulders in Poplar Portage. Larry hoped that his father was right about HEPCO needing help. If Robert was driving in the bush near home, he might even get home for supper.

As HEPCO set its sights on expanding operations into the upper Winnipeg River drainage basin and encroached on Anishinaabe territory, residents of Kenora also prepared for the promised industrial boom. James George White, MPP for Kenora–Rainy River from 1948 to 1951, advocated for the electrification of rural districts.[1] The *Kenora Miner and News* encouraged readers to support White, suggesting that "hydro brings [the] development of communities and the added business of appliances in the new resorts and private camps."[2] Citing an American study, the editorial team suggested that new industry could put an additional $360,000 per year into local circulation.[3] HEPCO, residents of Kenora were encouraged to believe, would create jobs in energy production and thus stimulate retail business.

By December 1950, White had achieved his goal of having sections of his riding electrified. The *Kenora Miner and News* announced that hydro power had been "assured for the Kenora district, either through a possible development at Boundary Falls, or [through] a hook-up with the Thunder Bay circuit through Dryden and Atikoken."[4] When HEPCO began building the Caribou Falls Generating Station on the English River and the Whitedog Falls Generating Station on the Winnipeg River, both within a sixty-five-kilometre radius of Kenora, the postwar economic boom finally arrived. However, there was no guarantee that hydroelectric development would benefit First Nations.

HEPCO's presence, Anishinaabe families argued, could be a blessing or a curse to their communities.[5] Some Anishinaabe families adopted an isolationist stance when it came to industry. Others took up jobs at the generating stations in the 1950s in the hope that their earnings would support year-round life on reserves during an era when band members were often forced to leave in search of employment. Despite working for the commission, Anishinaabe labourers objected to the expropriation of their lands and attached higher value to work for pay than their wages. Paid employment helped to maintain year-round occupancy on reserves, reinforce family bonds, and by extension strengthen their communities. Their paid labour was in response to limited economic opportunities (aggravated, ironically, by riverine modifications), but it also represented a vision of a future in which Anishinaabe labourers could ensure the socio-economic stability of reserve life. Unfortunately, HEPCO made no attempt to hire general Anishinaabe labourers over the long term, nor was it legally required to do so. Consequently, the dream collapsed.[6]

Declining Food Security and Employment Opportunities

On-reserve underemployment and limited infrastructure created incentives for Anishinaabe men to work for pay in the 1950s. For example, Dalles 38C, One Man Lake, and Whitedog Indian Reserves lacked road, water, and sewage infrastructure that might have stimulated maintenance work. Sources of employment were slim. Many able-bodied Anishinaabe men accepted seasonal jobs as fishing guides for American and Canadian tourists. Indeed, Captain Frank Edwards, the Indian Agent of the Kenora and Savanne Agencies from 1920 to 1948, identified guiding as a "main occupation" among his wards.[7] But opportunities for paid employment as fishing guides were short-lived. Employment peaked between May and September (or between Victoria Day and Labour Day).

Anishinaabe visibility in the guiding business was tied to market demand. Edwards claimed that few entrepreneurs wanted to hire Anishinaabe labourers, but tourists demanded that they do so: "Most camps prefer to hire white men, although the Tourists like to have Indian guides."[8] Consumer preferences even led some camps—such as the CPR's Devil's Gap camp near Rat Portage Indian Reserve—to hire "Indians almost exclusively for this purpose."[9] Newspaper reports and magazine articles published across North America had increased vacationers' interest in the region, particularly Lake of the Woods. Tourists imagined lakes brimming with prize-winning fish.[10] Although visitors demanded access to Indigenous knowledge of nearby fishing grounds, seasonal demands for Anishinaabe labour did little to counter discriminatory hiring practices year-round (or within the tourism industry itself). Anishinaabe labourers were siloed into guiding jobs that ended with the tourist season. Seasonal pay created an incentive for Anishinaabe labourers to seek contracts in other industries. For this reason, some Anishinaabe families saw the arrival of HEPCO as an opportunity to earn year-round pay.[11]

Anishinaabe women also found waged work at tourist camps as domestic labourers. This was not unique to the region; Indigenous girls were trained as domestic helpers through federally funded residential schools across Canada.[12] Elder Helen Everson of Shoal Lake Indian Reserve, born in 1908, indicated that employment opportunities for Anishinaabe domestic workers peaked during the tourist season, from May to October.[13] When she was in her early twenties, Hattie Martin, a non–status Indian woman from Kenora, found work as a cleaner and cook at the Flag Island Resort (c.

Figure 17. Anishinaabe fishing guide with patrons.
Figure 18. CPR's Devil's Gap camp, Kenora, Ontario, c. 1925.

1933) on the Minnesota side of Lake of the Woods. The employee-employer agreement required that she travel approximately thirty-two kilometres from Flag Island Resort to clean at Portage Bay Camp. As a condition of her employment, Martin moved from Kenora to Northwest Angle, Lake of the Woods, for the tourist season.[14]

Anishinaabe women without camp employment produced handicrafts to sell to tourists during the summer months. Hattie Martin's mother, Matilda (Ogimaamaashiik), started to make moccasins with floral motifs to sell to "white people" in the early 1900s. By mid-century, however, handiwork generated less revenue in Kenora than in more densely populated regions in eastern Canada.[15] Ogimaamaashiik similarly remembered being unable to demand more than $2.50 for her beadwork as a young woman (c. 1900). For Anishinaabe women, waged work in the tourist industry—and income generated in spin-off industries such as handicraft production—were limited.

During the fall, many guides and domestic workers returned to their home reserves. Most Anishinaabe families living at Dalles 38C maintained at least two homes. Summer housing was often located near the shores of the Winnipeg River, where it was easier for women and children to maintain subsistence gardens. These gardens were required to supplement meagre seasonal wages from guiding or cleaning. Everson revealed that planting occurred after the muskrat-trapping season (April–May).[16] Planted gardens averaged about half an acre. Elder Charlie Fisher of One Man Lake stated that "everyone had a garden" during his growing-up years.[17] Families planted carrots, potatoes, onions, pumpkins, and corn for household consumption. Elder James Redsky of Shoal Lake , born in 1899, explained that "none of the vegetables were sold; they were all put away in a deep hole in the ground. ... Corn was braided on stems and hung up to dry."[18] Guides and domestic workers likely returned to their summer homes to help harvest and preserve the garden produce that would feed them during the off-season.[19]

After the harvest, many families left their riverside homes and moved inland so that able-bodied men could cut wood. Elder David Wagamese remembers moving from the river to the interior of Dalles 38C throughout his youth. Elder Larry Kabestra of Dalles 38C confirmed this migration pattern. He testified that "there was a [winter] community" occupied primarily by Anishinaabe men cutting wood and pulp and their families. Larry remembered at least seven families who actively logged on the reserve in the 1950s. Neither Larry nor Wagamese could name his father's employer.[20]

Edwards, however, reported that at least some men "[got] jobs cutting wood and freighting wood for the trading and mining companies" in the 1930s.[21]

Records suggest that Anishinaabe men started logging for pay as early as 1884. There is evidence of Anishinaabe bands "getting out railway ties" from Lake Nipissing southeast of Kenora.[22] What remained constant at Dalles 38C was the style of winter employment, even though the employer changed from year to year as new businesses opened and closed in the area. Winter employment paid off, according to Edwards, who suggested that "some tribes have sustained a very good remuneration from the sale of pulp wood at their Reserves."[23] Although Indigenous loggers did not always receive competitive rates for their timber, wood cutting ensured some pay during the slow winter months.

Water fluctuations at the Norman Dam increased Anishinaabe reliance on waged labour long before HEPCO constructed the Whitedog Falls Generating Station. Prior to 1898, before Ontario used the Norman Dam to regulate lake levels, Crown agents associated manomin harvesting with Anishinaabe independence. In 1868, for example, Treaty Commissioner Simon J. Dawson noted that women's careful management of manomin (and garden produce) meant that Anishinaabe families suffered "not so much from the scarcity of food, although game sometimes fails, as from the want of clothing."[24] Anishinaabe researcher Kathi Avery Kinew found evidence suggesting that manomin harvests declined in direct response to water regulation as early as 1887. The Rollerway Dam (which predated the Norman Dam) at the western outlet of Lake of the Woods raised water levels along the north shore by 0.30 metre. In 1887, Indian Agent George McPherson reported that "the wild rice crop failed in the Lake of the Woods and Shoal Lake rice grounds. In the Lake of the Woods the failure is attributable to the high water in the early part of the summer.... The floods were caused by the damming up of the channel of the Winnipeg River at the foot of the Lake of the Woods [i.e., the western outlet]."[25] Families became increasingly reliant on waged labour after the International Joint Commission issued its recommendations in 1917 for water regulation on Lake of the Woods. Manomin yields declined as a result of these recommendations.[26]

Manomin is highly sensitive to water fluctuations. Avery Kinew and journalist Thomas Pawlick explain that "water depth is one of the main determinants in the growth of wild rice. It affects the amount of sunlight which reaches the plants and, if too high at certain points—such as the

floating leaf stage in June and July—the plant expends all its energy in elon-
gation and does not produce seed. Some plants fail to make it above water
at all and die."[27] Anishinaabe harvesters argue that water levels on Lake of
the Woods must be maintained between 1,058 and 1,059 feet (322.48 and
322.78 metres) above sea level for optimum manomin growth.[28] Records
indicate that at no point between 1951 and 1955—approximately five years
before HEPCO's arrival—were water levels at the Norman Dam regulated
to allow for optimum manomin growth.

Information on water levels between 1945 and 1950 is not readily accessible, but records indicate that Lake of the Woods was kept above 1,059 feet
(322.78 metres) during June and July (the floating leaf stage) from 1941 to
1945.[29] Similar conditions led Edwards to note that, "owing to the raising of
the Lake at the Norman Dam, for commercial purposes, this article of food
is becoming very scarce." As early as 1938, Edwards reported that "there is
no wild rice on the Lake of the Woods proper."[30] With international sanc-
tion, the Norman Dam likely drowned manomin crops to regulate lake
levels after (if not before) 1917. The decline in regional yield would have
affected families at Dalles 38C (and elsewhere on the river) as they intermarried with communities on Lake of the Woods and migrated between
fields. When HEPCO arrived in Anishinaabe territory at mid-century,
Anishinaabe families had been struggling to win both economic and food
security for years. Meagre wages and low manomin yields were common
among band members.[31]

Edwards suggested that the gradual erosion of treaty rights by Ontario
exacerbated the economic challenges (e.g., seasonal underemployment,
inability to manage native crops) faced by Anishinaabe families. Provincial
game laws "made it harder for the Indian" to subsist and prevented families
from using country foods year-round. Edwards reported that poverty could
be managed if they could "put up fish and meat for the winter, as they were
wont to do in bygone days," but "the Ontario Game Laws make this an impos-
sibility."[32] Provincial game laws were not only enacted but also enforced
in the Kenora District. Edwards claimed that the Anishinabeg received
"various convictions ... in the Local Police Court" for trapping violations
during his tenure as Indian Agent.[33] Legal historian Jamie Benidickson indicates that "Ontario pursued prosecutions, notwithstanding legislation that
appeared to respect Aboriginal wildlife interests" in the late 1890s and early
1900s. Benidickson ties prosecution to civilian pressure on the province.

Urban sportsmen and conservationists bemoaned year-round access to
fish and game in rural areas, demanding stricter regulations by government officials.[34] Likewise, Frank Tough suggests that Indigenous hunting
and trapping incomes declined in northern Manitoba in the 1900s because
of competition from white hunters and trappers. They were not sportsmen but worked in the fur trade. Near Churchill, Manitoba, for example,
"the railway and mineral exploration . . . led to an increasing involvement of
white labour in fur production [by the late 1920s]."[35] In Subarctic Canada,
it seems, resource competition (resulting in depleted animal populations)
also contributed to economic decline in Indigenous communities.

Game wardens were "zealous" in and around Kenora. The provincial
crackdown on Anishinaabe trapping included searching *tikinaguns*—cradleboards used by Anishinaabe women—for "illegal" furs during the winter
months. Game wardens searched for "preheated muskrat skins [placed]
around a child's feet in the bottom of the tikinagun."[36] Anishinaabe women
used muskrat skins to keep their children warm on trips to town, but this
child-care practice declined by mid-century as women feared "being hauled
before the magistrate for being caught with an out-of-season pelt."[37] Zealous
officials made it difficult for Anishinaabe families to trap in response to
need. It is no wonder that able-bodied Anishinaabe men sought logging
work during the winter months, for their families might now have required
wages to purchase items that previously were homemade.

Fishing activities on the Winnipeg River do not appear to have been
seriously jeopardized until the Whitedog Falls Generating Station began
operating in 1958. The ability to fish commercially, however, might have
been complicated by preferential licensing. Edwards explained that "few
tribes have commercial licences."[38] Without such a licence, one's ability
to turn a profit was limited: "Fish dealers are not allowed to purchase
from Indians, unless the Indians have a licence."[39] Acquisition of a licence
did not alleviate competition with non-Indigenous fishers for premium
fishing grounds. Competition was fierce in and around reserves. Edwards
complained that "licences are issued to white men to fish in waters, which
are really Indian reserve waters."[40]

Members of Dalles 38C Indian Reserve also faced unexpected competition for territory from the Ontario Fish Hatchery, which opened in the
early 1920s and closed in 1961. Employee testimony reveals that the hatchery set two nets near Dalles Rapids on the Winnipeg River each spring.

Provincial employees netted pickerel at these sites from April or May to June.[41] Biography and oral testimony suggest that the Lindsay family had previously fished in this area.[42] Not only did provincial agents displace Anishinaabe fishers for up to three months per year, but no remuneration was offered to band members for reserve access. In 1938, Edwards complained that "the local fish hatchery takes pickerel spawn from Indian waters (Dalles Reserve) without paying anything to the Indians for it."[43] Waged work, though discriminatory, provided necessary income in an era of increased resource competition, "zealous" game law enforcement, and declining manomin yields.

Unfortunately, the chances of full-time employment in Kenora were slim. Preferential hiring practices made it difficult for Anishinaabe men and women to work in town. Complaints that Kenora-based businesses did not hire Anishinaabe workers date back to the 1930s. Edwards suggested that Anishinaabe pupils graduated from residential school with little hope of employment. Reflecting on high rates of unemployment, he asked, "What effort have we made to assimilate them into our civilization after bringing them up in it?"[44]

Discriminatory hiring practices continued well into the 1960s. One accomplished Indigenous typist simply stated that Kenora businesses "didn't hire Indians."[45] Records of the Mayor's Indian Committee from 1968 indicate that few entrepreneurs responded to municipal requests to establish summer employment programs for Indigenous youth.[46] Anishinaabe complaints concerning discriminatory hiring are substantiated by records from the Ministry of Communication and Social Services. In 1974, the ministry identified Indigenous underemployment as a big problem in Kenora. Racism was the root cause: "Native people are often not considered to be 'good' employees."[47] Writing in 1969, Cree activist Harold Cardinal argued that such race-based hiring bars did, indeed, exist and were endemic across Canada.[48]

The Indian Affairs Branch did little to relieve on-reserve poverty that had been aggravated by discriminatory hiring practices in town, resource competition, low manomin yields, and seasonal underemployment. Federal relief, adhering to the principles of less eligibility, was so meagre that needy Anishinaabe families would rather have worked the lowest-paying jobs than depend on Indian Affairs for support. The 1966 Hawthorn Report revealed that Indian Affairs did not consider relief "the right of any Indian" at mid-century. Instead, relief was to be distributed "at the pleasure of the Branch to prevent suffering."[49]

The sympathy that Edwards displayed for his wards contravened federal norms. Indian Agents in the postwar era found little pleasure in providing relief to able-bodied men.[50] R.A. Hoey, the superintendent of welfare and training, for example, believed that "Indians must turn increasingly to agriculture in an attempt to become more self-supporting and less dependent upon the Government.... [It is] difficult to justify relief allowances on reserves with land available for cultivation and able-bodied Indians available for such work."[51] Difficulty in accessing relief was evident in the Kenora District despite Edwards's concern for Anishinaabe well-being. Elder Larry Kabestra claimed that his father "never depended on welfare." He further explained that "there was no such thing as welfare on this reserve."[52] Elder Alice Kelly (1946–2019) substantiated Larry's claim. She believed that her family garden was essential to survival because "they used to have a hard time to get welfare assistance. They have to work. It was hard for them."[53]

Federal relief distributed in the immediate aftermath of the Second World War was most likely to be distributed in-kind. Policy documents written by Colonel H.M. Jones, the superintendent of the Welfare Division of Indian Affairs, recommended that "relief [be made] payable ... through provision of food, fuel, clothing[, and] household equipment."[54] But even these in-kind payments were restricted "in areas where game and fish are plentiful" or if the applicant was "physically capable of hunting or fishing."[55] This policy did not seriously consider provincial game laws (or, in the Kenora District, provincial competition for fishing grounds). Poverty was widespread on reserves during the first half of the twentieth century; it was a symptom of prejudice as well as government policies that reduced Anishinaabe access to resources.

Working for HEPCO

In response to endemic on-reserve poverty, Robert Kabestra (1920–95) of Dalles 38C Indian Reserve routinely asked his wife, "What are we going to do?"[56] HEPCO provided at least one possible answer: work for pay on the development of the Whitedog Falls Generating Station. Faced with few jobs, limited relief, and complicated harvesting activities, the Anishinabeg turned to dam labour for a chance at economic security. Building the Whitedog Falls and Caribou Falls Generating Stations created an employment boom in Anishinaabe territory. By 1956, HEPCO's surveying team had been joined by approximately 310 men who worked on an all-weather road between Pistol Lake (three kilometres west of Minaki and close to Dalles 38C Indian Reserve) and the Whitedog Falls (four kilometres from Whitedog Indian Reserve).

The same stretch of land (and river) was used by band members. Those from Dalles 38C travelled downstream to witness important life events such as baptisms and to marry.[57] Conversely, those from Whitedog travelled upstream to trade.[58] The two groups also came together at Ena Lake and Corn Lake for berry picking.[59] When Anishinaabe families saw their lands being surveyed and cleared by HEPCO, they saw employment opportunities. Work for pay was available nearby—just a boat ride away from the reserve. This was at a time when people travelled by motorboat, canoe, or foot. The accessibility of employment was a major factor in attracting men to HEPCO construction sites. Paid work with the commission did not require the men to leave their reserves and their families for the tourist season.

The *Kenora Daily Miner and News* published HEPCO's development program in the spring of 1956. The commission emphasized the immensity of the project: over 150,000 horsepower was to be installed in the Northwestern Division. Roads needed to be cleared. Dams needed to be built. And, once the Whitedog Falls and Caribou Falls Generating Stations were installed, transmission lines needed to be erected to carry the electricity. HEPCO broke this immense project down into three mutually dependent units:

Whitedog Falls
Access Road, Camp Construction, Cofferdams and Diversion Channel, Dewatering, Power House

Caribou Falls
Access Road, Preliminary Investigations, Clearing, Cofferdams and Block Dams, Power House

Planning the Construction Job
Sidings, warehouses, accommodation, crushing plants, concrete plants, concrete, placing, mechanic shop, carpenter shop, temporary power

plants, hospitals, schools, cafeteria, commissary, recreation, fire and police protection, office and accounting

Field Engineering
Planning and Cost Control
Safety[60]

This newspaper announcement suggested job availability in both dam work and community construction. Readers could imagine where they might fit in the program. The announcement allowed able-bodied men to envision their contributions to HEPCO.

Anishinaabe men laboured in all three units, but they did not often apply for work in response to newspaper announcements. They heard about jobs through word of mouth and sought employment through kin networks. For example, Elder Bert Fontaine was about eighteen when HEPCO began its expansion project. He needed wages to fund his return to Sagkeeng First Nation from residential school in Kenora (a distance of approximately 220 kilometres). Fontaine explained that, "out of school, you need money, you know." He recollected, "I think it was somebody mentioned there was two dams coming up. So I went to the office."[61] Fontaine applied at HEPCO in response to the local buzz—rather than local reporting—about the project.

Robert Kabestra's situation was different. Robert had completed some schooling at St. Mary's Residential School and was settled at Dalles 38C. He likely hailed from Shoal Lake Indian Reserve but had married Flora McLeod from Dalles 38C in July 1940.[62] The married couple settled along the Winnipeg River, perhaps to be near McLeod's family, and started their own family. It is unlikely that newspaper announcements prompted his job-seeking activities. The announcements page of the *Kenora Daily Miner and News* targeted Kenora proper, Keewatin, and Jaffray Melick— all settler-dominated areas. Robert, it seems, responded to the proximity of hydro work. The idea of approaching HEPCO to secure a temporary contract resulted in his eventual employment.

Having secured a position, Robert worked to "get some of the guys [from Dalles 38C] in there to work." Likely the first link in a chain of reserve workers, he arranged work-for-pay opportunities for family members. Robert first secured employment for relatives of his wife. Larry Kabestra explained that "the McLeods, most of them [got jobs] at Whitedog Dam."[63] Work opportunities snowballed for Anishinaabe men from Dalles 38C in this manner: perform as an individual and then vouch for a relative. In contrast, non-Indigenous labourers relied more on professional networks such as the union dispatch to secure employment.[64] Given that Anishinaabe labour was overwhelmingly seasonal in nature, few able-bodied men were registered to benefit from these professional organizations.

Walk-ins and kin networks functioned as effective job-seeking strategies for Anishinaabe men because HEPCO did not have a rigorous hiring process for general labourers (Anishinabeg or non-Indigenous). Fontaine did not remember a formal interview process. He explained that "you just tell them what you can do, and you do it."[65] His description of this casual hiring process was echoed by other employees. In the postwar era, HEPCO showed greater interest in bodies (male and able) than in credentials for labour jobs.[66] Indeed, the commission expected that labourers would learn by doing. Necessary skills were to be developed on the job. Little time was lost between job application and job performance.[67] The commission's emphasis on learning by doing made it possible for men such as Fontaine and Robert to take on jobs immediately.

Anishinaabe men filled a variety of positions. The earliest available labour job was clearing the bush for roadwork. During the clearing phase, trees were felled. Anishinaabe men might have owned the necessary equipment to participate in the process from pulp-cutting contracts. In this scenario, HEPCO would not have needed to purchase extra equipment to hire extra hands: it made financial sense to employ Anishinaabe men to fell trees. Grubbing—that is, the removal of stumps and debris—followed. Newspaper records indicate that over 300 men were employed for road construction.[68]

Clearing work was also required to help create dam reservoirs. The *Kenora Daily Miner and News* published more specific details about the Caribou Falls Generating Station than the Whitedog Falls Generating Station. Journalists noted that "one unusual aspect of the new development [is] the clearance of some 19,000 acres of land for the headpond" or reservoir. HEPCO needed hands to complete "the most extensive [clearing] operation of its kind ever undertaken by the Commission."[69] Anishinaabe men were likely active in this phase of the project. Elder Charlie Fisher of One Man Lake Indian Reserve complained that the commission hired Anishinaabe men exclusively to fell trees, closing off alternative forms of employment. He also thought that Anishinaabe labour was confined to reserves: "We tried to get [talking about the project], but they just slashed the reserve, cutting

Figure 19. HEPCO shacker's camp, c. 1956.
Figure 20. Clearing work for the Caribou Falls Generating Station, c. 1956.

the trees down. . . . That's all we got to do. Just the reserve part. Other than that, we didn't get any, any jobs."[70] Fisher thought that his job options with HEPCO were heavily restricted: as an Anishinaabe worker, he was confined to felling trees at One Man Lake.

Barriers to Indigenous employment for the two generating stations do not appear to have been universally applied. HEPCO's big project required big machinery. The *Kenora Daily Miner and News* reported that "twenty hired trucks, ten bulldozers, [and] six power shovels [were] working on the road and various types of machinery, such as rubber-tired tractors, all makes and sizes of trucks, jeeps, compressors and equipment to no end[, could] be seen at the campsites."[71] J.A. Sherrett of the Kenora Chamber of Commerce was impressed by the "huge cranes, fifteen ton capacity trucks, bulldozers [and] road graders" being used at the Whitedog Falls Generating Station.[72] Progress reports published by the Kenora newspaper featured cranes and sheep-foot rollers.[73] What is missing from these reports is a description of the drivers. Larry Kabestra claims that his father, Robert, drove trucks for HEPCO.[74] This appears to have been Robert's primary form of employment. Fontaine, in contrast, drove only once, as he explained:

I'll tell you a funny one. One day this boss comes up to me. He says, "Hey, Fontaine, can you drive a big truck?"

Just joking, I says, "Yeah."

"Well, see that big truck over there? Bring it up!"

So I put [it] in gear—and I didn't know the first thing about big trucks. I made it up.[75]

Fontaine's driving experience appears to have been in response to an acute labour shortage; no truck drivers were available on site. Anishinaabe men remember (or are remembered) driving the machines, full time or infrequently, that helped to construct the two generating stations.

Big machinery required maintenance. The *Kenora Daily Miner and News* claimed that "one of the main requirements [of a remote construction project] is to have a machine shop with facilities adequate to handle almost any repair or fabrication jobs imaginable."[76] Importing new equipment was both difficult and costly. Before the access road was completed, equipment had to be shipped to Minaki by train and then barged to the construction site.[77] In this environment, maintenance men were essential to cost management: they helped to ensure continuous operations by repairing equipment on site. HEPCO invested considerable sums of money into building cutting-edge facilities for the mechanics. They were provided with "a fully functioning modern machine shop for all repairs" and had access to the best tools.[78] Fontaine's brother appears to have worked under the mechanical superintendent and was primarily responsible for oiling the cranes. Fontaine, in contrast, worked on smaller machines monitoring the manual oxygen supply for divers. His uncle successfully became a tradesman. He worked as a pipe fitter and plumber at the Caribou Falls Generating Station main camp.[79] He was the most skilled Anishinaabe labourer identified by interviewees.

Machines maintained by Fontaine's brother and driven by Robert remade the Winnipeg and English Rivers. The *Kenora Daily Miner and News* noted that the "road passes through some fairly rough country with numerous rock cuts."[80] Blasting regularly predated construction at many sites in the Canadian Shield, creating a heavy burden of waste. An estimated "188,000 cubic yards of rock" were moved during the construction of Whitedog Falls and Caribou Falls Generating Stations.[81] Fontaine facilitated the disposal of this blasted rock. As he explained, "[I was] spotting these trucks at night, where they dumped—like rock." "'Dump here!'" was a call that Fontaine made on the job.[82]

Once the road was cleared and the dam was constructed, HEPCO needed to transmit electricity to the Kenora Switching Station. Anishinaabe labour was used both to clear ground for the transmission lines and to construct transmission towers. Fontaine worked on a six-man team to "assemble towers for hydro, the hydro line."[83] Most of his workmates were Hungarian immigrants. He appears to have been the only Anishinaabe crew member. Larry Kabestra remembered an Anishinaabe work crew installing transmission towers through Dalles 38C Indian Reserve. He identified none of these crew members by name. Yet Fontaine's and Larry's testimonies uncover an Anishinaabe presence across all units of HEPCO's work program. From clearing bush to maintaining machines, Anishinaabe labourers formed part of the team that helped to construct the generating stations.

Figure 21. Blasted rock at the Norman Dam site, 16 July 1925.

Living and Working at the Dam Site

Seasonal vagaries complicated jobs worked by Anishinaabe men and non-Indigenous men alike. The majority of less-valued labour jobs, for which Anishinaabe men were primarily hired, occurred outdoors, in a climate that dipped below zero degrees Celsius for up to six months of the year. Bill Miller, who worked with a travelling line maintenance crew in the Northwestern Division in the 1950s, remembered winters so cold that "you'd hear the poplar trees crack."[84] Freezing weather was required to complete certain construction jobs. For example, HEPCO scheduled much of the initial transmission line work during the winter months. The commission needed its crews to work during the winter so that the line could be erected through swampland.[85] Winter work reduced the risk of sinking (and potentially drowning) in bio-silt. Freshwater marshes average 0.3 to 1.8 metres in depth. With the ground frozen, Anishinaabe men could move more freely through the construction site.

Work on the transmission line proceeded in December 1956 as planned: "Roads have been bulldozed through the snow in order to complete the work...before the frost leaves the ground."[86] Winter 1956 was particularly harsh. The average maximum temperature was -12 degrees Celsius, and the average minimum temperature was -22.5 degrees Celsius (without accounting for the wind chill). When line construction began, the bulldozer needed to clear thirty-six centimetres of snow from the ground. By February, an additional thirty-five centimetres had accumulated. A total of seventy-one centimetres was on the ground while Fontaine worked toward line completion. Extreme cold was a workplace reality for many Anishinaabe labourers and their peers. The previous season, even managerial staff acknowledged that hydro crews worked under "extremely difficult conditions" to meet "ready-for-service dates."[87]

Work was both environmentally and physically challenging for general labourers. Shifts could last for up to ten hours per day, and men worked an average of fifty hours per week. Given delays caused by harsh winter conditions in 1956, A. Gusen, a program planning and control engineer, asked R.G. Wykes, a construction engineer, "to [step] up the construction program to advance the in-service date" of the Whitedog Falls Generating Station. Wykes declined to do so. His work crew was already taxed. He explained that the workers were already working fifty-three hours a week. General labourers could be scheduled to work day or night. Wykes indicated that he had a "night shift on the most critical parts."[88] HEPCO officials approved of shift rotations, claiming that maximum production could be achieved by running two ten-hour shifts per day.[89] As a result, construction sites were active "24-hours per day for several days at a time" when concrete was being poured into the dam.[90] Anishinaabe men accepted shifts around the clock. Fontaine recalled spotting trucks at night, and Larry Kabestra remembered his father leaving for work in the mornings.[91]

Many jobs, worked over long hours, were dangerous—even in the summer months. Anishinaabe men regularly worked near open water and, according to some reports, on steep riverbanks.[92] The water below was deep, unusually so, for dam works. The *Kenora Daily Miner and News* noted that "the cofferdams are somewhat unusual in that they are being placed in very deep water."[93]

During the early stages of construction, supervisors lacked sufficient information to describe river conditions accurately to their staff. Engineers struggled to gauge the depth of the Winnipeg River. They experimented with new technologies to sound the river bottom. Eventually, they confirmed that the water was between fifteen and eighteen metres deep at Whitedog Falls.[94] Although HEPCO acknowledged the dangers of dam work, less-valued labourers were provided with limited safety training. Fontaine chuckled when asked to describe safety protocol. He summarized it: "Don't go near the rapids."[95] Safety practices—much like work-related skills—were picked up on the job. The power of water, for example, was reinforced when Fontaine's cousin Clifford fell in. Luckily, "he had a life jacket."[96] This accident showed both water danger and the importance of personal flotation devices. This lesson, however, was not universally shared among staff members.

The *Kenora Daily Miner and News* reported on two drownings between 1955 and 1958. Richard H. Bachmeier, age forty-nine, died at work at the Caribou Falls Generating Station. An anonymous journalist speculated that Bachmeier had fallen off a "spray machine on the upstream side of the dam."[97] Unlike Clifford, Bachmeier had not been fished out of the river, and it is unclear whether he had been wearing a flotation device. Later that year Robert Neil Farling, age thirty-one, "lost his life by drowning at the falls." The report suggested that Farling had died during his leisure time: "His abandoned boat was found on a beach."[98] Although HEPCO was not responsible for its employees after hours, no reference was made to safety provisions for or expectations of staff. Indeed, it seems that individuals developed safety practices (e.g., the use of life jackets) specific to their roles because the commission placed the onus for safety on individual labourers.

This tendency was reinforced when W.I. Clifton of the Accident Prevention Division visited the Whitedog Falls and Caribou Falls Generating Stations to conduct a workplace review. His review might have been prompted by the deaths of Bachmeier and Farling. Clifton recommended, in part, that a "dangerous water" sign be installed.[99] It appears that superiors did not discuss water safety with staff members. Instead, labourers were to acknowledge the sign and act accordingly. By installing signs, the commission transferred responsibility for workplace safety to individual labourers, believing that observant employees could (and should) manage the risks that they faced.

This division of responsibility was further reflected by the distribution of safety awards. HEPCO introduced the awards program in the Northwestern Division in 1952, a few years before construction began at the generating stations. Headquarters developed the program as an incentive to reduce on-the-job injuries, reinforcing once again that employee choices influenced safety outcomes. The award, a plaque, was provided to the "foreman and his crew for having completed a calendar year without a lost time injury." Distribution of the award reinforced that safety was to be ensured from the bottom up. R.M. MacDonald, whose crew received four successive awards (1952–56), reinforced the idea that each worker was responsible for his safety. In his acknowledgement speech, MacDonald "remind[ed] them [his workers] that it was through their efforts that he was able to receive the safety award." Safety, according to HEPCO, was determined more by employees' safe conduct than by the work environment.[100]

Safety norms for dam labourers do not seem to have improved substantively over the next decade. In 1968, when Larry Kabestra began working on the Norman Dam, employees were told to act responsibly. As Larry explained, "that's how you are trained—to be really careful where you step and how you approach the screen." Although the Norman Dam was owned by the Ontario-Minnesota Pulp and Paper Company, not HEPCO, his testimony revealed that employees continued to learn best practices on the job. Larry stated that "you get used to it."[101]

Labourers learned how to move through the site, and confidence increased with exposure. An emphasis on experiential learning is also reflected in the dangers that dam labourers raised. Fontaine, reflecting on Clifford's near drowning, discussed the importance of keeping a safe distance from the water (and of wearing a life jacket).[102] Larry downplayed the risk of drowning and emphasized the threat of being crushed inside the dam. As he explained, "well, to go against that screen—you'd have a hard time getting out of there! Bang [moving his hand to imitate moving water]! You'd be stuck in there."[103] The potential of water to kill was clear to both men, but Larry identified water pressure as the greatest risk, whereas Fontaine focused more on current. Their recollections reflect the onus on the labourer for maintaining his own safety in the energy industry. For undervalued labourers such as Fontaine and Larry, there was no universal safety standard. How general labourers defined and managed risk related directly to their lived experiences.

Employment Objectives and Benefits

There were risks associated with general labour, but the benefits outweighed them. HEPCO offered more than an income opportunity. For youth living away from home, such as Bert Fontaine, the commission provided the wages needed for family reunification. For local labourers such as Robert Kabestra, HEPCO provided the wages needed to subsist on reserves. Anishinaabe families thus attached higher meanings to their jobs.

When Fontaine arrived at the temporary camp near the site of the Caribou Falls Generating Station, geographical isolation meant that municipal services were unavailable. The workers lived in tents.[104] Administrators bemoaned staff conditions, emphasizing a "lack of accommodation and necessary sanitary facilities to house and feed the estimated man power requirements" during the early stages of development.[105] For many non-Indigenous labourers, moving into these remote work camps meant "leaving friends and family behind."[106] A counter-narrative emerges from Anishinaabe labourers such as Fontaine. Some of his relatives—brothers and cousins— were also in Kenora. He was stationed with his cousin Clifford on the English River. Although Fontaine rarely saw his uncle, he knew that his uncle could be found working at the main camp of the Caribou Falls Generating Station. Fontaine also had family at Whitedog Falls. He explained that "most of my brothers were [working] in Kenora."[107] Two of his brothers worked at the Whitedog Falls Generating Station. The hydro camp provided a space for relatives to reconnect—an alternative to home where familial bonds could be strengthened. For Fontaine, work was valued as a vehicle both for family reunification and to earn money.

For local Anishinaabe labourers such as Robert, working for HEPCO ensured the continuous occupation of reserve lands. Robert believed that labour agreements would help to maintain the territorial integrity of Dalles 38C Indian Reserve. Poor economic conditions had forced band members to leave the reserve in search of seasonal employment (e.g., fishing guides often left from late spring to early fall). Sometimes poor economic conditions resulted in long-term displacements. John Kipling Jr., for example, migrated from Dalles 38C to Winnipeg for waged employment. Kipling later secured a permanent position with the Ontario-Minnesota Pulp and Paper Company in Kenora. His family would not return to Dalles 38C as full-time residents.

The prolonged absence of band members facilitated the claiming of reserve lands by settler-colonists. When band members left Dalles 38C Indian Reserve, they risked losing their ancestral lands. Robert Kabestra, for example, returned from his trapline to discover that a Manitoba cottager had asserted ownership of his summer grounds. Settler-colonists had long taken advantage of seasonal rounds to claim Anishinaabe territories as their own. This practice heightened Robert's fear that prolonged absences by band members would compromise the territorial integrity of Dalles 38C. Paid work with HEPCO, however, allowed Anishinaabe men to occupy reserve lands continuously. If we accept that boundaries are performed, that to occupy space is to claim space, then the performance of daily life, at root, is an act of sovereignty. Robert believed that employment was the most effective means of keeping the reserve alive.[108] Local work had a higher meaning than pay; it was a strategy to protect Anishinaabe homelands.

For a time, paid work with HEPCO allowed Anishinaabe families to subsist on reserves. Larry Kabestra remembered that Anishinaabe labourers made "good money," but documents shared by Ontario Power Generation do not specify how much Anishinaabe labourers earned. They did earn enough income, however, to allow Robert to "coax some of them [band members] to stay, to try to stay," on the reserve and work at the Whitedog Falls Generating Station.[109]

Work also created new opportunities to socialize. Anishinaabe labourers from Dalles 38C worked similar shifts (approximately ten hours per day for up to fifty-three hours per week). As a result of their shared schedules, they began travelling to and from work together. Larry remembered the men from his community piling into the same boat each morning. They travelled, united, to the work site. Bert Fontaine also remembered travel as a communal activity. He and Clifford used to go to work together "on the barge."[110] These journeys, shared daily, created (and later reinforced) a sense of shared purpose: Robert and his team were affirming their territorial grasp on reserve lands, whereas Fontaine and his cousin were financing their return home.

The immediate benefits that Anishinaabe families received from HEPCO depended, in part, on whether they were from the Winnipeg River drainage basin or had been displaced by the Indian Affairs Branch. The commission established camps for its overwhelmingly transient male workforce. Its permanent camp at Whitedog Falls featured a "cafeteria, fire hall, school, hospital, [and] and recreation facilities."[111] Modern, clean, and orderly, it included bowling alleys, pool tables, and movies.[112] Despite these amenities, Kenora residents anticipated that HEPCO workers would become bored, and businesses prepared for them "to come out to the larger shopping centre on occasional weekends" for excitement.[113] Youth such as Fontaine living away from home were more likely to live in and use these built communities because they were unable to commute home. Labourers living on nearby reserves were less likely to use the recreational facilities; their presence at HEPCO campsites was temporary and driven by need, but some Anishinaabe families did purchase groceries from the commission's camp store.[114]

The Fontaine family likely had access to "the huge cafeteria dining room" while on contract. HEPCO committed to providing its labour force with "substantial meals."[115] They were served cafeteria style. Given the heavy caloric demand of labour jobs, meals were carbohydrate and protein heavy. A sample meal included soup, a choice of three kinds of meat, vegetables, gravy, raisin pie, and coffee. The bakery alone produced 1,000 loaves of bread a day.[116] There is no indication, however, that general labourers hired from Dalles 38C were provided with cafeteria access. Given their daily commute to and from the work site, they likely ate meals at home and purchased groceries from local stores. Indeed, local Anishinaabe labourers operated at the periphery of the camp community. Integration and the right to access food and entertainment facilities depended on whether one had lived in the camp.

Men who lived on site discovered a camp divided by class (i.e., education and perceived skill) more than race. When he visited the Whitedog Falls

TEMPORARY CAMP ON WEST SIDE OF FALLS

Figure 22. Camp village at the Caribou Falls Generating Station, c. 1956.

Generating Station, J.A. Sherrett, a representative of the Kenora Chamber of Commerce, was "immediately impressed with the quiet efficiency, orderliness, and immensity of this large power development."[117] HEPCO designated housing according to position. It provided 1,100-square-foot houses to the construction manager, construction superintendent, and field engineer(s). Families with three or more children were provided with 750-square-feet homes, whereas families with fewer than three children lived in trailers.[118] Because the commission hired Anishinaabe labourers for less-valued jobs, no status Indians lived in the big houses at the Whitedog Falls and Caribou Falls Generating Stations. They were more likely to be accommodated with other general workers in tent villages or staff houses.

Employment, even if it was low-ranking, fuelled Anishinaabe visions of socio-economic stability on reserves. Labourers such as Robert Kabestra envisaged a future in which able-bodied men would participate more actively in the wage economy; they hoped for the gift of continual employment. Larry Kabestra, born in 1948, proudly remembered his father working for HEPCO. He recalled band members hard at work: "They were out. They used to be all standing there. They were really [something]—some of them used to build those towers, and they'd climb them."[119] Larry identified Anishinaabe labourers as brave and agile. He identified these characteristics as both masculine and worth emulating. As a child, he learned that able-bodied men could use their strength and agility to earn wages that would protect ancestral lands. Anishinaabe labourers provided the youth with a new vision of masculine work.

As an adult, Larry sought employment with the Department of Lands and Forests. He worked primarily as a firefighter but also cleaned the screens on the Norman Dam. He saw himself as participating in a family tradition at the dam. He walked along a road that his father had blazed. When Larry cleaned the screens, he displayed the same bravery as his forefathers, the linemen, who hung from transmission towers. Larry overlooked the Winnipeg River with nothing more than a rope to prevent his fall.[120] He was not alone in seeking work with the Department of Lands and Forests. He worked alongside his brother Paul. He was also joined by other Anishinaabe youth, such as "[the] Ogemahs. . . . Leo Ogemah, Charlie Ogemah, Fred Ogemah, Langton Ogemah. . . . And . . . Andy White . . . was there with his brothers. . . . Andersons."[121] Larry emphasized that, though not all Anishinaabe labourers worked on the Norman Dam, he had been surrounded by Anishinaabe youth who saw screen cleaning at the dam as valuable, professional work. It was, he suggested, a good job. It was, he suggested, a family tradition.

Collapsing Dreams

HEPCO began to dismantle its labour camps in September 1958. The *Kenora Daily Miner and News* predicted that bustling hydro communities would become "ghost towns" as commission labourers "moved to other projects."[122] Relocation was not a viable option for Anishinaabe labourers who took work for pay to stay on reserves. Men such as Robert Kabestra feared relocation and sought local jobs to prevent land grabs by settler-colonists. HEPCO, however, was determined to provide provincial energy security and was not directly interested in stimulating local employment. The commission and general Anishinaabe labourers had developed, in relative isolation, conflicting long-term goals.

Anishinaabe labour also helped to reshape the river environment. Socio-economic stability on reserves, so earnestly desired by Anishinaabe labourers, was ultimately undermined by environmental changes, which HEPCO had not clearly communicated to band members. It is unlikely that Anishinaabe labourers anticipated the extent of flood damages that their labour facilitated. The Whitedog Falls Generating Station permanently raised water levels upstream on the Winnipeg River, collapsing a fragile subsistence economy at Dalles 38C Indian Reserve. The station compromised already reduced manomin yields between Whitedog Falls and the northern outlet of Lake of the Woods. As early as 1959, One Man Lake and Whitedog Indian Reserves claimed an annual loss of $10,500 in ricing income.[123] Members of Dalles 38C testified that they have been unable to harvest a commercially viable crop from the Winnipeg River for generations. Elder Alice Kelly explained that "the water comes both ways."[124] Water is occasionally released from Lake of the Woods into the Winnipeg River by the Norman Dam, leading to flash flooding downstream (toward the reserve). Unfortunately, the reserve is located upstream—the reservoir side—of the Whitedog Falls Generating Station, which means that water levels have been continuously higher than natural since the mid-1950s.

Carol Lawson, born to John Kipling Jr. in 1937, described declining crops through dietary change. In the late 1940s, when Lawson lived with her grandmother Matilda Martin (Ogimaamaashiik), she remembered eating manomin on almost a daily basis. Her grandmother's pantry was stocked full of manomin, which Lawson promised herself she would never eat as an adult. Thinking back, she stated, "I could eat my words."[125] Since large-scale aquaculture has collapsed on the Winnipeg River, Lawson no longer has the option of stocking her pantry with pounds of manomin. Her consumption of alternative carbohydrates—potatoes, rice, yams—is no longer a matter of choice. In response to flooding, manomin harvesting has become "more of a reason for a weekend outing" than a reliable source of income (or subsistence).[126]

The economic viability of trapping was also compromised by flooding. In former Chief Simon Fobister's words,

> the flooding changed the natural flow, the natural water cycle [near Grassy Narrows Indian Reserve]. For instance, historically, the water levels would go high in the summer and would eventually drop. Then the water would level, and the beavers and the muskrats would build their houses at that certain water level. When it became winter, the water levels would not go up. They [muskrats and beaver] would be safe; their houses would be above water. Although the river would be frozen, the house would remain on top of the ice. And then, when they built these hydro dams, the water cycle was opposite. The water levels would go up in the summer time, and they would increasingly rise in level. So the beavers and muskrats would build their houses at a certain level. But then, in the winter time, water levels would be released upriver, . . . and then the water levels would be going up again—the beaver houses and the muskrat houses would be totally flooded, and the animals would simply drown. That impacted on the income of the trapper, as the beaver population would be destroyed. And the muskrats—there would hardly be any.[127]

Federal adviser Anastasia Shkilnyk reinforced Fobister's report, suggesting that, after the 1958 flooding caused by the Caribou Falls Generating Station, muskrat catches declined and have fluctuated around a much lower average ever since.[128] Even though the price of furs increased in the mid-1960s, income potential failed to stimulate increased catches at Grassy Narrows First

Nation. As Shkilnyk concluded, "muskrat catching never again reached the levels of production recorded on the old reserve."[129]

The collapse of manomin cropping and muskrat trapping on the Winnipeg River confirms historian John Lutz's observation that "Aboriginal people were drawn into . . . paid-work relationships [that] made them unwitting participants in the very process that was transforming and displacing their own communities."[130] Anishinaabe labourers unknowingly helped to modify the river that had sustained their "unemployed" (or seasonally employed) relatives and their ancestors. Anishinaabe labourers unknowingly helped to modify the river that they hoped would sustain their descendants.

The stress placed on the subsistence economy by the Whitedog Falls Generating Station led to unpredictable—and notably diminishing—returns. As both yields and employment opportunities declined, resource competition among band members increased. This competition is evident in at least two competing narratives about Anishinaabe families who worked for HEPCO. According to one tale, Anishinaabe labourers succumbed to "the greediness and the selfishness of the white man."[131] Work-for-pay activities are seen as self- rather than community-motivated. The descendants of Anishinaabe labourers tell an alternative story. Larry, for example, argues that his father was motivated to "keep it [the reserve] alive" by stimulating employment opportunities nearby. Robert did not predict the extensive flooding of his homeland. Larry is pained by how some band members misinterpreted the intentions of Anishinaabe labourers: "Each generation is taught to hate, you know. And why do we do that?"[132] This hatred, Larry believes, is fuelled by the conflation of outcome (i.e., flooding) with process (i.e., work for pay). Hatred is bred from the misinterpretation of Anishinaabe labourers' intentions (i.e., socio-economic stability on the reserve) and community explanations of endemic on-reserve poverty (i.e., collapse of the subsistence economy as well as commercial ricing, trapping, and fishing). It is important, however, to separate process from outcome in telling the history of water development in the Lake of the Woods watershed. An examination of process reveals that Anishinaabe labourers envisioned an alternative future—one in which paid work would facilitate the continuous occupation of reserves.

CHAPTER 5

WASTE ACCUMULATION IN A CHANGED RIVER

Nobody remembered Elder Clarence Henry working at the Norman Dam.[1] Nobody remembered Henry working at the Whitedog Falls Generating Station either. Henry fished. As a child, he likely followed his family onto the river, participating in the sturgeon harvest between May and August. It took a team to successfully bring hooked (or netted) sturgeon to shore—at least four people and two canoes for a grandfather fish. Henry recalled the Winnipeg River teeming with fish and a vibrant reserve community. When a large sturgeon was caught, the entire camp divided the meat.[2] Henry feasted and danced and grew up beside the Jameson, Savage, and Nabish families.

Then, in the 1950s, everything changed. Rapids, once deep and wild, were blasted to widen the Winnipeg River and to relieve flood conditions in Kenora.[3] The Hydro-Electric Power Commission of Ontario started to survey lands near Henry's fishing grounds and incorporated Dalles Channel into its plans for the reservoir of the Whitedog Falls Generating Station. Within twenty years, Henry was catching garbage in his nets and finding sturgeon belly-up on the river. He had never seen anything like it. When he looked for possible explanations, his eyes turned south to Kenora. He saw new subdivisions that pumped human waste into Lake of the Woods, and he knew that the lake drained into the Winnipeg River. He also saw the Ontario-Minnesota Pulp and Paper Company dump industrial waste into Rideout Bay.[4] Waste accumulated between Dalles 38C Indian Reserve and Rideout Bay, but waste disposal alone did not explain declining water quality on the reserve. Water regulation by HEPCO was keeping solid waste suspended in the Winnipeg River. Unless it opened its gates at the Whitedog Falls Generating Station, human and industrial waste had nowhere to go.

In the mid-1950s, Mayor Peter Ratuski and members of the Kenora town council seemed to be blissfully unaware of Henry's garbage-laden nets and the dead fish on the Winnipeg River. During Ratuski's term, Kenora residents celebrated National Electric Week and arranged a speech competition to address how electricity made "life more interesting, more comfortable and pleasant." That water regulation could suspend human and industrial waste near someone's home seemed to be unlikely.[5] Indeed, letters published by the *Kenora Daily Miner and News* suggested that Lake of the Woods carried waste away from municipal intake sites: waterways operated to benefit Kenora residents.[6] Scientific publications acknowledged (albeit discouraged) dilution as an effective waste management system for low-density regions such as Kenora.[7]

The problem, however, lay in Ratuski's and his constituents' definition of community and how town council designed and approved waste systems to serve community needs. Hydroelectric and waste systems were developed to serve Kenora, Norman, and Keewatin. Community boundaries were determined by colonial settlement and industrial production.[8] Unfortunately, social boundaries conflicted with environmental boundaries: Kenora and Dalles 38C Indian Reserve belonged to the same drainage system. Although the two communities (settler and Indigenous) were connected by water, they were disconnected in municipal thought and practice: reserves such as Dalles 38C fell under federal jurisdiction.

In the Winnipeg River drainage basin, as elsewhere, when social boundaries conflicted with environmental boundaries, First Nations suffered. The municipality's failure to consider the natural and managed flows of the Winnipeg River in the development of waste management systems compromised the biological and social health of the community downstream at Dalles 38C. Seemingly rational decisions to facilitate growth and manage waste in town relied on an irrational conception of space that simply relocated pollutants to areas inhabited by the Anishinabeg rather than settler-colonists. What follows is a story about power structures—both hydroelectric and governmental—and the unintended consequences of controlling nature for economic profit.

Waste Management and Riverine Flow

The earliest known written descriptions of the Winnipeg River empha-size the swiftness of unregulated water flow. In the 1790s, explorer David Thompson experienced a "surly" river characterized by "raging rapids and thunderous waterfalls."[9] Years later, when Major Stephen H. Long's men pulled their canoes up onto "perpendicular precipices of granite" to avoid further thrashing by the Winnipeg River, Long mused that "our paddles had a comparatively easy task all day except at one place, where they attempted to paddle up the stream. . . . This place, called the 'Grandes Dalles,' presents the most rapid current against which we have ever seen a canoe paddled. It is a narrow strait, not exceeding forty yards [36.58 metres] in breadth. . . . Great exertions are required on the part of the canoe-men in order to ascend this, and one of the canoes, after two unavailing attempts to stem the current with paddles, was towed up with a line."[10] Community practice among the Anishinabeg likewise indicated a need to manage water risk. Before taking to the waters by boat, Anishinaabe travellers would visit "the sacred rocks where they made offerings for a safe trip."[11]

In the early 1900s, Dalles Rapids appeared on a chart of "Water Powers in Ontario and Manitoba" as a dominion property holding. The anonymous surveyor deemed their potential horsepower "unimportant" but provided information about their shape: they had a 4.5-metre head (the difference in elevation from the peak of the rapids to the base).[12] Although considered of little industrial importance, the wild water impressed itself on Ontario Land Surveyor T.D. Green. In the 1910s, he took notes of the land and water near Dalles 38C Indian Reserve as he produced a map of the Winnipeg River. Green identified Dalles Rapids—relatively unmarked by settler-colonists— as a notable feature of the landscape.[13] Travelogues, ceremonies, charts, and cartographic records memorialized the rapids as wild water, substantiating Henry's testimony that "before this channel was buil[t]. . . . The water was high and flowed rapidly."[14]

The natural flow of Dalles Rapids along a thirteen-kilometre stretch of the Winnipeg River explains the lack of complaint about water quality prior to 1950. Until the mid-twentieth century, this stretch of water near the reserve was in moderate health: the waterway sustained native vegetation and aquatic species despite the continued dumping of human and sawmill wastes by Kenora, Norman, and Keewatin since at least 1879. Aerobic bacteria thrived in the turbulent waters, and naturally occurring rapids helped to aerate the water, providing the oxygen needed for microbial decomposition. Aerobic bacteria used dissolved oxygen to break down organic material dumped into Lake of the Woods and Rideout Bay by settler-colonists. Grandes Dalles thus helped to maintain the equilibrium between oxygen content and organic inputs such as excreta and wood cellulose fibre prior to environmental modifications.

Rapids are caused by varying combinations of gradient, constriction, obstruction, and flow. In 1950, however, the *Kenora Miner and News* reported that Dalles Rapids would be blasted open to relieve flooding conditions in town. Town planners predicted that a wider channel would allow rising waters in Lake of the Woods to flow downstream more quickly, thus reducing urban property damage. On 12 May 1950, an unnamed journalist reported that the "Escape Channel" had been "Blown Open." The rock, the constriction causing the rapids, had been excavated through a draw to create the channel. The new channel was described as "150 feet wide, 1600 feet long and 30 to 40 feet deep."[15] Blasting reduced the difference in head down the channel. Subsequent reports affirmed that blasting had "dramatically changed the current around the community."[16] Although blasting increased the surface area of the water (increasing surface air-to-water contact), total aeration likely decreased with modifications to Dalles Rapids since the churning and spraying of waters ceased. Nevertheless, human and industrial wastes continued to flow downstream, preventing an accumulation of excreta and wood cellulose fibre near Dalles 38C. Until 1955, pollutants flowed into and out of the so-called escape channel.

However, when HEPCO modified the flow through the channel in 1955 with work on its "not-too-secret Whitedog Falls project,"[17] it allowed for an increased buildup of organic material in the Winnipeg River which increased the biological oxygen demand on the system. Unit 1 of the Whitedog Falls Generating Station began operations in February 1958. Unit 2 entered service about one month later, and Unit 3 followed in June 1958. Prior to construction, the Winnipeg River functioned like a drain: water flowed from Lake of the Woods through the river and toward the south arm of Lake Winnipeg. Units 1–3 worked to plug the drain forty-eight kilometres northwest of Kenora.[18] The upper Winnipeg River was no longer a rapidly flowing river, but a reservoir for the Whitedog Falls Generating Station. HEPCO generated power at Whitedog Falls by releasing stored water through the dam machinery before allowing the water to continue its journey toward Lake Winnipeg.

Turning the upper Winnipeg River into a reservoir for hydroelectric power production, however, meant that the Whitedog Falls Generating Station also plugged the escape channel with waste. High organic loading can compromise aquatic life in waterways because bacteria responsible for composting waste demand more oxygen for oxidation and synthesis.[19] Furthermore, damming compromised the seasonal flushing of wastes, whereby the tremendous spring discharge receded to a trickle in the fall and ended with the winter freeze-up.[20] Alongside annual spring discharges, Lake of the Woods was characterized by cyclical flooding prior to both blasting and blocking.[21] By capturing and storing spring flow in Dalles Channel, HEPCO prevented the river from flushing the system and diluting (if not redistributing) waste—both raw sewage and industrial pollutants—from reserve lands and waterways. As waste settled near Dalles 38C Indian Reserve, dissolved oxygen in the system also decreased: microorganisms used available oxygen to consume organic inputs from the mill.

When HEPCO was developing the Whitedog Falls Generating Station, engineers acknowledged the positive correlation between damming and declining water quality.[22] Community members also commented on the relationship. Elder Robert Kabestra explained that "water gets into these bays and doesn't get out—[it's] trapped there."[23] Without oxygen, anaerobic bacteria begin the process of anaerobic decomposition. They produce chemical compounds such as hydrogen sulphide that are toxic to fish, beneficial bacteria, and insects. Because the heat produced is much less than that of aerobic composting, anaerobic decomposition takes longer for organic inputs such as excreta and wood cellulose fibre.[24] River modification, both blasting and damming, reduces the amount of oxygen dissolved by the water and, by extension, the rate of waste stabilization. In reducing oxygen absorption by the river and preventing the flow of wastes downstream, the Whitedog Falls Generating Station unintentionally worked to suspend waste along Dalles 38C.

Figure 23. Contemporary imagining of rapids near the First Falls, c. 1893.
Figure 24. Municipal sewage disposal into Lake of the Woods, c. 1930.

Kenora's Sewage and Waste Problem

But other factors were at play. Prior to the economic growth initiated by dam and mill construction, the *Kenora-Keewatin Daily Miner and News* published the truism that "economic expansion is reflected usually in general community growth, with increases in population, school enrollment, and all the rest."[25] Locals had long associated population growth with industrial expansion, predicting that hydroelectric development would "grow" their town.[26] News reporting thus encouraged the belief in a causal link between power production and urban development.

By the mid-1950s, the population of Kenora had increased as men began construction of the Whitedog Falls Generating Station and families arrived in connection with mill work.[27] Local employment seemed to be guaranteed: in 1957, headlines declared "New MANDO Machine Adds 150 to Local Payroll—250 to Timber Department." Mill-related jobs also cropped up along Kenora's periphery as additional wood requirements promised "jobs for some 50 men in the company's logging camps and provide[d] a market for about 200 extra independent operators and tree farmers."[28] Urban growth mirrored mill expansion, which in turn mirrored hydroelectric development. An economic ecosystem developed in Kenora whereby the growth of one industry (or municipality) depended on the provision of electricity by HEPCO.

The population growth that followed the damming of the Winnipeg River, however, meant that more people were producing not only more paper but also more waste. About a year after the Ontario-Minnesota Pulp and Paper Company announced its expansion program, it was reported that "permits of new dwelling construction for the first seven months of 1956 total 61—a figure equal to the average annual new-house construction of the past several years."[29] By Christmas 1956, three additional new building permits had been issued by the Town of Kenora.

Although locals celebrated the "building boom," the newspaper reported that "the sewage question has become more acute."[30] The question centred on processing human waste that had long been privately disposed, for example through outside privies.[31] The Kenora Chamber of Commerce complained that people were using Laurenson's Creek, particularly "in the vicinity of bridges," to sink "old tires, bicycles and other objects." Originally believed to be the result of child's play, material dragged up by the Department of Public Works revealed that adults were also using local waterways for waste disposal: "Baby carriages—not doll carriages—tires, mattresses, axles, drill steels, as well as lumber slabs and loose rocks [were] removed." As Laurenson's Creek became normalized as a dumping site, waste accumulated on the creek bed, stopping water traffic. Dredging by Public Works allowed for "approximately three feet" of clearance and permitted small boat travel.[32] Although there was no direct reference to excrement, news reporters concluded that many Kenora residents "willful[ly] disregard . . . ordinary safety and cleanliness rules."[33]

The earliest known complaint about private dumping into local waterways was issued in 1893. An anonymous person had "dumped refuse" into Lake of the Woods. Mr. Fletcher, the health inspector for Rat Portage, considered dumping into Lake of the Woods near D.L. Mather's wharf an act of "gross carelessness" since locals consumed water from the area.[34] By 1910, Walter Atkinson was hired by the Town of Kenora to work with H. King, the sanitary inspector. Town records suggest that locals used Lake of the Woods to dispose of their waste—both human and household—at the time. During the summer of 1910, Atkinson was paid to remove a "pig from creek," "a dead dog from lake," "rotten beef and dead fowls from lake," "meat and cats from lake shore," and a "box of rubbish from lake shore."[35] Local use of Lake of the Woods to dispose of waste did not become an acute problem, however, until the population explosion of the 1950s.

In May 1955, Kenora announced a sewer and water project to "solve" some of the waste problems in the Central Park area. Council agreed to lay a sanitary sewer line to serve residents living near Central Park and "residents of Railway Street between 7th and 8th Avenues." Yet no system for sewage treatment was announced. Instead, human wastes were to be picked up and carried to the creek, which in turn would flow through the northern outlets of Lake of the Woods before becoming trapped in the now slow-moving waters of the Dalles Channel.[36] Within six months, pressure from the Ontario Department of Health prompted town council to hold a vote on a more complex three-stage sewage disposal program.[37] The proposed treatment solution serviced only Kenora's higher-density centre and retained dumping practices that moved waste to Dalles Channel: "Stage 1 involves the connecting up a [sic] sewage outfalls in the Creek and carrying the effluent out into fast-moving water in the vicinity of the hospitals, from where it would be carried down the [Winnipeg] [R]iver."[38]

Local resistance to the proposed treatment program was voiced in the *Kenora Daily Miner and News,* but complaints did not include concerns about downstream water quality. Instead, E. Hutchinson argued that "water runs down to the lake carrying the sewage at present. Would not a sewer line connecting existing outlets to the creek . . . laid down to the creek and out to deep water function without a pumping station?"[39] Concerns focused on the cost of establishing a pumping station when the creek appeared to manage waste at limited expense. Resistance, however, was rare. Few residents seemed to question Stage 1. Expressions of pride included the publication of statistics such as the fact that 1,750 of Kenora's 2,500 households had been provided with town-operated water and sewer facilities.[40]

Excreta continued to flow untreated (and in increased quantity) downstream while urban residents lauded "automatic telephones, paved streets, new schools and soon . . . adequate water and sewer systems" as markers of positive growth.[41] Local desires to maximize on the Ontario-Minnesota Pulp and Paper Mill's income potential and quickly to provide quality housing to working families pushed town council to rely on simple, inexpensive systems of aerobic composting long after the socio-environmental conditions that had assured its efficacy had changed. The inability of the Winnipeg River to handle increased municipal inputs became visible in solid waste accumulation. Between 1955 and 1958, Kenora's population grew from 9,813 to 10,538. The average person releases 511 litres of urine per year and 145 kilograms of feces.[42] Had all of Kenora's population been connected to the municipal sewer system, an additional 370,475 litres of urine and an additional 105,125 kilograms of feces would have flowed down the Winnipeg River per year.

Elders from Dalles 38C, about thirteen kilometres downstream from town, did not share in Kenora's celebration of "progressive" waste management. They associated the building boom with suspended solids instead. Henry recalled that "there was so many things we found in our nets—toilet paper for example."[43] Elder Jacob Lindsay also recalled "raw sewage coming down the river—shit, hate to mention the word—as well as 'rubber things' [condoms] snagged in nets." The ubiquity of waste in Dalles Channel led to jokes about urban waste. Lindsay explained that, "when someone caught or snagged 'those things' in the net, we used to laugh at them."[44] Suspension of waste was linked only in part to the slow process of anaerobic composting. While members of Dalles 38C experienced a river unable to process municipal waste, limited communication between town and reserve affirmed urbanites' assumption that dilution worked: waste became "stuck" only once outside municipal boundaries that artificially divided the Winnipeg River drainage basin into settler and Indigenous lands.

Poor Water Quality and Anishinaabe Health Concerns

Dilution as a method of treatment for raw sewage was declining in the 1950s, particularly when outfall caused a nuisance or endangered health.[45] Chemical precipitation, sewage farming, and experimentation with sand filtration existed as accepted alternatives, but municipalities situated along large bodies of water such as Kenora continued to discharge human waste into those waters.[46] The push toward sewage treatment amplified over the years "for the prevention of disease transmission."[47] By the mid-1950s, many Canadian municipalities had adopted "biofiltration and activated sludge type facilities ... and some use [had] been made of sewage lagoons."[48] But dilution—the least preferable form of sewage treatment—had not been professionally condemned for low-density regions, where waste could be "carried away by tide [or wave] action."[49]

By confining "community" to colonial settlements rather than including Anishinaabe settlements and the drainage basin, Kenora's town council appeared to meet industry standards: the Winnipeg River removed waste from high-density regions into Kenora's nether regions. Such a treatment strategy was behind Canadian trends in waste disposal but not condemnable. At a time when Kenora may have dumped in excess of 90,700 kilograms of feces into the Winnipeg River, fewer than half of Ontario residents received partial or full treatment of their sewage.[50] Social boundaries that conflicted with physical geographies allowed town council to serve local citizens to the detriment of "invisible" Anishinaabe neighbours.

Although it was acceptable by general Canadian standards, the accumulation of waste in the upper reach of the Winnipeg River was problematic in the context of local standards for disposal and national practices for drinking water. By 1958, Kenora had moved toward the final stage of its sewage program, and, as the *Kenora Daily Miner and News* reported, a "Portion of Mill Site [Was] Allotted for Sewage Disposal Plant."[51] Engineers ratified a plan to establish a treatment plant with 60 percent purification.[52] The Kenora Chamber of Commerce voiced dissatisfaction with the announced treatment plan, concerned that "40% [waste] will take place in the bay," a site that had become popular for tourists interested in visiting the Ontario-Minnesota Pulp and Paper Mill.[53] The chamber pitched relocation, asking the Town of Kenora to move the plant to "Hospital Bridge [where] the 40% remaining will run directly into the river."[54]

Members of Kenora's business community demanded a treatment program that would remove waste from high-traffic areas. Their relocation plan would not prevent waste from settling in the Winnipeg River and simply allowed waste to follow a northwesterly path that skirted Rideout Bay. The Chamber of Commerce petition sought to preserve mill tours to satisfy tourists in the community. Town council did not demand the full treatment of waste; instead, it asked that waste remain less visible. Pure(r) waters in Rideout Bay were demanded to maintain tourism, not to protect band members. The municipality forged ahead with the mill site, and the amount of waste accumulating at Dalles 38C was higher than would have been deemed acceptable in town.

The quality of drinking water also became a concern, particularly when it was linked to sewage and contamination. Writing about the Great Lakes, Joseph W. Ellms noted as early as 1931 that "the water in the Great Lakes is usually of excellent quality for public water supplies when unpolluted by sewage."[55] Even dilution—though an acceptable treatment solution at the time for human waste—was considered unsafe if drinking water was to be drawn from nearby outfall sites. Ellms noted that "dilution of sewage and trade waste discharges with the purer water of the lake, . . . [though] tending to diminish the concentration of polluting matter, is an uncertain factor of safety, owing to the erratic and irregular diffusion of these discharges."[56]

The risks associated with pollution (industrial and human) included water-borne disease. In the 1950s, for example, substantive debate continued about the transmission of tuberculosis (TB) through waterways, especially those contaminated by sewage. Although TB was known to affect Anishinaabe children who attended federally operated residential schools in town, health officials made no known attempt to associate municipal dumping with summertime exposure to untreated water.[57]

Standards for quality drinking water in the early to mid-twentieth century did not include clarity. As Dr. A.E. Berry, active in the Kenora region throughout the 1950s, explained, "in safe water all bacteria have been killed and do not pose a direct hazard to life. Good quality water contains no sediment discolouration. When I first started that often could be found in safe water . . . but the tests didn't show anything of a hazardous nature, such as cholera or other organisms."[58] By this standard, the accumulation of sawdust upstream of Dalles 38C may not have made water unfit for consumption on the reserve, though urban residents occasionally complained about foreign matter in municipal water supplies.[59] However, the accumulation of toilet paper, "shit," and "rubber things" near the reserve meant that band members were done a great disservice by the municipality, which compromised Anishinaabe water quality and failed to acknowledge (or plan for) the accumulation of waste on reserve lands.

Kenora's lack of interest in Dalles 38C did not reflect a lack of awareness of water-quality issues on the outskirts of town. For instance, residents of Kenora's so-called North End, which extended from 15th to 19th Avenue North, were off the town grid because rocky outcroppings made it impossible for the town to hook North Enders up to its rudimentary water system. Residents without privately owned wells found it necessary to carry water for more than two blocks, and other residents depended on the town to deliver water once a week. Alderman B. Paterson refused North Enders water service, citing the cost of installation "due to the nature of the terrain."[60] Inconveniently located—not tainted—water sources, however, entitled North Enders to a municipally organized truck delivery service. Town council extended this service to TransCanada Pipeline employees whose enclosed village was established near Rideout Bay. In October 1968, M.J.W. German of the Ontario Water Resources Commission confirmed that "unserviced sections of the town receive water by tank truck or from wells."[61]

Redditt, an unorganized settler community north of Dalles 38C, was also considered a region of concern by Kenora residents. Much like the North End, the municipality refused Redditt water services as it was too far from town to be connected. Prior to 1950, the Canadian National Railway (CNR) provided water service to its citizens. When the CNR cut service to Redditt in May 1950, the *Kenora Miner and News* suggested that the railway had committed an injustice, for water service was "beyond the means of the community to provide." Journalists called for the Department of Health to "find some regulation in the statutes" and to mandate a waiting period during which alternative services could be established before cut-off. Limited service was also identified as a "real health menace."[62]

Dalles 38C fell under federal jurisdiction, so Kenora cannot be faulted for failing to consider water provision to it. However, continued dumping of sewage in the context of active service provision to unorganized settler communities suggests an awareness of compromised water quality in northwestern Ontario. Residents of Kenora advocated for water service north of Dalles 38C but demanded no provisional solution for the reserve, an Indigenous territory and, by extension, a site of federal concern.

Band members came to associate ailments with polluted water in Dalles Channel. As Elder Jacob Lindsay explained, "water from the river gave us diarrhea."[63] Others testified that Indian Affairs failed to investigate health complaints in the 1960s. Although federal health statistics on water-borne illnesses at Dalles 38C have yet to be found, reports of diarrhea match scientific studies of the relationship between untreated human feces and infections of the gastrointestinal tract. Donald Wigle of the World Health Organization identified *Giardia intestinalis* (or *G. lamblia*) as a "globally important cause of waterborne diarrheal disease and the most common protozoan infection of the human small intestine" in the developed world, making it a likely explanation of Lindsay's health complaints.[64] *G. lamblia* is transmitted through fecal-oral routes, often through fecally contaminated water and food. Other common causes of diarrhea in developed regions of Canada and the United States include rotavirus and enteric adenovirus; however, they are primarily responsible for infantile diarrhea and were thus unlikely causes of Lindsay's gastrointestinal complaint given that his recollections focused on his youth at Dalles 38C.[65] Such explanations remain speculative. Plausibility lies in commonality: in northern Ontario, studies confirmed *G. lamblia* in nearly 10 percent of stool samples in First Nations communities into the 1980s.[66]

Linda Wasakkejick, an off-reserve member, reported that "we weren't even told the water was contaminated after flooding. We used to wash and bathe in it. My sisters developed disease from this."[67] Scientific studies have shown that a rash can be a symptom of infection by an enteric pathogen of fecal-to-oral transmission such as the coxsackie virus, a known cause of disease in Canada and the United States.[68] Wasakkejick's complaint also makes sense given that incidents of the virus reached "epidemic proportions" in the late 1950s and early 1960s.[69] Whether or not "dirty water" was indeed the cause of diarrhea and rash, the dumping of untreated sewage from Kenora exposed band members of Dalles 38C to unnecessary risk and possible infection.

The Town of Kenora's attempt to establish a waste treatment system was resisted by taxpayers. When they defeated a motion to modernize the waste system in 1954, town council asked them to vote on the sewage question again the following year.[70] Dissent galvanized Kenora's East Enders: "We of the East [E]nd of town are taxpayers and are also going to be asked to vote on this project, yet . . . there is no hope for us."[71] Geography prevented municipal hook-up there. Residents of the East End saw little value in supporting municipal wastewater extension since tax increases would not provide any immediate benefit to them. As the phrase "little hope" suggests, East Enders feared that a wastewater system would drain not their wastewater but their pockets.

Indeed, working-class homeowners saw no benefit in waste treatment, particularly when Lake of the Woods funnelled it northwest. Questions mailed in to the newspaper focused on fears of the rising cost of home ownership. "What will the tax be?" citizens asked in "Letters to the Editor."[72] Mayor J.V. Fregeau published his estimate in the *Kenora Daily Miner and News* but clarified that residents would be called to vote on the sewer system as a utility and not "to vote on the capital cost question."[73] The Town of Kenora tried to shift the debate away from cost and toward service, but rhetorical wrangling proved to be ineffective.

In 1956, when the sewage question cropped up in Norman, concerns focused again on cost: "Kenora ratepayers are going to be asked a $276,000 question on December 10th—should a water and sewer system be installed in Norman?"[74] Residents wondered how they would balance their personal budgets while financing a new utility, knowing that, "for every $1000 assessment, it would increase taxes by $1.00."[75] More often than not, taxation was perceived as a detriment to the individual. The Town of Kenora therefore did not try to sell waste treatment to residents as a health need. Instead, it emphasized neighbourly duty, arguing that Norman "had always supported money by-laws for the town" and that similar support was owed to the suburb.[76] The debate indicates that residents outside the urban centre valued personal savings over waste treatment.

It is unlikely that many residents of Kenora knew of the suspension of solid wastes in Dalles Channel. Municipal concern about Kenora's economic vitality, a belief in the principle of dilution, and a desire to lower taxes worked against the early establishment of a sewage treatment plant. In an attempt to provide cost-effective services to ratepayers and quick housing to a growing population of working families, town council centralized the dumping of sewage into Lake of the Woods. Excreta made their way into the dammed river to save money in the town but at the cost of Anishinaabe health.

Wood Cellulose Inputs and Food Insecurity

The Town of Kenora was not solely responsible for declining water quality in the Winnipeg River. The Ontario-Minnesota Pulp and Paper Company compromised water quality by adding nutrients to it. The mill likely doubled wood cellulose inputs into Rideout Bay in the mid-1950s, a change made possible by hydroelectric power production at the Whitedog Falls Generating Station.

Within weeks of signing a contract with HEPCO, the mill announced a $17 million enlargement program that included a new barker, eight new grinders, new screening facilities, and a new steam boiler.[77] The mill anticipated that the "modernization project," announced in March 1955, would be completed by 1958.[78] A guaranteed supply of power from the Whitedog Falls Generating Station allowed the mill to "more than [double] present newsprint production which is now in the neighborhood of 350 tons a day" to "more than 700 tons."[79] Indeed, local news reporters deemed expansion unlikely without hydroelectric development since "the new paper machine requires an additional 17,000 kilowatts of power increasing the present total for the mill, the town and rural areas from 30,000 to 47,000 kilowatts."[80] This was a power load that the mill's privately owned generating station, the Norman Dam, could not supply.[81] Increased production at the mill was a direct result of power production at the Whitedog Falls station; increasing pollution, a result of doubled production and unchanged industrial waste systems, was the indirect and largely unrecognized result of damming the Winnipeg River.

Although corporate records include few descriptions of the type or quality of waste, records of chemical inputs prior to expansion include an estimate of "96,000 tons of coal and lignite [and] 3,200 tons of sulphur."[82] An environmental site assessment conducted by Golder Associates in 2008 revealed "elevated concentrations of several metals in the groundwater near Rideout Bay," including barium (soil-based) and boron, chromium, copper, lead, nickel, vanadium, and zinc (water-based).[83] Of greatest concern was wood waste dumped from the wooden waste conduit into the river and wood fibre rubbed off trees during shipment since they triggered mercury methylation and thus compromised Anishinaabe food sources.

Until 1970, when the Ontario Water Resources Commission ordered the mill to reduce outputs into the river, the mill regularly dumped in excess of 25,000 pounds of waste into Rideout Bay daily.[84] Descriptions of the "modernization" program in the 1950s do not include waste treatment facilities or relocation of the wooden waste conduit. Indeed, the new facilities were designed so that the new barker drum aligned with the Winnipeg River.[85] That the mill used the Winnipeg River to funnel its waste was no secret. Peter Playfair, the director of the Northwestern Health Unit, reported that "the Ontario Minnesota Pulp and Paper Company dumps its industrial wastes into Rideout Bay[, which] flow[s] into the Winnipeg River."[86]

Dumping, however, was not the only source of pollution associated with mill operations. Considerable bark loss occurred through the repeated handling of logs during booming, transportation, and storage along Lake of the Woods and the Winnipeg River. It is impossible to estimate exactly how much bark rubbed off trees during shipment since variables including size and species influenced loss. We do know, however, that the mill processed between 120,000 and 162,000 cords of wood in 1955, suggesting that, after 1958, 240,000 to 324,000 cords of wood passed through the company per year because of increased capacity.[87] By the 1970s, whether from dumping or transportation, wood cellulose fibre "deeper than a standing human" had settled along the bottom of the Winnipeg River.[88] Such benthic deposits are rare where river current is strong but common to industrial dumping areas where water flow is slow.[89]

Residents of Dalles 38C recalled how wood waste piled up between Rideout Bay and Dalles Channel following industrial expansion. Elder Jacob Lindsay explained that, "close to Kenora, you could see 'bubbles' in the water. . . . a whole chunk of sawdust and all that crap coming up to the surface."[90] "All that crap" interfered with travel to and from the reserve. Elder Robert Kabestra indicated that there was "so much muck going downstream . . . the boat would stall every time you hit a bunch of sawdust or crap. The motor would be so thick of sawdust."[91]

Elder Clarence Henry complained that his fishing nets collected mill waste in the 1950s: "The stuff off the paper mill would be stuck on our nets. . . . We would pull our nets and clean that stuff out. . . . But the stuff from the mill ruined our nets. It stuck right on to our nets."[92] Prior to the 1950s, the fishing nets had not acted as sieves for mill waste because there was little to catch: unregulated water flow had allowed for waste dispersal, preventing the accumulation of wood debris near the reserve. This testimony reveals that Henry maintained fishing practices that he had established prior to the Whitedog Falls Generating Station and mill expansion. It was not until those two industries operated in tandem that he needed to change his fishing practices.

Although wood fibre enters healthy river systems through erosion, it can exert a biochemical demand on holding waters and upset oxygen levels. R.A. McKenzie noted the relationship between oxygen levels and mill waste as early as 1930: "It has been found that the coarse material, bark, limbs, and chips settle out in [the] deeper and less rapid part of the stream. . . . As a result of the decomposition of this fine material, the oxygen content of the bottom water appears to become lowered."[93] When oxygen levels change, the health of freshwater fish is affected. Indeed, a prolonged reduction in dissolved oxygen can cause species-based or water-wide mortality.

Of the fish consumed by the Anishinabeg (including whitefish, walleye, and northern pike), sturgeon was the least tolerant of hypoxia.[94] As oxygen levels declined in the Winnipeg River, so did the availability of sturgeon for commercial and household use. Elders emphasized the collapse of the sturgeon population in their accounts of on-reserve life in the 1950s. According to transcriber Verna Perrault, Elder Janet Green "recalled how plentiful the wildlife used to be and how good the fishing was, but they gradually lost everything due to the blasting and the dirty water."[95]

Sturgeon had formed part of the diet at Dalles 38C for generations prior to hydroelectric development. Reflecting on his traverse of Dalles Rapids in 1823, Major Stephen H. Long wrote that, "while we were resting on one of the islands, an Indian came up in his canoe with his family and supplied us with fresh sturgeon and with dried huckleberries."[96] Sturgeon was eaten fresh but also made into a product like bison pemmican "consisting of a special blend of sturgeon oil and dried and pounded sturgeon meat packed into sturgeon skin bags," making it a valuable food source in all seasons.[97]

In October 1992, Lindsay informed interviewer Cuyler Cotton that "fish were affected by pollution. . . . Sturgeon were dying for some reason. Maybe by pollution in the water."[98] Henry affirmed Green's and Lindsay's

Figure 25. Log boom, c. 1932.

suspicions and identified a strong causal link between declining sturgeon populations and mill operations. Henry reported to Cotton that "the fish feed off the bottom of the river, where this stuff from the mill is. The fish are killed off by this stuff they are eating in the bottom.... I've seen the fish floating around, even fish like suckers (mallets)—they suck the water from the bottom. When I was a young man ... there were still sturgeon around, quite a lot of them."[99] According to Elders, a combination of modifications to the river and urban pollutants compromised band members' access to a prized dietary staple.

By 1969, officials from the Ontario Water Resources Commission and the Department of Trade and Development had acknowledged the deleterious results of paper production in northwestern Ontario. In a memorandum to Stanley Randall, the minister of trade and development, D.J. Collins of the Ontario Water Resources Commission considered the cost benefit of waste treatment in the region. Using the Rainy River example, Collins argued that a treatment facility from $3 to $4 million was the most desirable. Effluent released by the Ontario-Minnesota Pulp and Paper Company into Rainy River had "grossly impaired" alternative water use.[100] Collins indicated that mill pollution had been known to destroy "fish life sometimes for up to 30 miles [about 50 kilometres] downstream" in parts of Canada.[101]

George Kerr, the minister of energy and resources management, would also weigh in on modernization debates. Kerr noted that modernization, particularly at Fort Frances and Kenora, would cause "improvement in the present unsatisfactory water pollution problems." He advised against "making concessions" for the Ontario-Minnesota Pulp and Paper Company despite slow growth in the industry. By the late 1960s, it is clear that provincial officials knew that mill wastes had created anaerobic environments in otherwise healthy river systems. Men like Kerr were no longer willing to put "a premium on inefficiency." [102] Such arguments came late.

Industrial Enthusiasm, Poor Planning, and Federal Inaction

Although it could be argued that the accumulation of industrial waste at Dalles Channel was "normative" by contemporary standards, given that Canada's environmental movement did not gain momentum until the 1970s, the reality is that industry standards had changed by the mid-1950s. Professionals published findings that denounced the relative merits of dilution for this type of waste. In 1954, *Sewage and Industrial Wastes* published the transcript of the Twenty-Sixth Annual Meeting of the Federation of Sewages and Wastes Associations. A panel participant for "Water Dilution Factors and Industrial Wastes" argued that, "where it applies to an individual plant, dilution is probably not an answer to the wastes problem." He identified an exception whereby clean water used for dilution "must be disposed of anyway."[103] Co-participant Frank W. Jones agreed, suggesting that "dilution *per se* doesn't always accomplish what it is intended to." Yet Jones, too, identified an exception: "If there is enough water to take away the visual evidence of sewage and to give the fish enough oxygen to live on without coddling them too much, the benefits of dilution are factual and real."[104]

Although dilution was recognized as a viable strategy for waste reduction, Kenora's mill surpassed the acceptable limits for waste stipulated by Jones. He explained that "certain things can be tolerated in some streams, but a park stream where children play should be of the best quality." It became particularly important to monitor discharge for downstream communities since factors beyond corporate control could jeopardize water quality. Jones noted that, "if a sudden downpour came . . . not giving sufficient time for purification and dilution, that festering mass from upstream was carried down into the clear [recreational] section."[105] According to him, nature could compromise best practices if industry relied on dilution for waste disposal. Given that Elders Robert Kabestra and Clarence Henry reported that mill waste interfered with motoring and fishing activities, dilution as practised by the pulp and paper mill failed to meet industrial standards as set by professionals at the time of (and indeed prior to) expansion.

Collapse of the sturgeon fishery in the Winnipeg River drainage basin failed to spark a municipal or provincial reassessment of waste management or water regulation. René Brunelle, the minister of lands and forests (1966–72), estimated that the forest industry accounted for 69 percent of all manufacturing employment in northwestern Ontario in the late 1960s. Given that the "pulp and paper [industry was] responsible directly or indirectly for one dollar out of every eight earned by all Canadians" and that Kenora operations alone "provided employment for over 800 men and women during the year," there was limited interest in Kenora in pollution abatement.[106] Demands for waste management plummeted throughout the 1960s as Ontario's "once favourable competitive position eroded through rising wood costs, increasing power rates, and greater transportation charges." In

1969, Brunelle advocated for Ontario's forest industry, suggesting that "it is highly desirable that we create a suitable economic environment to stimulate forest industry growth in these areas."[107] Although Brunelle made no direct reference to industrial pollution, he desired concessions from the Department of Trade and Development that would reduce operating costs.

Band members at Dalles 38C suffered from unabated industrial waste to keep the Ontario-Minnesota Pulp and Paper Mill's engines running. Costs were saved by postponing the modernization of waste disposal systems. Municipal priorities and provincial development goals, which excluded Dalles 38C (not out of malicious intent but because of jurisdictional limits), thus ensured the continued flow of waste into Dalles Channel.

It was not until the twenty-first century that biologists confirmed Elders' suspicions and attributed an accumulation of wood fibre on the riverbed to declining sturgeon populations. Reporting on the release of 50,000 freshly hatched sturgeon fry into the Winnipeg River, journalist Dan Gauthier suggested that "water flow and level fluctuations" had negatively affected the sturgeon population. He agreed with Scott McAughey, a biologist for the Ministry of Natural Resources, who had suggested that Ontario Power Generation, the Ministry of Natural Resources, and the Lake of the Woods Control Board ought to agree to reduce fluctuations during the spawning period to help the population recover.[108]

In contrast, journalist Jon Thompson focused less on water fluctuations and more on the "anoxic mush" at the bottom of the Winnipeg River. He provided a visual description of accumulated waste, noting that decomposed bark was at least two metres deep in the 1970s.[109] His position suggests an awareness of the risks associated with high organic loading. The amount of oxygen released from photosynthesis compared with the amount of oxygen removed by animal and microbial respiration determines any waterway's oxygen content. "If," as Scott Brennan and Jay Withgott explain, "nutrients flow into water bodies faster than they flow out or are broken down, the water bodies become increasingly laden with plant material and lower in dissolved oxygen."[110] As shown earlier, woody material sunk on its way to and from Kenora's mill: inputs exceeded outflows in Dalles Channel, forcing sturgeon to compete with bacterial colonies for oxygen. Disrupted flow between Rideout Bay and the Whitedog Falls Generating Station caused by blasting and damming reduced the amount of oxygen that could be dissolved by the river. No wonder the central question that Thompson posed was "is there enough food and oxygen to support [sturgeon] now?"[111]

Industrial enthusiasm and poor planning ensured the flow of waste into Rideout Bay, but federal inaction affirmed environmental inequalities resulting from careless municipal dumping practices. Federal officials in Ottawa, removed by almost 2,000 kilometres from the contaminated site, had no political pressure to act on behalf of Dalles 38C Indian Reserve, for in the mid-1950s no environmental law explicitly protected water quality in Dalles Channel. The Boundary Water Treaty of 1909 provided limited protection of Canadian waterways and read as follows: "The waters herein defined as boundary waters and waters flowing across the [American-Canadian] boundary shall not be polluted on either side to the injury of health or property on the other."[112] Pollutants moved away from the international boundary on Lake of the Woods and into waters claimed by Canada as they journeyed toward Hudson Bay. As a result of the northwesterly flow, members of Dalles 38C struggled to convince Canada to maintain the same standards for First Nations that they legislated for Canadians generally.

CHAPTER 6

MOTHER WORK AND MANAGING ENVIRONMENTAL CHANGE

The women of Dalles 38C Indian Reserve experienced the Whitedog Falls Generating Station differently from their male counterparts.[1] Reflecting on her years growing up on Dalles 38C between 1885 and 1908, Anishinaabe Elder Matilda Martin (Ogimaamaashiik) remembered working alongside her grandmother, Jane Lindsay, to maintain their family home.[2] During the fall, Martin helped to prepare a winter supply of whitefish under Lindsay's supervision. As they worked side by side gutting the fish from caudal fin to gill, Lindsay passed down women's knowledge of family care. Martin might have learned that expectant mothers who consumed whitefish produced breast milk of the highest quality—a lesson that she passed down to her granddaughter Carol Kipling years later.[3] Lindsay likely taught Martin to recognize whitefish soup as an alternative to breast milk that could be bottle-fed to infants. As a mother in the early 1900s, Martin would catch, prepare, and consume whitefish in an attempt to ensure her children's health. Although her husband's paid labour promised the family economic stability, Martin's unpaid mother work ensured the physical well-being of household members. Her experience as a key contributor to household welfare was not unique to

Dalles 38C. Anishinaabe women throughout Treaty 3 territory in the early twentieth century worked in partnership with men to raise healthy families.

In the 1950s, however, hydroelectric development along the Winnipeg River jeopardized Anishinaabe women's access to the local resources essential for mother work. The Whitedog Falls Generating Station disrupted the flow of the Winnipeg River past Dalles 38C and thus facilitated an accumulation of sewage and pulp waste in nearby fishing waters. High levels of organic loading by the Town of Kenora and Ontario-Minnesota Pulp and Paper Company raised the biochemical oxygen demand and exacerbated hypoxia. As oxygen levels in the upper Winnipeg River declined, so did sturgeon populations. Although other fish populations (e.g., walleye, whitefish, and northern pike) survived, they became highly toxic to humans. As micro-organisms digested pulp waste in and around Dalles Channel, naturally occurring methyl mercury was released into the Winnipeg River and accumulated up the food chain. Martin's great-grandchildren feared poisoning their infants with methyl mercury if they relied on country foods such as whitefish while pregnant or breastfeeding.

Hydroelectric power generation on the Winnipeg River not only disrupted the ability of the environment to provide resources necessary to maintain women's reproductive health (especially breast milk) but also led to food shortages that continually compromised Anishinaabe women's ability to maintain the household economy and to raise families in accordance with cultural expectations. There is also some suggestion that food shortages led families to consider residential schooling for their children. The history of methyl mercury contamination at Dalles 38C, when considered alongside more egregious examples such as Grassy Narrows and Whitedog First Nations, illustrates some of the ways in which colonization and land alteration negatively affected the health of Indigenous communities in Canada in the twentieth century.[4]

Cultural Expectations and Activities
According to Dan Pine, an Anishinaabe Elder from Garden River First Nation, women were traditionally responsible for household maintenance. He explains that "Kina gewii kinoomaajgaazo wa shkniigkwe nikeyaa ezhi-nokiimgag kina ge-goo ezhi-bmingaademgag maa biindig" (a young woman is taught everything, how everything works inside, how everything is

managed).["5] Inside tasks included child-rearing. During the first few years of a child's life, Anishinaabe women were primarily responsible for food provision, dominated by breast milk. To produce the best-quality breast milk, Anishinaabe girls and women avoided objects that they believed would harm or impede their breasts, such as bows and constricting bras, to ensure that their breasts could continue to feed their children.[6] Pregnant and lactating women followed strict dietary regimes to ensure that high-quality food—believed to have medicinal qualities—would be provided to their nursing infants.[7] If women could not nurse, then they used local resources, such as manomin and whitefish, to feed their children.

Anishinaabe girls such as Martin learned how to perform "womanly duties" from their mothers and grandmothers. Writing in the early 1900s, American ethnographer Frances Densmore found that "a Chippewa girl . . . learned many household tasks by watching and helping her mother."[8] Gendered teachings continued to shape Anishinaabe women's expectations and activities well into the 1940s and 1950s along the Winnipeg River. For example, an unidentified older woman from Dalles 38C Indian Reserve remembered being sent to her grandmother to learn about family provision: "Your grandmother would teach you, your great-grandmother. But mostly your mother turn[ed] you over to your grandmother. Because, you know, your mother, you wouldn't listen to her . . . but you respected your grandmother [and] listen[ed] to an Elder tell stories."[9] School attendance, particularly at day school, did not interfere with lessons on appropriate women's work. Elder Alice Kelly, born at Dalles 38C in 1946, credited her mother for teaching her how to maintain a happy home life. As a schoolgirl, Kelly would "come home," "do homework," and then "do chores inside or whatever." By the time she married, around the mid-1960s, she "knew everything" about providing for her family. In her words, "it was good."[10]

Milk Medicine and Infant Care

The bodies of Anishinaabe women were (and indeed still are) imbued with medicinal power by their communities. Like the Earth, pregnant women displayed the ability to (re)generate life. The conceptual links between pregnancy and medicinal power were made manifest in Anishinaabe healing places, particularly the sweat lodge. In Treaty 3 territory, there was a long history of political alliance and intermarriage between Anishinaabe and

Cree families,[11] and the testimony of Cree knowledge keepers reveals that female bodies were medicine bodies.[12] Cree knowledge keepers Eric Robinson and Henry Bird Quinney suggest that sweat lodges were initially designed to mimic "the belly of a pregnant woman" and explain that Indigenous men "use[d] the Sweat Lodge to go through the womb of a mother to try to understand the Creation process of Women and Mother Earth."[13] By passing through the symbolic womb, Indigenous men sought to renew their bodies—the sweat bath was used as both a general curative and a relief for stressed muscles. Indigenous women, in contrast, did not enter sweat lodges as often since female bodies cleansed themselves monthly and had the inherent ability to create life.[14]

Given Anishinaabe women's perceived medicine power, it is perhaps not surprising that breast milk was believed to be both "a gift [from the Creator] and a medicine a mother gives her child."[15] Recognized as a healing liquid, breast milk was the most highly valued food for infants.[16] Anishinaabe women recommended breast milk to lactating mothers over known alternatives such as whitefish and manomin soup. Breasts were seen as medicinal tools that both strengthened infants and maintained overall family health by limiting family size. Martin strongly associated pregnancy with the weaning of previous children, suggesting that breastfeeding might have been considered a form of contraception.[17]

Today breastfeeding, when used as a form of contraception, is known as the lactational amenorrhea method (LAM). LAM depends on hormonal changes experienced by lactating mothers, particularly the reduced production of hormones associated with ovulation. It is most effective within six months of giving birth.[18] LAM also works best if the mother "feeds her baby at least every four hours during the day and every six hours at night."[19] Anishinaabe mothers realized that suckling was not always a successful method of birth control. At Lac Courte Oreille, Minnesota, an informant told anthropologist Mary Inez Hilger that toddlers and their infant siblings sometimes nursed together.[20] Women observed that breastfeeding did not necessarily prevent multiple births. If breastfeeding was a reliable contraceptive, then siblings at different life stages would not have shared the breast.

Anishinaabe girls born on Dalles 38C Indian Reserve prior to the development of the Whitedog Falls Generating Station were raised under the assumption that they, too, would breastfeed. Oral testimony reveals that girls born in the 1940s were educated in breast care by their mothers. Rules existed discouraging the use of hunting tools and constrictive bras to facilitate the future flow of milk medicine. Elder Alice Kelly explained:

> My mom used to say, "Don't ever touch"—I don't know what they call those . . . slingshots and . . . a bow and arrow—"don't touch those."
>
> "Why?"
>
> "Your breasts. They gonna drag your breasts."

Kelly mapped the "drag" on her body, gesturing from her collarbone to her lower ribs. She explained that girls, to protect their breasts, were not allowed to touch "the boys' stuff."[21]

Whether Anishinaabe mothers feared that their daughters would develop boy-like chests, harm their breasts, or prematurely age them (and hence be unable to lactate) by using "boys' stuff" is unclear. What is clear, however, is that Anishinaabe mothers believed that dragging breasts could make them incapable of lactation. It is important to note that, though postmenopausal women were no longer able to produce milk medicine, they did not lose their medicine powers at large. Female Elders harvested herbal medicines and produced herbal decoctions and poultices.[22] In later life, among some postmenopausal women, their botanical knowledge supplemented their former reproductive power.

Clothing the Body for Mother Work

When Kelly became pregnant in the early 1960s, her mother provided further advice to encourage the flow of milk medicine and warned her against using "white women's stuff." Settler-colonist women had long displayed their breasts differently from Anishinaabe women. Throughout the nineteenth century, middle- and upper-class white women used corsets to bind their torsos. This constraining undergarment "impressed apparently natural virtues upon the shape of a woman's body" by creating an hourglass figure.[23] A bound waist accentuated the bust. By making the torso appear to be slender, the breasts seemed to be larger in contrast. The straight-front corset made "the monobosom" fashionable until the First World War.[24] Indeed, many non-Indigenous North Americans associated the monobosom with feminine beauty. Non-Indigenous women manipulated their bodies not only to enhance physical appearance but also to represent feminine virtue. Wendy Dasler Johnson notes that North Americans associated the torso with morality and "the chest as the seat of emotions." She argues that, "in a nineteenth-century corset, a woman's moral zone [was] 'thrown into prominence' while her appetites [associated with the abdomen] would be kept well under control."[25] Binding thus helped non-Indigenous women to control their waistlines and to display virtue for non-Indigenous men.

Anishinaabe women did not traditionally bind the waist to accentuate the bust. As cultural educator Basil Johnston suggests, an Anishinaabe "woman's worth was not measured by a lithe body [or] full breasts."[26] An Anishinaabe woman was valued for her industry and her skill.[27] Traditional teachings warned Anishinaabe youth against choosing a partner for his or her appearance. For example, one Anishinaabe man rejected suitable brides within his village and travelled until "he found a yellow-haired woman of great beauty." Her beauty, however, did little to ensure his well-being—this woman did not cook or sew. Over time, her beauty faded, and she became a burden. The young man had married Dandelion.[28] In this story, good looks are no virtue.

Given that breasts had limited sex appeal in Anishinaabe culture, women had little pressure (or indeed incentive) to showcase their busts with restrictive clothing. Before transatlantic trade, Anishinaabe women wore loose-fitting deerskin skirts and dresses.[29] Frances Densmore notes that "in early times the clothing of a woman consisted of a single garment made of two deerskins, one forming the front and the other the back of the garment, the two parts being fastened together at the shoulders and held in place with a belt."[30] The belt was functional rather than fashionable. To demonstrate their worth, Anishinaabe women adorned their clothing with beads made out of animal bone, stone, and shell. Over time, the women replaced handcrafted beads with glass, ceramic, and metal beads acquired through trade.[31]

Anishinaabe women also fashioned trade blankets into clothing. The adoption of European cloth did not cause the suppression of Anishinaabe chests or torsos. Densmore explains that "the blanket was wrapped around the limbs like a tight skirt and fastened with a belt; the upper part of the blanket was then thrown loosely around the arms and shoulders." This style of dress eased mother work: "A woman could put her baby in the blanket [or] drop the upper part of the blanket entirely, drawing it around the waist."[32] Blanket skirts did not showcase the bust; instead, they made it easier for Anishinaabe women to free their breasts to nurse. Clothing designed specifically for the chest was also functional. Densmore indicates that "a muskrat skin, tanned with the hair on it, was worn [seasonally] as a 'chest protector.'"[33] It was worn by both genders but more commonly by men on hunting expeditions.[34] It was placed inside blanket coats, perhaps to cut the wind. Unisex clothing such as the chest protector reinforces that the bust was not eroticized in Anishinaabe communities, and undergarments were designed not to enhance the chest but to protect it from the elements.

As trade increased, Anishinaabe women replaced loose-fitting deerskin dresses and skirts with ready-made fabric. In the 1860s and before, traders exchanged broadcloth with the Anishinabeg for furs. Much like deerskin dresses, broadcloth dresses were "held in place by strips over the shoulders and confined at the waist by a belt or a sash." Although Anishinaabe women adopted the new material, they rejected Western pressure to bind the torso. Intercultural exchange did influence how women showcased (and, perhaps, envisioned) their assets in the 1860s. Anishinaabe women added "front pieces" to their dresses around this time. The front piece extended across the chest and "was the first part of a woman's dress to be decorated in color."[35] Worsted braids sewn onto the front piece, instead of constricting undergarments, drew attention to the chest. In the early 1900s, Anishinaabe women used pointed waistlines to create an hourglass figure. They also adopted some European-influenced undergarments. Martin made bloomers from flannelette and used cotton to make slips.[36] Cost and the day-to-day reality of Anishinaabe women's lives, however, made corseting impractical.

Although Anishinaabe women refused the corset, they were familiar with body binding. Infants were bound to encourage healthy development. The tikinagun, or cradleboard, is perhaps the most famous example. In the Winnipeg River drainage basin, cradleboards were commonly "2½ feet long, fitted with a U-shaped shelf to contain the baby, and over which a drawstring-fitted cloth covering is placed."[37] This cloth is known as a *dikineyaab*. It was used by Anishinaabe mothers to keep infants securely attached to the cradleboard.[38] Indian enthusiast Frank Belmore claimed that infants appeared to be "so tightly packed in that [they] can scarcely move."[39] The head and arms, however, remained free. Children were protected from falls by "a stiff circle of wood" attached at "a convenient distance above the head."[40] Anishinaabe mothers bound children to protect them from harm. Belmore explained that "it prevents [children] from getting burned at the fire, cutting [themselves] on the sharp skinning knife." He determined that the tikinagun was an Anishinaabe tool that "defied improvement." Binding also allowed Anishinaabe women to carry "small children on dog-team and canoe trips."[41] Martin suggested that the tikinagun enabled women to work by freeing their arms. It allowed Martin to paddle and pick berries. By constricting their children, Anishinaabe women freed themselves for labour.[42]

Anishinaabe parents also used the tikinagun to direct growth. For example, they sometimes attached miniature moccasins to the "stiff circle of wood" in the hope of raising a good runner. Miniature bows and arrows, likewise, were used to encourage the development of a good hunter.[43] Bonnets were also used to direct growth. Elder Jane Lindsay instructed Martin to "put the bonnet on after the baby is born because their heads are not a very good shape." Lindsay was born two generations before Martin and believed that a "tight bonnet" would encourage healthy bone development. Martin observed that other Anishinaabe families, not just her own, used restrictive garments to shape babies' heads in the early 1900s.[44]

American and Canadian styles of breast management changed significantly after the First World War, though women continued to manipulate their chests for fashion purposes. By the 1920s, the brassiere had replaced the corset. Early bras offered little support—their sole purpose was to restrict movement. Some women opted to bind their breasts by repurposing old sheets to achieve "the look" without the cost.[45] Ideas of feminine beauty had changed: the hourglass figure was replaced by a tubular silhouette. Non-Indigenous North Americans now preferred a bound chest over a protruding monobosom. This form of binding was short-lived.

Uplift became fashionable in the 1930s, but it was not until 1947 that the first padded bra became popular among Canadian and American women. Manufacturers used foam rubber or felt to help women augment their chests.[46] In 1948, breasts throughout North America "got a lift" with the first mass-produced push-up bra, the Rising Star.[47] Many non-Indigenous North Americans associated an ample bust with attractiveness, particularly to the opposite sex. Young women expressed "anxiety about breast size, more than any other body part."[48] Industry responded. In addition to padding and underwire, American and Canadian women purchased vitamins, bust creams, hydro massage, and suction devices to increase breast size.[49]

But Anishinaabe women were taught to ignore the trend for high, formed breasts. Kelly's mother warned "don't put your [breasts] like this [lifts them as if in an underwire bra]. Let them be down."[50] Anishinaabe women, unlike settler-colonists, did not believe that men desired an ample bust. Language (Anishinaabemowin) taught them that men wanted companions. The word for relationship, *weedjeewaugun*, roughly translates as "he who goes with" or "she who walks with."[51] Ritual words spoken during marriage ceremonies encouraged husband and wife to "be kind to one another" and to "be kind to [their] children."[52] Oral stories emphasized that good parents nourished their children.[53] Clothing that improved breast function was thus more valuable than clothing that increased breast size. On a practical level, push-up bras might have complicated mother work by making the breasts less accessible to suckling infants. Kelly believed that her mother's advice worked, conceptually linking her milk supply to intergenerational guidance: "When I was carrying my kids, I could feel the milk already. . . . [It was] dripping when my baby was just about to come out." She associated her maternal success with unrestrictive clothing. Kelly then reiterated her mother's advice, reassuring me, an interviewer of childbearing age, that "milk will start coming all the time" if one's breasts are not artificially pushed up.[54]

Pre- and Postnatal Diets

Best practices for lactating mothers extended from dress to pre- and postnatal diets. Diets recommended to lactating mothers at Dalles 38C Indian Reserve reinforced the value of "wild foods," those found naturally in the local environment. Many Anishinaabe women believed that wild foods were essential to increasing milk supply without draining the mother of essential nutrients. Métis historian Kim Anderson found that northern Algonquian peoples designed prenatal diets under the assumption that "whatever the pregnant woman took in would be ingested by the baby."[55] Kelly suggested that a similar belief shaped postnatal diets in Treaty 3 territory: "My mom eat the wild food, and whatever she eat we suck her *[laughter]*. Breastfeeding."[56] Given that infant health depended heavily on quality breast milk, it was important that the mother ate selected, nutrient-rich crops, fish, and game.

In Minnesota, contemporary Anishinaabe knowledge keepers highly recommend manomin for mothers.[57] This is a long-standing practice. American ethnographer Mary Inez Hilger found that lactating "Chippewa" mothers in Minnesota, Wisconsin, and Michigan were encouraged to eat manomin during the 1930s. Other wild foods—such as venison, lake trout, and whitefish—were also valued for and by mothers.[58] In Treaty 3 territory,

Elder testimony revealed that whitefish soup was similarly a key component of postnatal diets. As Kelly explained, "my mom breastfeed us, all of us.
All she use is whitefish soup to have milk on her breast." The use of beaver
soup to encourage lactation, however, appears to have been unique to the
Anishinabeg in Treaty 3 territory.[59]

Anishinaabe women carefully monitored and regulated their diets to
encourage the production of milk medicine. The possibility of jeopardizing
it through an improper diet is evident by Anishinaabe dietary restrictions for
potential mothers. Kelly stated that turtle soup was believed to be capable of
compromising one's reproductive health: "But we weren't allowed to eat it
[turtle soup]. Just the old people. We used to peek and watch them, me and
my friends, my relatives. They looked, but don't eat it. . . . 'You'll kill your
virgin [reproductive health].' That's what my mom told me. Whatever we
have in our—I don't know, you ruin where the baby is. . . . That's the only
thing they never let us eat. The turtle soup."[60]

Kelly did not provide the rationale behind this dietary restriction. Hilger
suggested that the turtle, a recognized emissary of the spirit world, was
banned during pregnancy—for Anishinaabe mothers and fathers—in Mille
Lacs, Minnesota. Eating turtle was believed to cause the baby to "stretch
all the time."[61] Extrapolating from Cree testimonies, it is likely that taboos
around the turtle involved "taking the baby back"[62] or stretching the child
between worlds. Anderson found that it was considered "particularly dangerous to take the newborn into environments where he or she might come
into contact with negative energy, or where there may be spirits waiting to
take the baby back."[63] Capable of living both on land and in water, of living
between worlds, the turtle might have tempted the child's spirit to follow it
through the physical world. Cree knowledge keepers Robinson and Quinney
suggested that infants, being "closest to the Creator's Creation and Spirit
World having come more recently from the Womb," face greater tempta-
tion to leave the physical plane.[64] Anderson indicated that many northern
Algonquian people believe that this openness to the spirit world comes from
the fontanelle or "soft spot" in the baby's head.[65]

Although Anishinaabe restrictions on material culture and diet were
designed to ensure the production of milk medicine, labour demands or
bodily stresses sometimes prevented mothers from breastfeeding their children. Oral testimonies demonstrate how Anishinaabe mothers in Treaty 3
territory were encouraged to use alternatives such as whitefish, sturgeon,

and manomin soup. For example, Kelly testified that, when her mother left to harvest, a bottle of whitefish soup was left with her caregiver. Her mother explained that "'whitefish soup, that's what I feed you [when] I couldn't do it because I had to go look for food for you.'" Bottles were made from recycled goods to feed an infant while the mother was at work. Kelly described these homemade bottles: "They have these kind of old, old-fashioned nipples. I used to laugh at my mom. They used to have these old pop bottles, . . . and they used to put the nipples like this *[motions putting nipple over bottle-neck]*." Sometimes, particularly while mothers were at work, "the milk was fish soup."[66]

Supporting evidence for fish-based alternatives to breast milk predate Kelly's birth. Martin recalled how Anishinaabe mothers made bottles of rabbit bone and fish gut: "I heard one time a woman have no milk and, mind you, she make that baby drink that, small baby you know. She made something to suck it, to suck it out of, jackfish guts, you know, out of jackfish guts. I think she cooked the jackfish guts, and she made a hole in here and then she put a rabbit bone there. . . . That's the way that baby suck that fish bouilla."[67] Fish soup (or bouillon) was a long-standing solution for women unable to lactate.

Anishinaabe mothers valued wild food alternatives to manufactured baby foods. Commercial infant formulas were introduced to the market in 1867 with the development of Justus von Liebig's appropriately named Liebig's Soluble Food for Babies. By the turn of the twentieth century, Nestle's Milk, Mellin's Infant Food, and Ridge's Food functioned as formula alternatives to Liebig's.[68] Much like their Anishinaabe neighbours, Anglo mothers were encouraged to fortify their blood for nursing. In the 1910s, the *Kenora Miner and News* carried regular advertisements for Maltum Stout, a caramelized malt powder for nursing mothers. Mothers could order this "wholesome, positively non-intoxicating" powder from Winnipeg suppliers through their local grocers.[69] Commercial infant formula first became available in Kenora around 1923. Klim Powdered Whole Milk, "pure, fresh liquid milk . . . with only the water removed," could be ordered from Canadian Milk Products in Winnipeg. Advertisements urged Anglo mothers to order Klim, calling it "safe milk." Considerable social pressure existed to replace breastfeeding with formula feeding as Canadian doctors argued that formula—such as Klim—was "best for babies."[70]

But long before Klim entered the northwestern market, Anishinaabe mothers resisted cash incentives to bottle-feed their infants. As early as 1905, for example, Councillor C.W. Chadwick of Kenora was promoting the perceived benefits of goat's milk for nursing infants.[71] He entered five goats in the livestock show at the Kenora Agricultural Fair and displayed his animals "in the grounds to the rear of the Hudson's Bay store,"[72] a known Anishinaabe gathering site. Indeed, Martin remembered routinely boiling a pot of tea behind the store.[73] There Chadwick might have voiced his published opinion that goat's milk reduced indigestion in children: "The butter globules [in goat's milk] are so fine that curdling on a child's stomach is most improbable." In an attempt to improve the physical health of northern Ontarians, Chadwick offered cash incentives and money-back guarantees to families willing to incorporate goat products into their diets.[74]

Chadwick's efforts anticipated federal attempts to introduce goat's milk into Indigenous diets. In 1919, new "Indian" hospitals in Ontario began to replace cow's milk with goat's milk.[75] Oral testimony, however, suggests that Anishinaabe mothers rejected settler pressure to bottle-feed their infants. Martin did not recall any livestock rearing at Dalles 38C Indian Reserve.[76] Elder Charlie Fisher of One Man Lake, a neighbouring community (now flooded), similarly claimed that Anishinaabe families displayed limited interest in livestock rearing. He explained that families "couldn't really look after cattle at the same time [that they went trapping]."[77] As a result of their mobility requirements, Anishinaabe families might have rejected cash incentives to bottle-feed their babies. Anishinaabe mothers maintained that breast was best. Whitefish soup trailed close behind and was served in handcrafted bottles.

Given the perceived importance of whitefish soup to promoting milk supply and acting as a healthful alternative to milk medicine, it is unsurprising that Martin put extraordinary emphasis on teaching her granddaughter, Carol Kipling, how to make fish bouillon. Kipling remembers bringing Martin home to eat with her four boys: "There [were] some things that [were] her specialities—like, she loved her whitefish bouillon. And, uh, even in her later years, when she was in Pinecrest [Nursing Home], in the fall I would always go to the fish market and buy a big whitefish and go pick her up and bring her home." Although Martin might have acted as "head chef," Kipling was not allowed to be a passive observer in the kitchen. She remembers that she was carefully taught (and retaught) how to prepare whitefish

Figure 26. Chadwick family goat farm, c. 1920.

Figure 27. Matilda Martin (Ogimaamaashiik) with grandchildren Carol and Ray Kipling, c. 1945.

bouillon for her family: "She would always have to clean it right from the beginning to the end. . . . And every year it was like she'd never done it in front of me before or [like] I didn't know anything about making fish bouillon. She would have to show me step by step how to scale the fish, how you cut off the head. Now you do this. Now you do that. And so she would make this fish bouillon as if it was the very first time."[78] The dedication to teaching Kipling how to prepare whitefish bouillon reflects the importance that both Martin and her community attached to it. Although Kipling "married out" and raised her children off reserve, Martin provided her with the key to preserving infant health. She ensured that her granddaughter could prepare the best-known alternative to breast milk, though the river that they had long fished was beginning to change.

Environmental Contaminants in Country Foods

The construction and operation of the Whitedog Falls Generating Station curtailed Anishinaabe women's ability to provide milk medicine to their children at Dalles 38C Indian Reserve. Increased levels of methyl mercury in predatory fish (e.g., whitefish) were identified and made public by the Ministry of the Environment after HEPCO entered the region. The generating station has limited subsequent generations—such as my own—from raising children according to local cultural standards.

Although whitefish continued to live in the fishing territories of Dalles 38C, band members believed that mill operations negatively affected fish quality in terms of taste (not toxicity) in the 1950s. Indeed, whitefish remained a dietary staple. Nevertheless, band members closely associated mill production with fish health and taught their children to monitor industrial dumping. The children were taught that pulp waste directly influenced food quality. Kipling described a family fish fry during her youth: "[Dad would say,] 'Oh, you don't have any idea how good it used to taste before the mill came.'" She was taught to observe "the baths from the wood and the sludge that came from the mill and the sewer [that] would go right into the river." Her elders insisted that the fish "never tasted the same" and had become "tainted."[79]

As adults, these children noted an accumulation of mill wastes near the Dalles Channel, now a reservoir of HEPCO. Elder Robert Kabestra echoed Kipling family sentiments regarding pollution and flavour. He claimed in the 1990s that the "meat doesn't taste the same."[80] The change in flavour altered Anishinaabe perceptions of locally harvested foods and resulted in many families questioning their ability to feed their children from the river.

Many Elders believed that pollution from the pulp and paper mill changed not only the taste but also the healthfulness of country foods. Elder Clarence Henry observed that "fish got sick from the worms" near the mill.[81] Similarly, Robert and Elder Joe Wagamese testified that disease in fish and game was visible physically: "Blisters, spots [appear] on the liver, lungs, [and] kidneys [of game animals]. . . . It was the organs that were full of blisters."[82] Band members feared that human ingestion of "sick" fish and game might cause illness. Henry suggested that "a human would get sick if they got worms in their body."[83] Oral testimony indicates that Anishinaabe families discarded "sick" animals to prevent the transfer of disease between species. As Robert recalled, "Joe [Wagamese] mentioned cutting a duck's chest and discovering white veins in the chest. He threw it away."[84] Anishinaabe families clearly monitored consumption to maintain good health.

In the 1970s, the Ministry of the Environment confirmed Anishinaabe fears that country food could cause disease. Federal officials did not comment on worms, blisters, or spots, but they did report an invisible problem: mercury levels in excess of 0.5 parts per million in northern pike, smallmouth bass, sucker (redhorse and white), and walleye. This finding meant that large fish populations near Dalles 38C were deemed unfit for human consumption.[85] Minaki Lodge, a nearby tourist facility, announced its closure in 1971 to limit outsiders' exposure to mercury through the sport fishery.[86]

Federal and commercial recognition of fish toxicity raised fears about mercury poisoning at Dalles 38C. Regular interaction with Grassy Narrows—a neighbouring community that intermarried and shared harvesting grounds with Dalles 38C—alerted families to the risk of Minamata disease. Members of Dalles 38C were attuned to multiple symptoms displayed at Grassy Narrows, including, but not limited to, "numbness of the mouth, lips, tongue, hands, and feet; tunnel vision[;] impairment of hearing; speech disorders; difficulty in swallowing; loss of balance[;] disturbances in coordination[;] extreme fatigue[; and] mental depression."[87]

By 1973, Anishinabeg in and around Kenora feared that mercury was causing death. However, during the inquest into the death of Thomas Strong, H.B. Cotnam, supervising coroner for the Province of Ontario, argued against the popular Anishinaabe belief that Strong had died from mercury poisoning. Cotnam confirmed that Strong had died from "an acute coronary thrombosis" rather than "high levels of mercury."[88] His test provided limited reassurance to Anishinaabe families, however, since "expert evidence during the inquest revealed recent mercury analysis of blood and hair from Indians in the area were higher than normal, and some were in the known dangerous range." Strong's inquest led the Ministry of Health to establish preventative health measures for band members of Grassy Narrows, including a twice annual "mercury analysis of blood and hair samples" by Dr. J. Stopps of the Environmental Health Services Branch.[89] Stopps did not offer comparable testing at Dalles 38C. Family networks made band members aware of the hazards of consuming fish from nearby waters but provided them with none of the benefits of federal monitoring. Band members came to live in a constant state of apprehension, wondering if "dirty water" was poisoning their families.[90]

Historians have long discussed mercury methylation and its effect on fish populations. Yet this link has been discussed almost exclusively in relation to rising male unemployment and welfare rates in Indigenous communities as Indigenous men were unable to guide or to fish commercially. Little attention has been paid to how declining catches by male family members influenced Anishinaabe women's ability to care for their children.[91] Indeed, such changes are difficult to identify since child-care practices such as breastfeeding cannot be tracked in the same way as fishing licences.

Within Anishinaabe communities, however, such changes are writ large. For example, many women raised to care for their breasts in the hope of providing milk medicine were unable to follow Anishinaabe dietary recommendations for lactating mothers, which emphasized the importance of whitefish in breast milk production. One Elder from Dalles 38C remembered an unidentified medical official visiting her community around 1970. This was the first time that she was told "not to eat any more fish, not even muskrat, or beaver." She described the visit as follows: "I remember a nurse came with a doctor. They told us not to eat game, fish, not to eat any of those things anymore that we got from the river, that . . . they were polluted with mercury and waste from that paper mill. . . . It was terrible."[92]

In April 1973, Anishinaabe women at Grassy Narrows organized the Women's Mini Conference and invited women from other reserves in Treaty 3 territory to exchange knowledge and voice women's concerns.

They feared that federal agents might downplay mercury problem to maintain the milling economy.[93] Lacking confidence in federal representatives, Grand Council Treaty 3 sought alternative medical advice. *Council Fire*, an Anishinaabe circular, published Dr. A. Burnstein's warning to Treaty 3 subscribers: "If a pregnant mother has mercury, then the mercury will concentrate on the unborn baby. The mercury will cause improper growth to the child."[94] Burnstein implored pregnant Anishinaabe women in the Treaty 3 district to visit Winnipeg General Hospital and be tested for mercury intoxication, indicating an awareness of the challenges that they faced in finding acceptable protein substitutes in isolated communities. The women were faced with a choice: avoid whitefish or breastfeed without the sense of breast milk as milk medicine.

In response to health concerns, Anishinaabe women organized events such as the Women's Mini Conference to increase awareness of the risk of consuming wild foods while pregnant or breastfeeding. On-reserve schools also taught children that mercury pollution was bad for community health; for the first time, children were being taught at home that Anishinaabe waters and foods could be poisonous. A story by Tony Ashopenase revealed that children understood that the dangers of mercury were often invisible. He wrote:

> once there was a boy named Tony Ashopenase who Always Cleaned
> his back ground. finally One day He got a job. He worked for the treaty
> tree councle. He was to clean All Around the whole Reserve. He went
> Around every house and around back Grounds, Every day, He got
> Twenty five dollars a day. Ever where he goes He sees garbage, pop cans,
> Papers, bag boxes and bottles, Everything. Then soon Grassy narrows
> ont looked better. But theres stil mercury Pollution.[95]

Even in his childhood fantasy of being a well-paid employee of Treaty 3, Ashopenase could not remove mercury from his community. He could only improve how the reserve looked. Much like an Anishinaabe mother could not see the damage that her diet inflicted on her fetus, children were taught that they could not see the dangers in their river.

Children were taught, however, that this invisible danger was as real as a discarded pop can. An unsigned image published in the same newsletter

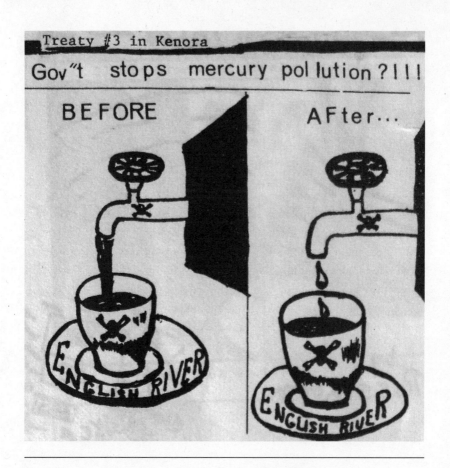

Figure 28. Anishinaabe representations of water quality, c. 1973.

as the Cleaning Up Grassy series depicts a tap filling a household tea cup. This tea cup is marked with a skull and crossbones, the standard symbol for poison. The image reveals that band members had come to recognize daily fare—such as a cup of tea—as potentially toxic.[96] Unlike their mothers, children growing up in the late 1960s and early 1970s were taught to avoid foods harvested from the river. Unlike their mothers, these children were not taught that whitefish had medicinal qualities; rather, they learned that whitefish could harm them. And, as Anishinaabe women worked to eliminate breastfeeding within their communities, the strict rules for breast care—avoiding the use, for example, of push-up bras and slingshots—declined.

Hungry Times, Residential School, and the Sixties Scoop

Children who grew up on Dalles 38C Indian Reserve after construction of the Whitedog Falls Generating Station do not share the memories of their older siblings, cousins, and neighbours. For many, life in the 1950s and early 1960s is remembered as a hungry time. Elder Roberta Jameson recalled her baby brother screaming out in hunger. Her father's nets had been ripped from the shore by deadheads, trees that had been uprooted by flooding but not removed from the water by HEPCO. Debris prevented her father from bringing home fish even before her mother learned that they had been poisoned. On the shelf sat one box of Pablum baby cereal. Her mother fed the screaming infant one spoonful at a time. Jameson and her older siblings watched, their tummies grumbling, unable to take from the baby.

According to Jameson, she was shipped to residential school shortly after her parents stopped being able to provide for the family. She attended Cecilia Jeffrey Residential School, where her parents believed that the Presbyterian Church would feed her.[97] Elder Alice Kelly also recalled being registered for residential school in the mid-1950s. Her mother enrolled her at St. Mary's Residential School when she started "having a tough time to support us." Prior to construction of the Whitedog Falls Generating Station, Kelly remembered that "we were eating fish and potatoes. Bannock, that's how I was grown up." However, as she entered her preteen years, that was "not the way they were feeding their kids." For Kelly, residential school started when fish and potatoes stopped.[98] At Dalles 38C today, Elders such as Jameson and Kelly clearly associate food insecurity with institutionalization.

Some Anishinaabe parents relied on federal institutions—such as residential schools—to feed their children because of the food shortage caused by hydroelectric development. The solution was temporary, for parents voluntarily split up their families in the hope of keeping their children well fed. At Dalles 38C, chubby children were desirable—parents believed that the healthiest children had meat on their bones. Carol Kipling explained that "[Grandma] wanted me to be fat. And, when I would bring friends home, girls who were on the chubby side, she'd say, 'Oh, they so good lookin!' She'd say, 'Why don't you put on some weight?' She wanted me to be fat too—that was a big thing with her. If you were fat, you were healthy, and that was good."[99]

In his research on Pikogan, Quebec, Roger Spielmann similarly found that additional weight was a desirable physical attribute, explaining that "someone who has plenty of meat on their bones is considered healthy and strong." He suggested that "part of the reason for this goes back to when people were living in the bush. . . . It was always important to have plenty of flesh on your bones to tide you through the time when game was scarce."[100] Parents in the Winnipeg River drainage basin could not raise "healthy" children on rationed teaspoons of Pablum.

The Children's Aid Service (CAS) took notice of parents' failure to feed their families. Throughout the 1960s, the CAS scooped up children from Dalles 38C Indian Reserve. Provincial intervention in Indigenous family life was not unique to northwestern Ontario. In 1966, H.I. Hawthorne published a report recommending the extension of provincial welfare services to reserves across Canada to close the gap between "Indians" and others. According to social workers Nancy MacDonald and Judy MacDonald, Indigenous children "quickly became over-represented" and made up to "40–50% of the total number of children in care" for many years after Hawthorne's report.[101] Patrick Johnston coined the phrase "Sixties Scoop" in *Native Children and the Welfare System* to describe the mass removal of Indigenous children from their natal homes into foster or adoptive care with, primarily, non-Indigenous families.[102] Many social workers believed that foster or adoptive care would save Indigenous youth from poverty, substandard housing, poor sanitation, and malnutrition on reserve.[103]

Unlike other victims of the Sixties Scoop, some children from Dalles 38C might have been placed with other status Indian families. If this speculation is accurate, then the CAS did not relocate these children to assimilate them. An unidentified Elder told sociologist Jennifer Leyson that "these

kids and everything got taken away by CAS, the Children's Aid. And there
are some sad stories there. . . . I'll give you an example of my brother there.
He was taken away and sent up north. . . . They put them in a plane, told
them they were gonna go for a plane ride and . . . would be . . . going home
later on. But what actually happened was . . . those kids got . . . flown up
and they landed somewhere in [another] community."[104] In cases in which
Anishinaabe mothers lost control—not only of their ability to feed their children but also of their ability to place them—families broke up permanently.
The Department of Indian Affairs assigned children adopted by Indigenous
families with new band numbers, creating significant challenges for birth
parents trying to track down their children through federal registries.[105]

Yet Anishinaabe mothers developed adaptive strategies to manage
environmental changes within their families. For example, they adopted
canned, condensed, and sweetened Carnation Milk as a substitute for breast
milk. Canned milk could be picked up at the Kenora Friendship Centre,
and some mothers even suggested in interviews that Indian Affairs distributed Carnation Milk to Anishinaabe families as a form of in-kind welfare.[106]
Although many Anishinaabe mothers can no longer provide milk medicine (fortified by whitefish consumption) to nursing infants, they have
fashioned Carnation Milk cans—which have become symbols of welfare
dependence—into healing regalia. Anishinaabe historian Brenda Child
notes that, "in the Ojibwe world, spiritual power moves through the air,
and sounds hold significance. The jingle dress is special because of the rows
of metal cones . . . that dangle from the garment and produce a pleasantly
dissonant rattle as they bound against one another [during dances]."[107] In
the Kenora District, some Anishinaabe women claim that Carnation Milk
cans make the best jingle cones for jingle dresses.[108]

Today female jingle dancers are provided with tobacco by community
members seeking healing prayers for themselves or their loved ones. Holistic
medicinal practices (e.g., jingle dancing) have come to reinforce and rein-
vigorate women's work. Although not all jingle dances serve a medicinal
purpose, the jingle dress originated from a medicine dream (c. 1900). In
Treaty 3 territory, it is believed that a *Midewinini* from Whitefish Bay First
Nation introduced the healing dress and dance. According to local history,
the Midewinini had a granddaughter who was gravely ill. He was gifted with
a vision of a spirit in a jingle dress. The spirit informed the Midewinini that
he could heal his granddaughter by recreating the dress and putting it on her.

The Midewinini accepted the spirit's advice. He recreated his vision dress, put it on his granddaughter, and carried her to the dance circle. His granddaughter then took three turns in the pow-wow circle. She was carried by the Midewinini for the first turn; she walked with the support of women for the second turn; she walked alone, healed, for the third turn. Convinced of its medicinal power, Anishinaabe women adapted the jingle dress as a healing dress thereafter. By saving the tops of Carnation Milk cans, by washing them and rolling them to fashion jingles, Anishinaabe mothers help their daughters to develop new forms of medicine power.[109]

SO THAT OUR NEXT GENERATION WILL KNOW

When I was younger, I asked my father—as most children are wont to do—why? In 1986, as Mom carried the weight of my brother, Michael, inside her, I wanted to know why. "Why is Mommy's tummy so big?" I asked. In 1990, shortly after my sister, Ashley, was born, I wanted to know, "Why do babies cry?" By the time that I reached adolescence, I wanted to know how our family had come to be part of the Dalles 38C Indian Reserve diaspora. Why had Michael, Ashley, and I been raised in town? How had we come to be third generation born and raised off the land?

What had made my great-grandfather John Kipling Jr. leave the place of his birth? As a toddler, John had pulled his tikinagun toward Ogimaamaashiik, my paternal great-great-grandmother, hoping to be carried through our ancestral territories. From his tikinagun, he had watched her paddle toward manomin fields. He had seen Ogimaamaashiik and her peers pick blueberries for home use and for sale. As a child, he had loved Dalles 38C and off-reserve harvesting grounds. Yet John had left. He had left permanently. His mother, Ogimaamaashiik, had responded to the name Matilda Martin throughout his adult life. Why?

To answer my questions, Dad drove me to the Norman Dam at the western outlet of Lake of the Woods. He parked the truck and asked me to

164DAMMED

walk alongside him. The dam, he explained, had changed how water flowed through the upper Winnipeg River drainage basin. I learned that my heart is composed of water (an estimated 73 percent). I learned that my blood is composed of water. Just as a clogged artery had caused my grandfather's heart to stop, the Norman Dam and Whitedog Falls Generating Station farther downstream had stopped the natural flow of water from Lake of the Woods toward Hudson Bay. Water regulation killed the four-leggeds and some swimmers too. Muskrat drowned as backed-up waters inundated their dens. Sturgeon suffocated as wood waste accumulated in the upper reach of the Winnipeg River. Anishinaabe mothers stopped producing best-quality breast milk as mercury levels increased in predatory fish.

John Kipling Jr. had wanted to give descendants such as me a full life: he had worked for pay in Kenora as the subsistence economy on reserve flat-lined. Other Anishinaabe families living along the Winnipeg River chose to relocate too. Dalles 38C was nearly abandoned after the Hydro-Electric Power Commission of Ontario incorporated the stretch of river between the Norman Dam and Whitedog Falls Generating Station into its reservoir system. In 2008, journalist Lloyd Mack reported that, "between 1956 and 1970, the population declined steadily until there was nobody left." Concerns about water quality and its effects on local wildlife had spurred massive out-migration.[1] The testimony of Elder Clarence Henry aligned with Mack's observation "Everything was dying away, just like that. Eventually there were hardly any people left. People my age [born around 1930] spread out."[2] Elder Alice Kelly testified that her mother, Catherine Hunter, had relocated her children to Whitefish Lake Indian Reserve near Sioux Narrows, Ontario, in response to food insecurity.[3] Historian Bryan Palmer has suggested that Indigenous Peoples across Canada—not just members of Dalles 38C—tried to escape from poverty through out-migration. According to Palmer, the percentage of status Indians in Canada who lived in urban centres rose approximately 10 percent between 1959 and 1972. The population on reserves decreased accordingly.[4]

In 1974, the Ministry of Transportation and Communication showed on a map (albeit unintentionally) the near abandonment of Dalles 38C. The Project Planning Branch produced a feasibility study in response to a request from the Indian Affairs Branch for a transportation service from Kenora to nearby reserves. Dalles 38C Indian Reserve is strikingly absent from the map. By 1974, there was no resident population to consider. One Man Lake Indian Reserve is also missing from this map. The Indian Affairs Branch had merged its band members with those of Whitedog Indian Reserve in response to rising water levels. Between 1950, when Dalles Channel was blasted open, and the 1970s, when the Ministry of the Environment identified methyl mercury in the Winnipeg River, the human geography of Anishinaabe territory had changed. Although a paucity of historical data makes it difficult to quantify the effects of hydroelectric development on Anishinaabe bodies, provincial maps allow us to see its effects on physical communities: band members left Dalles 38C in the hope of raising healthy families elsewhere. In 1984, I was born in the Lake of the Woods District Hospital. Living off reserve was my inheritance. John Kipling Jr. had decided to stay in Kenora after residential school. His children and their children had been born in town, part of an increasingly urban Anishinaabe and mixed-blood population.

HEPCO's expansionist program, which ultimately incentivized Kipling's decision to live in town, was not unique to northwestern Ontario. The Second World War is generally believed to have ushered in a period of "unparalleled economic growth" across Canada.[5] Historians J.M. Bumsted and Douglas Owram have linked an increase in per capita income with improved standards of living nationwide.[6] One of the crossing points that emerges from these pages, from the testimonies of Anishinaabe knowledge keepers, is that their families did not prosper alongside Canadians in general. Instead, they experienced a precipitous decline in living standards on reserve. While the Ontario-Minnesota Pulp and Paper Company used hydroelectricity to expand newsprint production, Anishinaabe employment decreased as HEPCO disassembled work camps once the Whitedog Falls Generating Station began operations. Prior to the establishment of the station, Anishinaabe labourers had supported their families by combining wage work with seasonal harvesting. While suburbanites used new electric appliances to lessen the burden of domestic labour in Kenora, Anishinaabe mothers downstream struggled to feed their infants with best-quality breast milk. Before the station began operations, they had resisted federal and municipal pressures to bottle-feed their infants. Indeed, hydroelectric development after the war exacerbated the socio-economic divide between settler-colonists and Anishinaabe families.

Histories of postwar Canada often miss the widening economic gap between Canadians and First Nations after 1945 because of two popular misconceptions, widely thought to be historical facts.[7] First, historians assumed that amendments to the Indian Act in 1951, which increased First Nations control over their affairs, also improved the economic standing of status Indians on reserves.[8] However, few historical studies compare this increased political control with the effects of concurrent federal programming in the areas of industrial expansion and employment. Canada gave First Nations increased control over their affairs at the same time that industry jeopardized the economic functioning of reserves. Indigenous Peoples gained limited control over their decreasing land and resource bases. Although federal programs were designed to help status Indians build sustainable communities in the postwar era, they obscured the role of industrial development in economic collapse.

Second, scholars tied endemic poverty on reserves to the allocation of reserve lands in the late nineteenth century and early twentieth century, emphasizing the role of isolation, poor soils, and Indian Affairs in preventing Indigenous Peoples from growing crops for home use or sale. Such arguments draw upon two seminal works in Indigenous history. In *Colonizing Bodies: Aboriginal Health and Healing in British Columbia, 1900–1950,* historian Mary-Ellen Kelm revealed that reserve life in British Columbia led to malnutrition because reduced access to traditional harvesting areas stymied Indigenous food production.[9] In *Lost Harvests: Prairie Indian Reserve Farmers and Government Policy,* historian Sarah Carter uncovered how federal policy curtailed Indigenous harvesting activities on reserve. She further argued that Canada reallocated seemingly un- or underused lands to settlers, shrinking Indigenous land holdings in what we now know as the Canadian prairies.[10] While scholars iterated on Kelm's and Carter's important findings, a gap in the literature emerged. What became of reserves that were economically sustainable until Canada's postwar boom? How did postwar expansion affect the size or usability of Indigenous territories? A failure to consider such alternatives may have led political scientist Tom Flanagan, in *First Nations? Second Thoughts,* to advocate for the dissolution of reserve lands as a solution to welfare dependency. He associated reserves with isolation and isolation with economic failure. Flanagan assumed that Indigenous Peoples had refused "to move to where jobs and investment opportunities exist."[11] He did not address the fact that job opportunities on reserves had only recently declined in regions such as the Winnipeg River drainage basin.

A second crossing point that emerges in *Dammed* is that Anishinaabe reserves were economically sustainable until the 1950s. The Winnipeg River example shows that endemic poverty was not the inevitable result of poor soil, geographic isolation, or a refusal to participate in the free-market economy.

Looking out from Anishinaabe territory, the negative and cumulative effects of government policy on Anishinaabe economies after 1945 become clear. Endemic poverty on reserves resulted from federal and provincial postwar policies undertaken for the "common good." This narrative was used to justify development on Indigenous lands and overshadowed alternative narratives of Indigenous Peoples who suffered to provide power for settler-colonists who resided in urban centres.[12]

Although historians have challenged the notion of the common good, few have challenged HEPCO's representation of space. Historians, like Canadian hydro companies, maintain that development served the "centre."[13] Postwar development is said to have occurred in "peripheral" spaces or spaces without social and economic systems valued by settler-colonists. This definition of space has assumed a shared citizenship across these two zones (centre and periphery), normalizing colonial conceptions of space that overwrote Indigenous homelands. It has also overlooked the fact that Indigenous Peoples live at the centres of their own communities.

By making Anishinaabe territory central, an alternative notion of space emerges. Anishinaabe families in the Winnipeg River drainage basin did not see themselves as peripheral. They lived under a separate jurisdiction shaped not by the common good but by the unequal distribution of benefits and damages. First Nations and Ontario citizens had little in common under the law. Anishinaabe families living on federally designated lands saw few benefits from postwar expansion. Canadian citizens, in contrast, saw little of the suffering just outside town limits.

Looking at hydroelectric development from Anishinaabe perspectives adds nuances to histories of environmental change. A third crossing point that emerges in these pages is that there was no single "Indian" experience of flooding in the Winnipeg River drainage basin even though Canadian law (i.e., the Indian Act) collapsed subsistence and wage labourers, men and women, children and youth from the Atlantic to the Pacific under that one label. Hydroelectric development caused Anishinaabe communities to fracture. Individuals had to make difficult choices about how to respond to HEPCO, and their options were shaped by their job, gender, and age.

Elder Robert Kabestra, a general labourer, planned to use his wages to sustain Dalles 38C Indian Reserve. Elder Clarence Henry, in contrast, continued to fish in the Winnipeg River. HEPCO informed neither Kabestra nor Henry of the anticipated impacts of the Whitedog Falls Generating Station.

When HEPCO builders left Treaty 3 territory, both men found themselves struggling to find steady employment. Hostilities against wage-earning families such as the Kabestras, however, increased. Some misinterpreted Kabestra's attempt to sustain the reserve by cooperating with HEPCO as collaboration with settler-colonists.

Flora McLeod, Robert's wife, did not work for HEPCO like her husband. She was busy maintaining the family home. Mothers such as McLeod experienced the Whitedog Falls Generating Station differently from their husbands or, indeed, postmenopausal women. After the station began operations and increased methyl mercury levels in the Winnipeg River became widely known, Anishinaabe mothers had to change their breastfeeding practices to maintain the health of their infants.

Looking at the history of hydroelectric development from Anishinaabe perspectives allows us to do more than challenge histories of prosperity and loss in Canada. What emerges is a fourth crossing point that challenges narratives about Indigenous activism after the Second World War. Long before 1969, when Indigenous Peoples united to oppose the Canadian government's proposal in its White Paper to dismantle the Indian Act, Indigenous communities responded to industrial intrusions by adapting to, cooperating with, or passively resisting settler-colonists. Prior to construction of the Whitedog Falls Generating Station, older stations had prompted important questions about Anishinaabe treaty lands in the area. The Norman Dam, constructed by the Keewatin Power Company, had jeopardized Anishinaabe mobility along the Winnipeg River since the 1890s. Water fluctuations had reduced the structural integrity of ice roads, which in turn had reduced safe access to traplines between Kenora and Dalles 38C, One Man Lake, or Whitedog Indian Reserve. Ice instability had also increased the risk of travelling to town for provisions or Western medical aid.

By the 1900s, Anishinaabe families knew that water regulation affected their ability to sustain themselves from the river. They responded creatively to environmental changes and adjusted labour and saving practices to maximize available resources to meet new circumstances. Anishinaabe families continued to sell blueberries to generate income during the summer months, but now occasionally they banked blueberry money in Kenora. They could draw on their capital during the winter months if their traplines failed. Writing on blueberry sales in the United States, Anishinaabe historian Brenda Child has identified "participat[ion] in the broader cash economy as an antidote to poverty."[14] Like Child, I argue that adaptation ought to be identified as a form of resistance to the expropriation of natural resources by settler-colonists. Adaptation allowed Anishinaabe people to endure despite increased incentives to abandon their reserves and assimilate into the Canadian body politic. Adaptation allowed Anishinaabe families to retain their special homeland.

By the 1950s, when HEPCO began work on the Whitedog Falls Generating Station, Anishinaabe families had every reason to assume that water regulation would once again change how they occupied their lands. They required a new strategy to ensure the continuous occupation of reserves such as Dalles 38C along the Winnipeg River. That some Indigenous men chose to cooperate, to accept new developments and try to turn them to their advantage, has been overshadowed by a tendency among scholars to focus on the economic losses of fishers, hunters, and trappers, not on the economic gains of labourers, another important theme in the testimonies of Anishinaabe men.

The story that emerges from Anishinaabe experiences is one of cultural continuity. Although Anishinaabe labourers might have been anomalous in their communities, they created social and cultural spaces for themselves and future generations at the dam site and in the wage economy more generally. Anishinaabe men earned wages clearing brush, driving trucks, and erecting transmission lines. This work allowed them to use locally earned dollars to support their families on reserves. Unfortunately, this strategy—which temporarily allowed Anishinaabe families to resist the pressures of assimilation—failed in the long run. HEPCO did not employ Anishinaabe men in the Winnipeg River drainage basin after 1958. As historian Frank Tough found in his study of northern Manitoba, the "lack of control [of Indigenous people] over land and their role as labourers meant that they were not in a position to secure long-term benefits."[15] The stress placed on the subsistence economy by the Whitedog Falls Generating Station led to unpredictable—and notably diminishing—returns. As both yields and employment opportunities declined, resource competition among band members increased.

Even as Anishinaabe attempts to sustain reserves through employment with the commission failed, men and women upheld a vision of a special homeland that conflicted with provincial redefinitions of treaty rights, reserve lands, and water use. Anishinaabe families passively resisted the flooding of their lands by HEPCO (and, indeed, by earlier water developers such as the Keewatin Power Company). Members of Whitedog Indian Reserve turned to settler advocates such as local MP William Moore Benedickson to demand that HEPCO consider Anishinaabe complaints about the loss of their trapping and ricing incomes. The letters that resulted stand as evidence of a non-violent response to environmental change. Because the commission controlled the Whitedog Falls Generating Station remotely from Kenora, the powerhouse had no resident attendant.[16] The decision to write to HEPCO and earlier attempts to build relationships with the commission through waged labour suggest that Anishinaabe families did not necessarily oppose hydroelectric development. Their strategies of resistance—adaptation, cooperation, and passive resistance—suggest that, given the new reality of hydro development on their ancestral lands, some band members desired a relationship with HEPCO that would allow them to help determine how water regulation would affect reserve lands and harvesting grounds.

To date, Canadian historians have largely ignored moderate responses to settler-colonialism. Moderate actors worked for change outside the Canadian legal system. They worked within their communities or their families to manage environmental change. A refusal to operate within the Canadian state might have been an Anishinaabe expression of sovereignty: moderate actors sought change from within their ancestral territories. Yet the year 1969 has been upheld as a watershed moment when Indigenous Peoples from British Columbia to Nova Scotia united to defend their treaty rights and to assert their special relationship with the Crown.[17] Historian Bryan Palmer argues that Indigenous Peoples entered a "period of self-discovery" in the 1960s. He attributes this socio-political awakening to "national and international currents of dissent" from Québécois nationalists' cries for sovereignty to African American demands for equality under the law.[18] Indigenous Peoples, he suggests, were inspired (if not radicalized) by external forces. Palmer describes a decidedly pan–Indian Red Power movement. This political ideology acknowledged the shared struggles of colonized peoples (e.g., Nehiyawak, Haudenosaunee, and Anishinabeg) and demanded change en masse (i.e., as "Indians" under the Indian Act). A "failure" to unite before 1969, however, need not be equated with submission. Anishinaabe histories challenge readers to rethink 1969 as a "period of self-discovery." Although moderate action was largely ineffective in achieving legislative change in Canada, it operated within and thus reinforced precolonial boundaries (an Anishinaabe homeland). Ironically, unified resistance in the 1960s required a suspension of unique interests—Anishinaabe activists demanded better treatment as "Indians" under the Indian Act, not as a treaty nation.[19]

The year 1969 marked a change in strategy that acknowledged federal legis-lation. Local moderate responses to HEPCO provide an alternative definition of Indigenous resistance. I argue that localized resistance requires (1) a strong sense of one's treaty rights, (2) a powerful, anti-colonial sense of one's terri-torial limits, and (3) an unwavering desire to maintain a special homeland by living in it. These tenets allow us to envision Indigenous resistance better on a continuum and in a way that acknowledges the experiences of average fami-lies, not just leaders of and participants in public protests.

By focusing on the day-to-day experiences of the Anishinabeg, flaws in Ontario's remedial process become clear and hold lessons for twenty-first-cen-tury energy users. Apologies issued by Ontario Power Generation (OPG, formerly known as HEPCO) suggest that reserves are economically unsus-tainable. In 2008, OPG presented Anishinaabe labour in the Winnipeg River drainage basin as traditional or anti-modern in a public statement about flood-ing at Dalles 38C. The apology began thus: "Long before Ontario Hydro . . . came to build hydro-electric facilities on the Winnipeg River . . . the people of [Dalles 38C] were a self-sufficient people." Readers are transported to a time before living memory. Self-sufficiency is located in the distant past—a time when Anishinaabe families "share[d] and care[d] for all of creation . . . the waters, water and fish life, plants, medicines, trees, animals, birds." Economic decline is associated (implicitly) with the arrival of settlers. OPG does not accept responsibility for negatively influencing the mixed economy (i.e., the loss of guiding jobs), for laying off Anishinaabe labourers, or for complicating women's reproductive labour in the 1950s. Instead, it presents hydroelectric flooding as a threat to "hunting, trapping, fishing and harvesting in balance and harmony with the land."[20]

Canadian historians have suggested that these economic activities had already been compromised by settler encroachment and federal surveys. The apology suggests that OPG contributed to, but did not cause, endemic poverty on reserves. The company claims to have "further impacted the resources and way of life of the people" of Dalles 38C. OPG thus participated in a metanarra-tive of endemic poverty on reserves that locates blame with Canada's colonial predecessors. Having located self-sufficiency in the distant past, the company minimized its blame for recent environmental damages. It apologized for "not resolving these past grievances [i.e., disruption of traditional ways] sooner."[21] Although it successfully negotiated a cash settlement with Dalles 38C in 2008, damages are ongoing. As recently as October 2015, band members asked

Ontario and Canada to provide compensation for the swamping of reserve lands. Band members argued that property values were declining because of water fluctuations caused by the Whitedog Falls Generating Station.

Unless we think critically about how continued energy use floods reserve lands, we risk thinking that an apology is a cure. Anishinaabe intellectual Leanne Betasamosake Simpson has noted that "the perception of most Canadians is that post-reconciliation, Indigenous Peoples no longer have a legitimate source of contention."[22] As energy users, we all need to understand how human (Indigenous and non-Indigenous) and natural systems interact. Cash settlements do not change how these systems interact, and the dominant narrative of postwar affluence in Canada does not teach the average citizen how to read for system overlap. It is my hope that this book will counter public apologies that shift the burden of responsibility from current energy users to past federal and provincial administrators.

Indeed, the experiences of the Anishinabeg in the Winnipeg River drainage basin reveal how the benefits of development were inequitably distributed in the past. *Dammed* shows how political, cultural, and economic systems functioned and interacted to the detriment of Anishinaabe families. Their experiences stand as a powerful lesson about the far-reaching implications of our day-to-day decisions about energy use. I take seriously historian Paige Raibmon's argument that Canadians need to take responsibility for privilege rather than seeking to blame "Indian" policy (or ancestral land grabs) for the socio-economic disadvantages of Indigenous Peoples. Raibmon argues that it was not simply nameless and faceless bureaucrats who dispossessed and disinherited Indigenous Peoples. Canadian citizens continue to benefit from earlier dispossessions.[23] Every time I turn on a light in Kenora, I place demand on an electrical grid that causes the periodic flooding of my ancestral home. It is my hope that the stories contained in this book will cause you to ask "where is electricity being generated?" It is my hope that you will ask "whose lands are being inundated for my convenience?"

If you listen carefully, then you might hear the water drum in answer to your questions. Anishinaabe families continue to resist the erosion of their homelands. Drum songs remind us that reserve lands are not inherently unsustainable. Uninformed energy consumption continues to make them so.

ACKNOWLEDGEMENTS

When the Canadian Historical Association awarded my doctoral thesis the John Bullen Prize, I was shocked. Pleasantly so. I had often considered leaving academe and seeking an alternative career in business management. I am grateful to Mom and Dad for encouraging me to continue my research journey. Mom and Dad, you reminded me that health—emotional and environmental—influences work quality. Thank you for teaching me how to set healthy parameters around work. I will teach mentees to do the same.

Carolyn Podruchny and Colin Coates, thank you for your ongoing kindness and support. You always delivered feedback with time to discuss it. You always explained your *why*, providing a clear sense of the improvement toward which I was working. From you, I have learned how to coach compassionately. You have set a high bar for me to reach during my supervisory career. Thank you for inspiring me. By emulating your model, I hope to serve students learning under me.

Ben Bryce and Andrew Watson, you provided meaningful feedback on every chapter in this book. Some you read more than once. I am lucky to call you both friends. You taught me the value of a writing network, of creating a safe space in which to make mistakes and discuss ideas. Thank you for helping me to laugh through the process of revision. By sharing our writing model with mentees, I hope that future scholars will forge impactful relationships and write stronger work while having fun in the process.

Lori Nelson and Lynn Riddell at Lake of the Woods Museum, thank you for your detailed responses to my innumerable questions, for digging up and recommending primary sources, and for providing me with a desk on which to work. Lori Jackson at the Kenora Public Library, I would like to thank you for teaching me how to work a microfilm reader. You treated each question, however small, as if it mattered. My research is better for it. Together, the three of you taught me that how we respond to questions influences confidence. I hope to follow in your footsteps, responding to questions with patience and kindness and, by so doing, building the research skill and capacity of future writers.

Karen Clark at the University of Regina Press, I am grateful for the kindness that you extended to me. You saw my research question as the foundation for a scholarly monograph. Because of you, I will encourage mentees to think about the many uses of their research, from blog post to full-length manuscript.

Lesley Erickson, you coached me through the process of turning my doctoral research into a book. Jill McConkey, at the University of Manitoba Press, you provided a home for this work. Together, you have reinforced the importance of teamwork in scholarly publication. I will remind future writers that the best work is born of conversation and revision.

To the Elders who sat down with me, *miigwetch* for sharing your rich histories. American poet and civil rights activist Maya Angelou famously wrote that "I can be changed by what happens to me. But I refuse to be reduced by it." You breathed life into these words. Your teachings are helping me to become a better Anishinaabe-kwe. I hope that, like you, I can continue the long march toward treaty recognition in Canada with grace and grit.

To the many others—Andy Sky, Boyd Cothran, Catherine Carstairs, Cuyler Cotton, Gabrielle Goldhar, Kristeen McKee, Leo Waisberg, Margaret Lehman, Myra Rutherdale, Peter Holdsworth, Samantha Mehltretter, Tim Holzkamm, Victoria Jackson, and Yvan Prkachin—whose input influenced my output, thank you for sharing your time and skill with me. To those who helped to create space for me to write, Elizabeth Dawes and Elizabeth Ewan, I am grateful for the timelines that you set. To my peer reviewers, *miigwetch* for your careful reading. You devoted extraordinary care to my manuscript. I am fortunate to have been paired with you. What follows is my attempt to improve in response to your words.

To all those who loved me on this journey, its many highs and lows, know that you too are loved. I am grateful for the moments that we shared.

Any mistakes that remain are my own and, I hope, opportunities for continued growth.

A NOTE ON SOURCES

In researching *Dammed*, I gathered evidence of Anishinaabe resistance from oral testimony of family-elected Elders who relayed family histories of hydroelectric flooding to me, local historian Cuyler Cotton, and translator Barry Henry. Cotton was working concurrently on a claim involving flood damages at Dalles 38C Indian Reserve. Whenever possible, we scheduled overlapping interviews to prevent Elder burnout, associated with physical and emotional fatigue caused by repeated interviews, particularly the need to recall personal traumas during the interviews.

The Anishinaabe Custom Council (ACC) inspired the call for interview participants. Dalles 38C established the council in the 1990s to combat political upheavals associated with the Indian Act. Under Section 78(1), Indigenous communities are legally required to hold biannual elections.[1] Appointments to the Anishinaabe Custom Council, in contrast, can endure as long as one is presumed competent (or able to represent family interests). The ACC monitors the Chief and council and is empowered to transfer funds to a third-party manager if foul play is suspected. This body thus represents (and helps to finance) community needs across election cycles. Each family group on the band list may appoint a representative to the council. This process helps to ensure equal representation in local politics. In recognition of the ACC's association with fair representation, each family group on the band list was issued an invitation to participate in the research. Eight Elders were recommended for interviews. The eight interviews, conducted in 2012, were supplemented by transcript summaries produced by Cotton after a series of interviews with

Dalles 38C band members in the 1990s. An additional nine interviewees were identified off reserve using the snowball technique.

At times, however, that technique failed. Chapter 4 demonstrates its limits. Elder Bert Fontaine of Sagkeeng First Nation worked for HEPCO in 1956. Elder Larry Kabestra testified about his father's experiences working with the commission during the 1950s. Larry also described his own work in the dam business, particularly cleaning screens at the Norman Dam.[2] Both Larry and Bert could name other Anishinaabe men who had been employed by HEPCO. However, I was unable to gather further testimony using these names. When I asked Bert to refer his past colleagues, he responded that "they're all dead."[3] This chapter was constrained by the much lower life expectancy of Anishinaabe men. As late as 2000, their average life expectancy was only 68.9 years.[4] When interviews were conducted in 2012, the Whitedog Falls Generating Station had already been in operation for fifty-four years. If we assume that the earliest age at which an Anishinaabe youth could seek work for pay was sixteen (the age at which school attendance was no longer compulsory),[5] then potential interviewees were statistical anomalies. Bert and Larry thus represented a much larger pool of working Anishinaabe men whose testimonies are now, literally, buried with them. I relied on textual sources to supplement oral testimonies.

The archives that I visited, however, were determined by the interviews with Elders. I was looking for publicly available texts that could be used to tell Anishinaabe history while respecting Elders' concerns about appropriation. Repeated references to family events (e.g., marriages and funerals) led me to parish records at Notre Dame Church (Catholic) and the Diocese of Keewatin (Anglican) in Kenora.[6] Church records helped me to envision active use territory and to track movements between reserves. These records deepened my understanding of Anishinaabe reliance on water (and ice) transit. Interviewees also drew my attention to written sources produced by Anishinaabe cultural educators. Autobiographical writings and policy proposals that originated from Dalles 38C Indian Reserve, Shoal Lake No. 39 and No. 40 Indian Reserves, and One Man Lake Indian Reserve were also incorporated into this study.

The complete collection of the *Kenora Daily Miner and News* held by the Kenora Public Library proved to be invaluable in building a general timeline of development in the upper Winnipeg River drainage basin. I mined newspapers for details about the Norman Dam, the hearings of the International Joint

Commission, and the Whitedog Falls Generating Station. My reading process was shaped by Elders' testimonies. Elders suggested that Anishinaabe concerns rarely made front-page news, so I turned my attention to the back pages of the newspaper. I focused on "Announcements," which often reported who came to town, how they passed their time, and when they left. Here I found evidence of Anishinaabe movements along and around the upper Winnipeg River. I paired newspaper records with texts (e.g., town plans) and artifacts (e.g., photographs) held by the Lake of the Woods District Museum in Kenora.

Three archives were foundational to my success. The Treaty #3 and Aboriginal Rights Research Centre (TARR) in Kenora opened its document collection to me, which allowed for extended stays in the field during the summer semester. From Kenora, I was able to identify the RG10 folders that I would need to consult from Library and Archives Canada (Ottawa). I was then able to contract Peter Holdsworth, a graduate of the Master's Program in Public History at Carleton University, to pull and scan material from these folders. This process enabled me to live in Treaty 3 territory, spending more time with Elders and near the Winnipeg River and less time in colonial institutions. Historians who want to use TARR's collection might require a band council resolution from their partner communities. A BCR is a federally recognized document recording the band council's decision ("by a majority vote of the councillors present") on issues raised during a band meeting.[7]

During fall and winter semesters, I returned to southern Ontario to study and, later, to teach. I scheduled visits to Toronto-based archives during that time. The Archives of Ontario provided key information about how the province understood and (re)valued water during the period under study. I paid particular attention to the records of Ontario Tourism and the Ontario Water Resources Commission. Although I chose to limit my discussion of sites of spiritual significance compromised by hydroelectric flooding, leaving those stories to spiritual leaders, the Royal Ontario Museum's archives provided me with a sense of pictograph use and loss in Treaty 3 territory in the mid-twentieth century.

This project would have been impossible without the support of Ontario Power Generation. Public access to its records is currently limited. In the summer of 2008, I was granted access to business records shortly after OPG settled with Dalles 38C Indian Reserve. Although the terms of the settlement between OPG and Dalles 38C are private, the company agreed to provide educational support to band members.[8] As the daughter of Allan

Luby (Ogemah), a registered band member and former Chief, I was granted educational support in the form of access to documents. Since that time, OPG has continued to uphold its educational promise to Dalles 38C and to interpret this promise broadly. In 2010, the company supported the erection of a memorial on the reserve to teach future generations about the struggles of band members whose lands were flooded by the Whitedog Falls Generating Station in the 1950s.[9] My research has been made possible by OPG's commitment to resolving the grievances in the Northwestern Division. My ability to tell this story, to access archival material, is the outcome of historical trauma experienced by my paternal ancestors.

The financial costs of my research were offset with very generous funding from the Social Sciences and Humanities Research Council, the Ontario Graduate Scholarship Program, the Graduate Program in History at York University, and the Faculty of Graduate Studies at York University.

NOTES

Foreword

1   The Kenora Powerhouse also sits upstream of Dalles 38C, though band members believe that it might have less of an impact on their living conditions. Researchers at the University of Guelph are currently investigating flow patterns, at the request of Chief and council, to determine the unique and combined effects of these three structures on the Winnipeg River.

Introduction: Looking Out from Anishinaabe Territory

1   Evelyn Gunne, "The Lake of the Woods," in *The Silver Trail* (Boston: Richard G. Badger; Gorham Press, 1906), 36.

2   I use the term "Anishinabeg" to identify the distinct socio-cultural and -political group of Treaty 3 First Nations. I use the terms "Indigenous" and "First Nations" interchangeably to maintain flow and avoid repetition. Collectively, First Nations, Inuit, and Métis peoples constitute the Indigenous Peoples of what is now known as Canada. As a term, "First Nations" tends to exclude persons of Inuit and Métis descent. I have adopted "Indigenous" as the preferred collective term, for it is acknowledged that the Anishinabeg (and other Indigenous Peoples) originate from and belong to their distinctive territories. "Indian" is still a legal term in Canada, and I therefore use it in reference to legal decisions. I recognize that the term has problematic racist connotations.
"Euro-Canadian" is commonly used as an identifier for "white people." However, I do not believe that this term accurately reflects Anishinaabe perceptions of non-Indigenous newcomers. "Euro-Canadian" normalizes Canada as the nation-state. It suggests that "Euro-Canadians" are the inhabitants of a legitimate sovereign territory (Canada) and descended from European immigrants. The Anishinabeg living in Treaty 3 territory did not recognize (and continue to challenge) Canada's claim to land in the upper Winnipeg River drainage basin. In recognition of the basin as an Anishinaabe homeland, I identify newcomers to Anishinaabe territory as "newcomers," "treaty partners," and "settler-colonists" or by trade (e.g., "industrialists" or "labourers").

3   Courtney Milne claims that "Original Man was lowered by rope from the sky to become
    the first inhabitant of Turtle Island" at Manito Ahbee. He further suggests that First Man
    received sacred teachings at this site to "guide the [Anishinabeg] in caring for the
    [E]arth." Courtney Milne, *Spirit of the Land: Sacred Places in Native North America*
    (Toronto: Penguin Books, 1994), 22. Edward Benton-Banai does not identify Manito
    Ahbee as a site of origin. He suggests that Gitchie Manitou used earth to create First Man.
    Upon completion, Gitchie Manitou lowered First Man to the Earth at an unidentified site.
    Benton-Banai suggests that our origins are revealed by our name, Anishinaabe. *Ani* means
    "whence," *nishina* means "lowered," and *abe* refers to "the male of the species." Edward
    Benton-Banai, *The Mishomis Book: The Voice of the Ojibway* (Minneapolis: University of
    Minnesota Press with Indian Country Communications, 1988), 3.

4   Archaeologist Paddy Reid claims that "the oldest recorded site around Kenora is on
    Tunnel Island and dates back 7000 years." He found evidence of Paleo-Indian activity
    around Rainy River, southeast of Kenora, dating back to 8000 BCE. For further informa-
    tion, see Rick Vandervliet, "Paddy Reid and Archaeology in Kenora and NW Ontario,"
    Lake of the Woods Vacation Area, accessed 1 September 2015, http://lakeofthewoods.com/
    stories-from-the-lake/paddy-reid-archaeology-in-kenora-nw-ontario/.

5   Benton-Banai, *The Mishomis Book*, 94.

6   Ibid., 100.

7   Lake of the Woods Writers' Group and Kenora Centennial Committee, *Through the Kenora
    Gateway*, ed. Florence Mead (Kenora, ON: Bilko Press, 1981), 9, 55.

8   James R. Stevens, editor's introduction to Redsky, *Great Leader of the Ojibway*, 9. See also
    the editor's note on page 28.

9   Ibid., 31, 72, 32.

10 Duane R. Lund, *Lake of the Woods Yesterday and Today* (Staples, MN: Nordell Graphic
    Communications, 1975), 9.

11 Written evidence of large-scale fishing by the Anishinabeg in what is known as north-
    western Ontario—extends back to 1660, when trader Pierre-Esprit Radisson claimed to
    have seen over 1,000 sturgeon being dried on the south shore of Lake Superior. See Tim
    Holzkamm and Leo Waisberg, "Native American Utilization of Sturgeon," in *Sturgeons and
    Paddlefish of North America*, ed. William Beamish, Greg LeBreton, and Scott McKinley
    (New York: Springer, 2004), 29–30.

12 As early as May 1973, Dr. A. Bernstein informed Anishinaabe women that "mercury [in
    fish] will cause improper growth" in developing fetuses. He advised pregnant women to
    moderate fish consumption and to undergo a physical examination at Winnipeg General
    Hospital to determine their level of risk. "Mercury Pollution Endangers Unborn Babies,"
    Treaty #3 Council Fire 2, no. 5 (1973): 3.

13 Lund, *Lake of the Woods Yesterday and Today*, 9.

14 Benton-Banai, *The Mishomis Book*, 100–01.

15 Martin-McKeever, *The Chief's Granddaughter*, 23.

16 Journalist Elsie Neufeld reported that Shoal Lake Wild Rice buys grains "from as far east
    as Marathon and as far west as the Saskatchewan/Alberta border to assure a stable supply."
    Neufeld quoted Ben Ratuski, owner-manager of Shoal Lake Wild Rice: "We wouldn't have

a supply if we relied on this area." Elsie Neufeld, "Another Wild Rice Season Draws to a Close," *Saturday Miner and News*, 28 October 2000, 10.

17 Lund, *Lake of the Woods Yesterday and Today*, 10.

18 Lake of the Woods Writers' Group and Kenora Centennial Committee, *Through the Kenora Gateway* claims that "the first business establishment in the area that is now Kenora was the Hudson's Bay Company post on Old Fort Island in 1836." In 1861, the company relocated from Tunnel Island to Rat Portage (now Kenora) proper. The Kenora Centennial Committee locates the 1861 site at the northeast corner of present-day First Street South and Main Street (43). See also Lake of the Woods Museum and Aulneau Adventure Tours, *The Explorer's Guide*, 21.

19 Kelly, "We Are All in the Ojibway Circle," 579–80.

20 Lake of the Woods Museum and Aulneau Adventure Tours, *The Explorer's Guide*, 23.

21 Lund, *Lake of the Woods Yesterday and Today*, 95. Lake of the Woods Writers' Group and Kenora Centennial Committee, *Through the Kenora Gateway*, 61, suggests that the Keewatin Lumber and Manufacturing Company (KLM) never constructed a powerhouse. In *Levelling the Lake*, Jamie Benidickson further explains that Ontario granted KLM "most of Tunnel Island and twenty-three additional acres near the lower falls" in 1891. The company promised to "invest $250,000 for power development" in return and to "lease power and lands for buildings and factories at rates to be fixed by a provincially appointed engineer" (66). KLM did not construct a powerhouse in the 1890s. Instead of using the Norman Dam to generate electricity, Ontario used KLM's property to control water levels in Lake of the Woods.

22 Ruth McLennan, "Ontario-Manitoba Boundary Dispute, 1880–1884," 13 April 1967, unpublished document, Kenora Public Library, 1, 3.

23 The Whitedog Falls Generating Station consists of three units. Unit 1 went into operation on 17 February 1958, Unit 2 on 25 March 1958, and Unit 3 on 16 June 1958. At this time, the generating station became fully operational. Ontario Power Generation, "Whitedog Falls Generating Station," 15 December 2015, http://www.opg.com/generating-power/hydro/northwest-ontario/Pages/whitedog-falls-station.aspx.

24 Lake of the Woods Control Board, "Winnipeg River in Ontario," 17 November 2014, https://www.lwcb.ca/reg-guide/rgp-PT2-WPGRVRON.html.

25 For example, in "Studying Canadian Military History," *Canadian Military History* 2, no. 21 (1993), Desmond Morton claims that "war has been a catalyst for every kind of political, social and economic change, from female suffrage in 1917 to post-1945 affluence" (139), a position he substantiates in *Canada and War: A Military and Political History* (Toronto: Butterworths, 1981). J.L. Granatstein and Desmond Morton echo this sentiment in "The War Changed Everything," in *Readings in Canadian History: Post-Confederation*, 6th ed., ed. R. Douglas Francis and Donald B. Smith (Toronto: Nelson Thomson Learning, 2002). They suggest that wartime atrocities prompted Canadians to re-evaluate which services the state offered to which of its citizens. They conclude that "Canada loosened up, lightened up, and became a kinder, gentler place" as a result of the Second World War (328).

26 For example, in *Planners and Politicians: Liberal Politics and Social Policy, 1957–1968* (Montreal and Kingston: McGill-Queen's University Press, 1997), Penny Bryden argues that Canada's welfare state was founded, in part, on political self-interest: the Liberal Party proposed Canadian welfare programs to compete with John Diefenbaker's working-class

appeal in an attempt to return to power. Bryden thus offers an interesting counterpoint to Morton and Granatstein.

27 I do not discount post–Second World War studies that acknowledge the uneven distri-
bution of wealth by gender, sexuality, or perceived ideological standing. See, for example,
Jennifer Stephen, *Pick One Intelligent Girl: Employability, Domesticity and the Gendering of
Canada's Welfare State* (Toronto: University of Toronto Press, 2007); Veronica Strong-
Boag, "Home Dreams: Women and the Suburban Experiment in Canada," *Canadian
Historical Review* 72, no. 4 (1991): 471–504; Mary Louise Adams, *The Trouble with
Normal: Postwar Youth and the Making of Heterosexuality* (Toronto: University of Toronto
Press, 1997); Gary Kinsman and Patrizia Gentile, *The Canadian War on Queers: National
Security as Sexual Regulation* (Vancouver: UBC Press, 2010); Gary Marcuse and Reginald
Whitaker, *Cold War Canada: The Making of a National Insecurity State, 1945–1957*
(Toronto: University of Toronto Press, 1994); and, Bryan Palmer, *Canada's 1960s: The
Ironies of Identity in a Rebellious Era* (Toronto: University of Toronto Press, 2009).

28 Two notable exceptions include Lutz, *Makúk*, and McCallum, *Indigenous Women, Work,
and History*. Lutz examines Indigenous contributions to industries such as fishing and
logging. He suggests that paid work fuelled a "moditional economy," a term that refers to a
hybrid system in which Indigenous workers combined subsistence activities with work for
pay (and, in later years, social assistance). Lutz seeks to revise Robin Fisher's argument in
Contact and Conflict: Indian-European Relations in British Columbia, 2nd ed. (Vancouver:
UBC Press, 1992), that Indigenous Peoples became economically irrelevant after the gold
rush (which coincided with reduced settler interest in fur trading). McCallum also takes
issue with the historical emphasis on fur trade economics (5). *Native Pathways*, edited by
Brian Hosmer and Colleen O'Neill, discusses alternative American Indigenous economies
in the twentieth century. Taken together, these works—American and Canadian—suggest
that other historians have conflated the concepts of capitalism and modernity. These
authors reveal that Indigenous Peoples participated in (and adapted) Western economies
in distinctively Indigenous ways after the Second World War.

29 J.M. Bumsted, *A History of the Canadian Peoples*, 4th ed. (Don Mills, ON: Oxford University
Press, 2011), 356–402.

30 Michael Bliss, *Northern Enterprise: Five Centuries of Canadian Business* (Toronto: McClelland
and Stewart, 1987), 481.

31 J.L. Granatstein and Desmond Morton, "The War Changed Everything," 327.

32 Within this statistic, individuals of British, Irish, and French descent formed the demographic majority. Canadian Human Rights Commission, "Population and People: 1
January 1950," in *Human Rights in Canada: A Historical Perspective*, https://www.chrc-
ccdp.gc.ca/historical-perspective/en/getBriefed/1950/population.asp.

33 Bumsted, *A History of the Canadian Peoples*, 377.

34 Chelsea Vowel, "We Can't Get Anywhere until We Flip the Narrative," Âpihtawikosisân,
22 August 2013, https://apihtawikosisan.com/2013/08/we-cant-get-anywhere-
until-we-flip-the-narrative/.

35 Alfred, *Heeding the Voice of Our Ancestors*, 9.

36 Simpson, *As We Have Always Done*, 6.

37 Potts and Brown, "Becoming an Anti-Oppressive Researcher," 19.

38 Phil Lane Jr. et al., *The Sacred Tree* (Twin Lakes, WI: Lotus Press, 1989), 36; Rheault, "Anishinaabe Mino-Bimaadiziwin," 36; Simpson, *As We Have Always Done,* 154; Marlene Brant Castellano, "Ethics of Aboriginal Research," *Journal of Aboriginal Health* 1, no. 1 (2004): 100.

39 Spiritual relations with non-human beings could also be forged through fasting and dreaming "or other means"; see Miller, *Ogimaag,* 11, 26.

40 Rheault, "Anishinaabe Mino-Bimaadiziwin," 38.

41 Lane et al., *The Sacred Tree,* 23.

42 Simpson, *Dancing on Our Turtle's Back,* 31.

43 Smith, *Decolonizing Methodologies,* 15–16, 166, 199.

44 Quoted in Doerfler, Sinclair, and Stark, eds., *Centering Anishinaabeg Studies,* 7.

45 Ibid., 6.

46 Richter, *Facing East from Indian Country,* 8–9. Michael Witgen extended the practice of "visual reorientation" into Anishinaabe territory in *An Infinity of Nations.*

Chapter 1: By Water We Inhabit This Place

1 Records indicate that Chief Powassan was alive in 1912. It is unclear whether he was living in 1915. The story presented here is an imagined one, intended to welcome readers into Anishinaabe relationships with water as well as plant and animal beings.

2 "A Triune City," [Rat Portage] *Weekly Record,* 9 January 1892, 1.

3 The MUSE-Lake of the Woods Museum, "Historical Timeline," 2019, https://themuse-kenora.ca/historical-timeline/. See also Robert M. Bone, *The Canadian North: Issues and Challenges,* 3rd ed. (Don Mills, ON: Oxford University Press, 2009), 99–100.

4 See Ontario, *Statutes of the Province of Ontario Passed in the Session Held in the Fifty-Fourth Year of the Reign of Her Majesty Queen Victoria, Being the First Session of the Seventh Legislature of Ontario* (Toronto: Warwick and Sons, 1891), 7–9. On 16 April 1894, Canada and Ontario came to a statutory agreement known as the 1894 Joint Agreement of the 1891 Legislative Acts. It affirmed that "the land covered with water lying between the projecting headlands of any lake or sheets of water not wholly surrounded by an Indian Reserve or Reserves shall be deemed to form part of such reserve [or reserves]"; quoted in McNab, "The Administration of Treaty 3," 149. In 1915, Ontario overturned its position with An Act to Confirm the Title of the Government of Canada to Certain Lands and Indian Lands. Section 2 of this document suggested that "land covered with water lying between the projecting headlands of any lake or sheets of water not wholly surrounded by an Indian reserve or reserves ... shall not be deemed to form part of such reserve [or reserves]"; quoted in M.A. Sanderson, "Reasons for Judgement: *Keewatin v. Ontario (Minister of Natural Resources),*" Ont. S.C.J., Court File No. 05-CV-281875PD, 16 August 2011, 214, http://caid.ca/KeeDec2011.pdf.

5 Notzke, *Aboriginal Peoples and Natural Resources in Canada,* 68–69.

6 Lake of the Woods Writers' Group and Kenora Centennial Committee, *Through the Kenora Gateway,* 10. This population estimate might have been pulled from Simon J. Dawson, who wrote that "the only localities where the Indians are at all numerous are at the Lake of the Woods and Rainy River, but the entire population does not greatly exceed three thousand."

Simon J. Dawson, "The Indian Element," *Report on the Line of Route between Lake Superior and the Red River Settlement* (Ottawa: Hunter, Rose and Company, 1868), 27.

7   McNab, "The Administration of Treaty 3," 145.

8   Germaine Warkentin, ed., *Pierre-Esprit Radisson: The Collected Writings, Volume 1, The Voyages* (Montreal and Kingston: McGill-Queen's University Press, 2012), 256.

9   Tim E. Holzkamm, Victor P. Lytwyn, and Leo G. Waisberg, "Rainy River Sturgeon: An Ojibway Resource in the Fur Trade Economy," *Canadian Geographer* 32, no. 3 (1988): 195. In his 1868 publication, Dawson noted that hundreds of Anishinabeg gathered at Rainy River to harvest large quantities of sturgeon: "I have seen as many as five or six hundreds of them collected at one time, at the rapids on Rainy River, engaged in catching sturgeon, the flesh of which they preserve by drying like Pemmican." Dawson, *Report on the Line of Route*, 27.

10   Holzkamm and Waisberg, "Native American Utilization of Sturgeon," 29.

11   Unidentified observer quoted in ibid., 30.

12   Theresa Schenck, "William W. Warren's *History of the Ojibway People*: Tradition, History, and Context," in *Reading beyond Words: Contexts for Native History*, ed. Jennifer S.H. Brown and Elizabeth Vibert, 2nd ed. (Toronto: Broadview Press, 2003), 199.

13   The fish clans are catfish, pike, sucker, sturgeon, and whitefish; Johnston, *Ojibway Heritage*, 53, 60. In 1885, historian William Warren identified the same clans. However, he specified that sucker, sturgeon, and whitefish "are only known on the remotest northern boundaries of Ojibway country." Warren also identifies "Merman" as a fish clan. Warren, *History of the Ojibway People*, 44–46.

14   Elder Alice Kelly, "Living with 'Dirty Water': Personal Recollections from on and off Dalles 38C Indian Reserve," paper presented at the Native American and Indigenous Studies Association, Uncasville, CT, 3 June 2012.

15   Johnston, *Ojibway Heritage*, 53.

16   Elder Kelly, "Living with 'Dirty Water.'"

17   Quoted in Andy Sky, "Draft: Giimiiniigoomin Manitou Gitigan," 2 September 2014, Treaty and Aboriginal Rights Research (TARR), Grand Council Treaty #3, Kenora, Ontario. Elder Skead lived from about 1922 to 1996.

18   Ibid.

19   Elder Theresa Jourdain, Elder Larry Kabestra, Elder Josephine Klein, and Elder Archie Wagamese, group interview with the author, Dalles 38C Indian Reserve, ON, 20 September 2019.

20   Robin Wall Kimmerer, "Returning the Gift," *Minding Nature* 7, no. 2 (2014): 18-24. See also: https://www.humansandnature.org/returning-the-gift.

21   The thirteen conditions, dated 22 January 1869, were attached to the report by Alexander Morris of the negotiations in 1873. Alexander Morris, "Demands made by the Indians as their terms for Treaty, 2 October 1873," Library and Archives Canada (hereafter LAC), RG10, vol. 1918, fol. F2790B.

22   Densmore, *Chippewa Customs*, 125.

23 Letter from Wemyss Simpson, S.J. Dawson, Robert Pither, Indian Commissioners to Joseph Howe, Secretary of State for the Provinces, 17 July 1872," LAC, RG 10, vol. 1868, file 577.

24 In *Bounty and Benevolence: A History of Saskatchewan Treaties* (Montreal and Kingston: McGill-Queen's University Press, 2000), 3–21, historians Arthur J. Ray, Jim Miller, and Frank Tough reveal that HBC traders maintained peaceable relationships through regular participation in ceremonies. In what would become Treaties 4, 5, 6, 8, and 10, Indigenous inhabitants expected annual gifts from the Hudson's Bay Company. They also expected relief for individuals who endured physical and/or material hardships. It is likely that the Hudson's Bay Company adopted similar practices in what would become Treaty 3. See also John Palliser, "Exploration of British North America," in *The Papers of the Palliser Expedition 1857–1860*, ed. Irène M. Spry (Toronto: Champlain Society, 1968), 76–78.

25 Simon J. Dawson, "General Report on the Progress of the Red River Expedition," in *Report on the Exploration of the Country between Lake Superior and the Red River Settlement and between the Latter Place and the Assiniboine and Saskatchewan* (Toronto: John Lovell,, 1859), 27.

26 It is important to note that mineral rights also featured in the 1871 negotiations. "Simon Dawson, Robert Pither, Wemyss Simpson, Report to Joseph Howe, Secretary of State, 17 July 1872," LAC, RG10, vol. 1868, file 577.

27 Simon J. Dawson, "The Indian Element [1 May 1869]," in *The Red River Country, Hudson's Bay and North-West Territories, Considered in Relation to Canada, with the Last Two Reports of S. J. Dawson . . . on the Line of Route between Lake Superior and the Red River Settlement*, ed. Alex J. Russell (Montreal: G.E. Desbarats, 1870), 170.

28 Holzkamm and Waisberg, "Native American Utilization of Sturgeon," 32.

29 Quoted in Tim Holzkamm and Leo Waisberg, *We Have Kept Our Part of the Treaty: The Anishinaabe Understanding of Treaty 3* (Kenora, ON: Grand Council Treaty #3, 3 October 1998), 6.

30 Canada, *Treaty 3 between Her Majesty the Queen and the Saulteaux Tribe of the Ojibbeway Indians at Northwest Angle on the Lake of the Woods with Adhesions*, https://www.aadnc-aandc.gc.ca/eng/1100100028675/1100100028679.

31 Ojibwa Chiefs of Treaty 3, Paypom Treaty, 4 October 1873, TARR. In this chapter, I actively incorporate the treaty, using it as corroboration of more familiar non-Indigenous documents in an attempt to increase public exposure to written Indigenous texts.

32 "Minister of the Interior David Laird to Department of the Interior, 24 June 1874," LAC, RG2, Series 1, PCOC 841(a).

33 "Unidentified to Honourable Geo Foster, Minister of Mines and Fisheries, 27 December 1886," LAC, RG10, vol. 3800, file 48–542.

34 "E.W. Dewdney, Superintendent General of Indian Affairs, to the Department of Indian Affairs, 17 December 1890," LAC, RG10, vol. 3830, file 62509-1 Black.

35 Ontario, "An Act for the settlement of questions between the Governments of Canada and Ontario respecting Indian Lands," *Statutes of the Province of Ontario Passed in the Session Held in the Fifty-Fourth Year of the Reign of Her Majesty Queen Victoria, Being the First Session of the Seventh Legislature of Ontario* (Toronto: Warwick and Sons, 1891), 7–9. Jamie Benidickson cautiously identifies a related argument in Benidickson, *Levelling the Lake,*

NOTES TO PAGES 24–29

26. He indicates that the headland principle can be linked to food security: "The objective [of concurrent 1891 federal and Ontario legislation] was presumably to secure food sources—fish and wild rice—for Indigenous communities." He traces this claim back to McNab, "The Administration of Treaty 3."

36 "Simon Dawson, Robert Pither, Wemyss Simpson, Report to Honourable Joseph Howe, Secretary of State, 11 July 1871," LAC, RG10, vol. 1864, fol. 375.

37 Douglas Harris, *Landing Native Fisheries: Indian Reserves and Fishing Rights in British Columbia, 1849–1925* (Vancouver: UBC Press, 2008), 187, 196, 198.

38 A.W. Ponton, *Treaty No. 3 Ontario: Survey of Indian Reserve No. 38C at "The Dalles" Winnipeg River* [map] (Ottawa: Dominion Land Survey, 1890).

39 Sheldon Ratuski, "Gathering Traditional Knowledge and Perspectives of Sturgeon on the Winnipeg River from Dalles Community Members," unpublished report, 2005, LOWM.

40 Simon J. Dawson, "Notes taken at Indian Treaty North West Angle, Lake of the Woods, from 30th Sept. 1873 to close of treaty," LAC, MG29, C67, 35.

41 "J.S. Dennis, Surveyor General, to David Laird, Superintendent General of Indian Affairs, 1 November 1875," LAC, RG10, red vol. 1918, file 2790D.

42 Bartlett, *Aboriginal Water Rights in Canada*, 49. Water courses were still considered public resources under the law. Riparian owners were simply entitled to receive the flow of water to their properties. For further reading, see Alastair R. Lucas, *Security of Title in Canadian Water Rights* (Calgary: Canadian Institute of Resource Law, 1990), 102.

43 Ontario Department of Agriculture, *The Pioneer Farm and the Wabigoon Country Rainy River District—A New Section Opened for Settlement, Information as to the Country and Its Capabilities, an Account of the Farm Established There by the Ontario Government* (Toronto: Ontario Department of Agriculture, 1896), Toronto Public Library, CIHM/ICMH Microfiche Series, no. 93747.

44 "Our North Country," *Rat Portage Miner and Semi-Weekly*, 16 May 1906, 1.

45 Nelles, *Politics of Development*, 217.

46 "Rat Portage and the Rainy River District: The Islands of the Lake of the Woods as a Summer Resort: The Lumber Industry of the District: The Rich and Fertile Farming Lands of the Rainy River: Mineral Wealth and Development," *Rat Portage Weekly Record*, 1888, J.J. Talman Library, AO, pamphlet 1888#26.

47 Ontario Department of Agriculture, *The Pioneer Farm and the Wabigoon Country Rainy River District*.

48 "Rat Portage and the Rainy River District . . . ," *Rat Portage Weekly Record*, 1888, J.J. Talman Library, AO, pamphlet 1888#26.

49 Population details were pulled from Town Planning Consultants, *Report on Existing Conditions Prepared as Base Material for Planning* (Kenora, ON: Town Planning Consultants, 1947), "Chart IV: Population, Town of Kenora, Anticipated Growth," 25.

50 Denison, *The People's Power*, 27.

51 Hay, *Electric Power in Ontario*, 5.

52 Ibid.

53 Nelles, *Politics of Development*, 321. In *Electric Power in Ontario*, Hay emphasized that Ontario depended on coal suppliers before the development of water power: "Coal [could] be shipped hundreds of miles from Alberta or imported from the United States." In 1897, during an American miners' strike, Ontario industrialists were forced to import coal from Wales (5).

54 Nelles, *Politics of Development*, 315.

55 Ibid., 241.

56 Quoted in William Rothwell Plewman, *Adam Beck and the Ontario Hydro* (Toronto: Ryerson Press, 1947), 39. Nelles also selected this quotation for discussion in *Politics of Development*, 241.

57 Plewman, *Adam Beck and the Ontario Hydro*, 39.

58 Nelles, *Politics of Development*, 257.

59 Quoted in Plewman, *Adam Beck and the Ontario Hydro*, 47. Hay, *Electric Power in Ontario*, 10, paraphrased Whitney's nationalist declarations as follows: "Whitney said clearly that the water power of Niagara was the property of the Canadian people and declared that the Ontario Government must make it possible for the people to enjoy this heritage without paying tribute to profit-seeking enterprise."

60 Nelles, *Politics of Development*, 257.

61 James Sturgis, *Adam Beck* (Don Mills, ON: Fitzhenry and Whiteside, 1982), 15.

62 Hay, *Electric Power in Ontario*, 14.

63 Sturgis, *Adam Beck*, 19.

64 McNab, "The Administration of Treaty 3," 147. Shortly after James Whitney took office, in 1905, the Hydro-Electric Power Commission of Enquiry was established. This commission resulted in "a comprehensive survey of the development and undeveloped water resources of Ontario"; Hay, *Electric Power in Ontario*, 11. It also raised awareness of and increased concern about the location of reserves throughout the province.

65 Bartlett, *Aboriginal Water Rights in Canada*, 50.

66 Canada, "Reserves," *Indian Act* (R.S.C., 1985, c. I-5), https://laws-lois.justice.gc.ca/eng/acts/i-5/.

67 John L. Tobias, "Protection, Civilization, Assimilation: An Outline History of Canada's Indian Policy," in *As Long as the Sun Shines and Water Flows: A Reader in Canadian Native Studies*, ed. Ian A.L. Getty and Antoine S. Lussier (Vancouver: UBC Press, 1983), 39–51.

68 "E.L. Newcombe, Deputy Minister of Justice, to Frank Pedley, Superintendent General of Indian Affairs, 6 February 1906," LAC, RG10, vol. 2314, fol. 62509-4, pt. 1.

69 Ibid.

70 "W.R. White, Deputy Minister of Lands, Forests, and Mines, to Duncan Campbell Scott, Deputy Superintendent General of Indian Affairs, 15 December 1915," LAC, RG10, vol. 2314, fol. 62509-5, pt. 1.

71 "Duncan Campbell Scott, Deputy Superintendent of Indian Affairs, to W.R. White, Deputy Minister of Lands, Forests, and Mines, 30 December 1914," LAC, RG10, vol. 2314, fol. 62509-5, pt. 1.

72 Ibid. In her analysis of the Moose River Basin, Jean L. Manore found that "the federal government would not defend Aboriginal peoples' right and title against hydroelectric exploitation, insisting only on compensation for those individuals and bands harmed by the loss of possessions or land"; Manore, *Cross-Currents*, 8. Scott's recommendation to provide dispossessed bands with a "percentage of the gross earnings" aligns with this claim. However, Scott did not insist on compensation. In later exchanges, he trusted that White would adhere to the compensatory scheme proposed by the Department of Indian Affairs. The subsequent failure of Indian Affairs to comment on the 1915 act suggests that Scott (a federal agent) did not insist on compensation on behalf of his wards. The federal government did not overtly challenge provincial breaches of power, in part (as Manore suggests) because "the federal government too supported the idea of development" (8).

73 Duncan Campbell Scott, Deputy Superintendent General, to Aubrey White, Deputy Minister of Lands, Forests, and Mines, re: Treaty No. 3 Reserves, March 19, 1915, LAC, RG10, vol. 2314, file 62509-5, pt. 1.

74 Ibid.

75 An Act to Confirm the Title of the Government of Canada to Certain Lands and Indian Lands, SO 1915, c. 12.

76 Benidickson, *Levelling the Lake*, 73–75.

77 The Indian Lands Act, SO 1924, c. 15. For more information on the mineral question that prompted this act, see Benidickson, *Levelling the Lake*, 49–57.

78 The Indian Lands Act, SO 1924, c. 15.

79 The Grand Medicine Society is a "traditional" spiritual association; see Michael Angel, *Preserving the Sacred: Historical Perspectives on the Ojibwa Midewiwin* (Winnipeg: University of Manitoba Press, 2002).

80 The Haudenosaunee also built water drums, often made of birch, for ceremonial use; see Carleton University and Canadian Heritage, "Iroquois Water Drum," in *Native Drums*, http://www.native-drums.ca/index.php/Drums/Water_Drum; Thomas Vennum, *The Ojibwa Dance Drum: Its History and Construction*," Smithsonian Folklife Series 2 (Washington, DC: Smithsonian Institution Press, 1982), 40.

81 Vennum, *The Ojibwa Dance Drum*, 228.

82 Ibid., 41.

83 Derrick Bresette, interview with Franziska von Rosen, Toronto, 7 November 2004, http://www.native-drums.ca/index.php/Interviews?tp=a&bg=1&ln=e.

84 Langdon Winner, "Do Artifacts Have Politics?," *Daedalus* 109, no. 1 (1980): 121–36.

85 Paul Nadjiwan, interview with Franziska von Rosen, Ojibwe Culture Centre, M'Chigeeng First Nation, ON, 10 November 2004, http://www.native-drums.ca/index.php/Interviews?tp=a&bg=1&ln=e.

86 King, *The Truth about Stories*, 24. In Miller, *Ogimaag*, 23, Cary Miller suggests that "a complete inversion of the sense of human domination over the natural world presented in western religion and philosophy" existed in Anishinaabe society. Miller links this inversion to "the Ojibwe extension of the category of personhood beyond human beings."

87   Al Hunter, "Water," in *Days of Obsidian, Days of Grace: Selected Poetry and Prose by Four Native American Writers*, by Al Hunter, Denise Sweet, Jim Northrup, and Adrian C. Louis (Duluth, MN: Poetry Harbor, 1994), 30.

88   Ibid., 30–31.

89   "Rat Portage, Keewatin and the Canadian Lake of the Woods," Special Supplementary Number of *The Colonist*, September 1893, 5.

90   "Norman: Suburban Notes," *Rat Portage Weekly Record*, 31 August 1894, 3.

91   Vennum, *The Ojibwa Dance Drum*, 41.

92   Ibid., 31.

93   Martin-McKeever, *The Chief's Granddaughter*, 39–40.

94   Elder Alice Kelly, interview with the author, Dalles 38C Indian Reserve, ON, 30 July 2012.

95   Ruth Landes, quoted in Vennum, *The Ojibwa Dance Drum*, 24.

96   Constance Backhouse, "'Bedecked in Gaudy Feathers': The Legal Prohibition of Aboriginal Dance: Wanduta's Trial, Manitoba, 1903," in *Colour-Coded: A Legal History of Racism in Canada, 1900–1950* (Toronto: University of Toronto Press, 1999), 63. To review the 1895 amendment to sec. 114, see Keith D. Smith, ed., *Strange Visitors: Documents in Indigenous-Settler Relations in Canada from 1876* (Toronto: University of Toronto Press, 2014), 96–97.

97   Backhouse, "'Bedecked in Gaudy Feathers,'" 65.

98   Ibid., 67.

99   R.S. McKenzie to Secretary of the Department of Indian Affairs, 3 October 1905, transcribed by Tim Holzkamm, the author's collection.

100 Chief Joe Pa-wa-wasin to Reverend Mr. Sermons, Winnipeg, 29 July 1911, facsimile provided by Tim Holzkamm, the author's collection.

101 Deputy Superintendent General of Indian Affairs circular to the Kenora and Fort Frances Indian Agents, 15 December 1921, transcribed by Tim Holzkamm, the author's collection.

102 Former Chief Allan Luby (Ogemah), telephone interview with the author, 1 December 2014. In September 2015, Luby indicated that ceremonies would be held from thirty to fifty kilometres away from Kenora at Lake of the Woods. The distance from town was to prevent Indian Agents from disrupting Anishinaabe ceremonies. Former Chief Allan Luby (Ogemah), "Regulating Capital, Creating Christians: Banning Indigenous Ceremonies, 1895–1951," e-lecture, Laurentian University, Sudbury, ON, 29 September 2015.

103 Martin-McKeever, *The Chief's Granddaughter*, 68.

104 Earl Chapin, quoted in Lake of the Woods Writers' Group and Kenora Centennial Committee, *Through the Kenora Gateway*, 5.

Chapter 2: Rising River, Receding Access

1   This is a fictional account of Matilda Martin's (Ogimaamaashiik's) life in town. It has been shaped by family narratives passed down orally, some of which are in Martin-McKeever, *The Chief's Granddaughter*, 55–57, 59–60, 67–68, 79.

2   In *Levelling the Lake*, Benidickson explains that John Mather of the Keewatin Lumbering and Manufacturing Company supervised construction of the Rollerway Dam "with cabinet approval and funding" in 1887; upon its completion, "lake levels were . . . held between one and a half and three feet higher" (62). Between 1893 and 1895, the Keewatin Power Company—also led by Mather—built the Norman Dam to replace the Rollerway Dam (127). Although Keewatin Power owned the dam, the Ontario Commission of Public Works determined water levels (134).

3   Ibid., 114.

4   Manton M. Wyvell, "Peace between Canada and the United States," *Advocate of Peace through Justice* 83, no. 7 (1921): 256.

5   Anishinaabe silence mirrored provincial claims that "Indians" had no claim to waters running through or around reserves, as discussed in Chapter 1; Anishinaabe exclusion also aligned with subsequent revisions to the Indian Act: in the 1920s, the federal government added s. 141 to bar status Indians from hiring a lawyer to pursue land claims.

6   "The Peoples' Forum," *Kenora Miner and News*, 18 October 1922, 2.

7   Former Chief Allan Luby (Ogemah), interview with the author, Kenora, ON, 28 December 2014.

8   In 1908, Matilda married Edward Martin, a non-Indigenous fisher and trapper from the Sand Lake area. Shortly after their marriage, they took up residence north of Dalles 38C. Until then, Matilda had lived primarily with her maternal grandparents at Dalles 38C. For more information, see Martin-McKeever, *The Chief's Granddaughter*, 44, 48. See also Elder Matilda Martin (Ogimaamaashiik), interview with the *Kenora Daily Miner and News*, 30 June 1972.

    George Beatty was a journalist for the *Kenora Daily Miner and News* who coordinated interviews with Elder Matilda Martin (Ogimaamaashiik) during the summer of 1972 to produce a series of articles on Anishinaabe life in the Kenora area. He worked with a female assistant believed to be Jillian Torrie. Dorothy Lavergne McLay later made copies of the interview transcripts. Dorothy Lavergne McLay, telephone interview with the author, 2 October 2011.

9   "Old Time Resident Fondly Recalls Walk from Dalles," *Kenora Miner and News*, n.d., n. pag., in file compiled by Lucille Burton, "Memoirs of Matilda Josephine Lavergne Kipling Martin," 1987, LOWM.

10 "Local Items," *Rat Portage Miner and Semi-Weekly News*, 15 December 1905, 4.

11 "Local Items," *Rat Portage Miner and Semi-Weekly News*, 26 December 1905, 4.

12 "Town Topics," *Rat Portage Weekly Record*, 10 February 1893, 2.

13 "Town Topics," *Rat Portage Weekly Record*, 8 December 1893, 2.

14 "Local Items," *Kenora Miner and News*, 2 February 1906, 4.

15 Nancy Miller, "Ice in, Ice Out," in *Lake of the Woods Vacation Area*, http://www.lakeofthe-woods.com/stories-from-the-lake/ice-in-ice-out/. Former Chief Allan Luby (Ogemah) further explained that "usually it didn't take long [to establish an ice road] once the weather got cold. It would only take a few weeks, and you could travel to a certain extent." Former Chief Luby (Ogemah), interview with the author, 28 December 2014.

16 Martin-McKeever, *The Chief's Granddaughter*, 8–11, 43–44.

17 Elder Kelly, interview with the author, 30 July 2012.

18 W.H. Williams, *Manitoba and the North-West: Journal of a Trip from Toronto to the Rocky Mountains* (Toronto: Hunter, Rose, 1882), 32.

19 Marilyn Peckett, "Anishinaabe Homeland History: Traditional Land and Resource Use of Riding Mountain, Manitoba," research report, Bagida'an Aboriginal Research and Partnership Services, 1998, 8–9.

20 Ibid., 41.

21 Elder Matilda Martin (Ogimaamaashiik), interview with the *Kenora Daily Miner and News*, 27 July 1972. Horse ownership appears to have increased in the 1940s. Elder Charlie Fisher testified that he cut wood at Dalles 38C Indian Reserve from 1939 to 1946. During this period, "Peter Savage had a horse that he would use to transport people and their belongings over the portage at the Dalles." Elder Charlie Fisher, interview with Cuyler Cotton, transcript, Dovetail Resources, Kenora, ON, 6 October 1992. The transcriptionist appears to have paraphrased interview text.

22 Morris, *The Treaties of Canada with the Indians of Manitoba and the North-West Territories*, 50.

23 In her interview, with the *Kenora Daily Miner and News*, summer 1972, n. pag., LOWM. Elder Martin did not identify the year that Chief Kawitaskung travelled to Winnipeg for eye care. According to Martin-McKeever, *The Chief's Granddaughter*, 27, Kawitaskung had a stroke and went blind in 1902. It is likely that the trip happened between 1902 and 1904 since Martin transported her grandfather to town by sled alone (without spousal support).

24 Grant Bogart, interview with John Batiuk, Kenora, ON, summer 1972.

25 Iain J. Davidson-Hunt, "Indigenous Lands Management, Cultural Landscapes and Anishinaabe People of Shoal Lake, Northwestern Ontario, Canada," *Environments* 31, no. 1 (2003): 33.

26 "Winter Trails on the Lake," *Rat Portage Miner and Semi-Weekly News*, 19 December 1905, 1.

27 Former Chief Allan Luby (Ogemah), email correspondence with the author, 31 January 2015.

28 George H. Henshaw, *On the Construction of Common Roads to which Is Appended Some Remarks on the Preservation of Winter Roads* (Montreal: John Lovell for the Office of the Minister of Agriculture, 1871), 31.

29 During the winter, overland travel remained challenging since snow did not eliminate the rocky and uneven terrain of the Canadian Shield. Ice roads (or the cross-over of canoe routes) thus provided the most effective means of winter travel. Treeline analysis might help future researchers to identify the planting of coniferous windbreaks by Anishinaabe road users. A study of Anishinaabe burning patterns might also help to determine the maintenance of windbreaks. Shoreline burns might have helped to "crack open" pine cones; although not a recognizable form of planting, it would have spurred new growth along shorelines.

30 "Winter Trails on the Lake," *Rat Portage Miner and Semi-Weekly News*, 19 December 1905, 1.

31 The U.S. Department of the Interior, "Putting a Stop to Stop Logs," in *Reclamation: Managing Water in the West*, http://www.usbr.gov/pn/video/transcript/minidokastoplogs.pdf, explains that the use of "wooden stop logs is a very traditional way of controlling the elevation of a river or reservoir." It further explains that "they are actually a series of logs that are stacked horizontally" and that the logs can "[hold] the water back." Managing

lake levels with stop logs was a labour-intensive process since "all ... stop logs would be manually changed, by hand."

32 "Hebe's Falls," *Rat Portage Weekly Record*, 5 December 1891, 2.

33 Ice stability is affected by a number of factors, including flow. For example, rapids and springs can erode ice from below. Although ice stability would have increased north of Hebe's Falls (as the current decreased), ice was not reliable for the entire stretch between Rideout Bay and Dalles 38C. It seems that Miller's Rapids (near Old Fort Island, ON) created a second notable weak spot. A break in the ice road near Miller's Rapids caused members of Dalles 38C to move off the ice and rest (or change) near present-day Barski's Hill, ON, before continuing into Rat Portage, ON, for trade. Elder Martin, interview with the *Kenora Daily Miner and News*, summer 1972.

34 "Local Items," *Kenora Miner and News*, 12 November 1924.

35 "Town Topics," *Rat Portage Weekly Record*, 24 November 1893, 2.

36 Former Chief Luby (Ogemah), interview with the author, 28 December 2014.

37 Elder Jacob Lindsay, interview with Cuyler Cotton, transcript, Dovetail Resources, Kenora, ON, 2 October 1992. The transcriptionist appears to have paraphrased interview text.

38 International Joint Commission, *Final Report*, 11.

39 Boundary Waters Treaty, quoted in ibid.

40 Michael Bliss reminds us that the Reciprocity Treaty of 1854 allowed Canadians to profit considerably from freer trade during the American Civil War. See Bliss, *Northern Enterprise: Five Centuries of Canadian Business*, 248–51.

41 International Joint Commission, *Final Report*, 19.

42 Ibid., 21.

43 Ibid., 3.

44 Ibid., 14.

45 Ibid., 11.

46 Record Detail, Charles Alexander Magrath (1860–1949), Galt Museum and Archives, Lethbridge.

47 Fleming, *Power at a Cost*, 14.

48 Between 1885 and 1900, Kenora's population more than quadrupled from 750 to 3,500. This influx of people reflected the expansion of mill operations. "Historical Timeline," MUSE-LOWM.

49 Nelles, *Politics of Development*, 495.

50 American Society of International Law, "Boundary Waters Between the United States and Canada," The *American Journal of International Law* 4, no. 3 (1910): 669.

51 Wyvell, "Peace between Canada and the United States," 255.

52 Milloy, "The Early Indian Act," 57.

53 International Joint Commission, *Final Report*, 13.

54 On 11 September 1913, the International Joint Commission announced that "any person having information or evidence bearing upon the question [of water levels in Lake of the Woods will be] granted permission to be heard." The commission called on persons capable of speaking to "agricultural interests, fishing interests, [and] harbor and navigation interests." The call was made public through the *Kenora Miner and News*. As wards of the dominion, though, the Anishinabeg did not qualify as persons in matters of rights. Under the Indian Act, reserve lands were federal lands. Thus, Indigenous Peoples affected by flooding or changed patterns of flow might not have been considered citizens of Ontario with agricultural, fishing, or navigation interests. "Joint Commission Here Monday," *Kenora Miner and News*, 11 September 1913, 1. For more information on the legal definition of a person under the British North America Act (c. 1867–1929), see Tabitha Marshall and David A. Cruickshank, "Persons Case," in *The Canadian Encyclopedia*, http://www.thecanadianencyclopedia.ca/en/article/persons-case/.

55 International Joint Commission, *Final Report*, 18. See also "International Joint Commission Will Hold Sessions Here," *Kenora Miner and News*, 11 September 1915, 1.

56 Arthur J. Ray, *I Have Lived Here since the World Began: An Illustrated History of Canada's Native People*, Revised Edition (Toronto: Key Porter Books, 2005), 203.

57 "Local Items," *Kenora Miner and News*, 30 October 1915, n. pag.

58 Ray, *I Have Lived Here since the World Began*, 205.

59 In 1914, E.D. George, who represented the Department of Indian Affairs, the Town of Fort Frances, and the Township of McIrvin, focused his discussion of damages incurred by the Anishinabeg to reserve lands. He explained that "the [shore] banks have washed away to an extent of 8 feet" and focused his complaint on the road allowance. International Joint Commission, *Progress Report on the International Joint Commission on the Reference by the United States and Canada in re Levels of the Lake of the Woods and Its Tributary Waters and Their Future Regulation and Control: Including Public Hearings at International Falls and Warroad, Minn., and Kenora, Ontario* (Washington, DC: Government Printing Office, 1914), 67.

60 International Joint Commission, *Final Report*, 12.

61 Arthur V. White and Adolph F. Meyer, "Southerly Shore: Lake of the Woods from Northwest Angle Inlet to Big Grassy River, 1913–1914," in *Atlas to Accompany Report to International Joint Commission Relating to Official Reference re. Lake of the Woods Levels* (Ottawa: Government Printing Department, 1915), Sheet No. 4.

62 Frances Densmore found that her informant, Mrs. Wawiekumig (Nawajibgokwe), "conformed to the shape of the piece of paper on which it (a map) was drawn, so that relative distances and points of the compass were not strictly maintained." Densmore, *Chippewa Customs*, 180.

63 Grace Rajnovich, *Reading Rock Art: Interpreting the Indian Rock Paintings of the Canadian Shield*, 2nd ed. (Toronto: Natural Heritage/Natural History, 2002), 92.

64 Densmore, *Chippewa Customs*, 176.

65 International Joint Commission, *Final Report*, 12.

66 "Captain J.T. Hooper to Arthur White, 14 April 1913," Lake of the Woods—Levels, LOWM.

67 According to the *Kenora Miner and News*, "Hooper stated with particular reference to the high water mark on the rocks that he had seen the water higher before the construction of

these dams than it has even been since." No indication of the regularity of such high-water levels is provided. "High Water Levels a Necessity," *Kenora Miner and News*, 15 September 1915, 1.

68 "Captain J.T. Hooper to Arthur White, 14 April 1913," Lake of the Woods—Levels, LOWM.

69 In another example from the Lake of the Woods watershed, E.D. George testified that "Indians have made complaint as to the pollution of water below the river and the destruction of fish." James A. Tawney, an American representative of the International Joint Commission, then asked for a prepared statement "setting forth their complaints." He explained that "if they . . . submit that statement in writing to the commission it will answer every purpose." International Joint Commission, *Progress Report on the International Joint Commission*, 70.

70 D.W. Moodie and Barry Kaye, "The Northern Limit of Indian Agriculture in North America," *Geographical Review* 59, no. 4 (1969): 528.

71 White and Meyer, *Atlas to Accompany Report to International Joint Commission*, Sheet No. 4.

72 "Frost-Proof Corn Grown by Indians," *Kenora Miner and News*, 25 October 1924, 2. According to Lake of the Woods Museum and Aulneau Adventure Tours, *The Explorer's Guide to Lake of the Woods* (Kenora, ON: n.p., 2000), 98, Garden Island was previously known as Cornfield. Presumably, this name appears "on maps that pre-date 1900." It is known that a "five acre cornfield and three acres of potatoes, squash and pumpkin" covered the island when the Dawson and Hind survey party passed through Lake of the Woods in 1858. Hind "ascertained that the island had been cultivated by the Lake of the Woods Ojibway Indians for generations." Henry Youle Hind, *Narrative of the Canadian Red River Exploring Expedition of 1857 and of the Assinniboine [sic] and Saskatchewan Expedition of 1858, Volume 1* (London: Longman, Green, Longman, and Roberts, 1860), 97–98.

73 International Joint Commission, *Final Report*, 27.

74 "Don't Risk Crossing Ice to Tunnel Island," *Kenora Miner and News*, 27 December 1924, 5.

75 Quoted in ibid.

76 Lake of the Woods Writers' Group and Kenora Centennial Committee, *Through the Kenora Gateway*, 61.

77 "Skating on Thin Ice," *Kenora Miner and News*, 11 November 1925, 3.

78 The Norman Dam likely had the greatest effect on ice stability upstream of Dalles Channel (formerly Dalles Rapids). It is less likely to have compromised the route for Anishinaabe travellers north of Dalles Channel. Hydroelectric development appears to have more seriously curtailed Anishinaabe access to town, rather than between communities downstream of Dalles 38C, in the early 1900s.

79 René R. Gadacz, "Rabbit Starvation," *The Canadian Encyclopedia*, 14 August 2006, https://www.thecanadianencyclopedia.ca/en/article/rabbit-starvation. In "'Ould Betsy and Her Daughter': Fur Trade Fisheries in Northern Ontario," in *Fishing Places, Fishing People: Traditions and Issues in Canadian Small-Scale Fisheries*, ed. Daniel Newell and Rosemary E. Ommer (Toronto: University of Toronto Press, 1999), 80–96, Arthur J. Ray identifies Indigenous food preferences in the central subarctic culture area before 1905. This area overlaps with the territories covered by Treaty 3. Ray notes that Indigenous Peoples, particularly the Cree, favoured large game such as caribou (83). Deer and moose, however, were more plentiful in Anishinaabe territory. Ray also notes that the Cree prized

beaver meat (83). Oral testimony introduced in Chapter 6 of *Dammed* suggests that beaver was also prized in the Winnipeg River drainage basin. Indigenous Peoples in the central subarctic culture area ate a wide variety of fish, as Ray identifies, throughout the year, such as sturgeon, whitefish, northern pike, and sucker (83). Oral testimony from the Winnipeg River drainage basin suggests that sturgeon was perceived as a "rich fish" instead of a lean fish; Ratuski, "Gathering Traditional Knowledge and Perspectives of Sturgeon on the Winnipeg River from Dalles Community Members," 3. An anonymous Elder explained that "sturgeon was mostly eaten in the summer but would also be stored for winter by digging deep holes . . . in the ground. . . . Ice stored in ice houses was sometimes used to help preserve the raw sturgeon" (3). Testimonies indicate that Anishinaabe families ate this rich fish in small portions (3, 5); others suggest that they used it medicinally (8, 14, 17) or on special occasions (9, 11). Sturgeon preserved for winter use would allow them to couple an oily fish with garden produce or stored manomin to help prevent rabbit starvation.

80 "The Peoples' Forum," *Kenora Miner and News*, 18 October 1922, 2.

81 Elder Kelly, interview with the author, 30 July 2012.

82 "Don't Risk Crossing Ice to Tunnel Island," *Kenora Miner and News*, 27 December 1924, 5; "Body Found at Minaki," *Kenora Miner and News*, 25 November 1925, 1.

83 "Low Water in Lake Kills Thousands of Muskrats," *Kenora Miner and News*, 22 April 1925, n. pag.

84 "Local Items: Indians Out of Work," *Kenora Miner and News*, 23 May 1925, n. pag.

85 "Indians Start Bank Accounts," *Kenora Miner and News*, 5 October 1921, 1.

86 Ibid.

87 Elder Kelly, interview with the author, 30 July 2012; Elder Marjorie Nabish, interview with the author, Dalles 38C Indian Reserve, ON, 9 August 2012.

88 "Profitable Blue Berries," *Rat Portage Miner and Rainy Lake Journal*, 10 July 1899, 3. See also International Joint Commission, *Final Report*, 17.

89 Elder Matilda Martin (Ogimaamaashiik), interview with the *Kenora Daily Miner and News*, 11 July 1972.

90 According to Section 32(2) of An Act to amend "The Indian Act, 1880," "any person who buys or otherwise acquires from any such Indian, or band, or irregular band of Indians, contrary to any provisions or regulations made by the Governor in Council under this Act, is guilty of an offence, and is punishable, upon summary conviction, by fine, not exceeding one hundred dollars, or by imprisonment for a period not exceeding three months, in any place of confinement other than a penitentiary, or by both fine and imprisonment." Canada, *An Act to amend "The Indian Act, 1880*," Indigenous and Northern Affairs Canada, modified 15 September 2010, https://www.aadnc-aandc.gc.ca/eng/1100100010280/1100100010282 (https://perma.cc/8355-C3TH).

91 "Local Items," *Kenora Miner and News*, 6 July 1915, 3.

92 "Blueberry Crop above Average," *Kenora Miner and News*, 29 July 1925, 1.

93 Elder Martin, interview with the *Kenora Daily Miner and News*, 11 July 1972.

94 The Inflation Calculator, a program available through the Bank of Canada, was used to estimate the average annual income in 1920 since Abdul Rashid used "current dollars

[1993]" in his estimates. Abdul Rashid, "Seven Decades of Wage Changes," *Perspectives on Labour and Income* 5, no. 2 (1993): 9–21.

95 "Indians Start Bank Accounts," *Kenora Miner and News*, 5 October 1921, 1.

96 A. Irving Hallowell, *Culture and Experience* (Philadelphia: University of Pennsylvania Press, 1955), 233–34.

97 Ibid., 234.

98 Ibid., 223.

99 Alternatively, it could be argued that the Norman Dam prompted Anishinaabe families in the Winnipeg River drainage basin to adopt a moditional economy as they relied increasingly on berry sales for capital. One's interpretation depends, perhaps, on whether annual berry sales are identified as a form of independent trade or informal contract labour.

100 "Indians Start Bank Accounts," *Kenora Miner and News*, 5 October 1921, 1.

Chapter 3: Power Lost and Power Gained

1   "Progress Scenes at Whitedog-Caribou Falls," *Kenora Daily Miner and News*, 4 September 1957, 1.

2   Bliss, *Northern Enterprise: Five Centuries of Canadian Business*, 454.

3   Ibid. Ontario also supported industrial expansion in the northwest. The Ontario-Minnesota Pulp and Paper Company received approximately $300,000 from the province to finance expansion. Provincial money allowed the company to install "4 new 3A Bird screens, Bauer stock cleaning equipment, new Valley head box and slice and a new mixing pump, plus related equipment." "O&M Production Will Increase," *Kenora-Keewatin Daily Miner and News*, 11 March 1955, 7.

4   Lake of the Woods Writers' Group and Kenora Centennial Committee, *Through the Kenora Gateway*, 63.

5   Beniah Bowman, Minister of Lands and Forests, and Edward W. Backus, Indenture Made in Triplicate, 30 September 1920, Whitedog Falls Generating Station, OPG, FP3-10101–8, V. 1, Item 114.

6   Assistant Solicitor (illegible, presumably W.S. Campbell) to E.T. Ireson, re. Winnipeg River—White Dog Power Site, 6 May 1955, Whitedog Falls Generating Station, OPG, FP3-10101–8, V. 1, Item 114.

7   Lake of the Woods Writers' Group and Kenora Centennial Committee, *Through the Kenora Gateway*, 61, 63. See also "Historical Timeline," MUSE-LOWM.

8   Lake of the Woods Writers' Group and Kenora Centennial Committee, *Through the Kenora Gateway*, 63. See also Benidickson, *Levelling the Lake*, 164, 167.

9   Paraphrased in "A Brief History of Dryden during the Depression," Dryden High School Online, Kenora Patricia District School Board, http://dhseagles.kpdsb.on.ca/about/theGreatDepression/TheGreatDepression.html.

10 The Ontario and Minnesota Paper Company amalgamated Kenora Paper Mills, Keewatin Power Company, Keewatin Lumbering and Manufacturing Company, and Fort Frances Pulp and Paper Company. "Reorganization of Local Paper Mill Is Announced: Will Be Known as Ontario and Minnesota Paper Company; Kenora and Fort Frances Plants Are in

the New Company," *Fort Frances Times and Rainy Lake Herald*, 1 May 1941, 1. There was a name change as a result of the amalgamation.

11 Doug Owram, *Born at the Right Time: A History of the Baby Boom Generation* (Toronto: University of Toronto Press, 1996). Journalist Robert J. Samuelson addressed the American case, arguing that Americans began "to take prosperity for granted" in the postwar era; Robert J. Samuelson, *The Good Life and Its Discontents: The American Dream in the Age of Entitlement* (New York: Vintage Books, 1997), 35.

12 Former Chief Allan Luby (Ogemah), email message to the author, 15 July 2015. In his submission to the Royal Commission on Aboriginal Peoples (1993), Sam Horton, then vice-president of Ontario Hydro's Aboriginal and Northern Affairs Branch, echoed these sentiments: "Ontario Hydro is really a company which failed to respect the Aboriginal people. . . . In short, we've pursued our own interests in our own ways and the result is that, while Ontario Hydro and its customers have enjoyed low cost hydro electric energy, the life sustaining capabilities of many of the watersheds have been destroyed in the process" (385–86). "Royal Commission on Aboriginal Peoples: Presentation by Sam Horton, Vice-President, Aboriginal and Northern Affairs Branch, Ontario Hydro," Our Legacy, 3 June 2003, http://digital.scaa.sk.ca/ourlegacy/solr?query=ID:31496&start=0&rows=10&mode=results.

13 Generation Engineer, to W.S. Campbell, re. Winnipeg River: Whitedog Power Site, 29 April 1955, Whitedog Falls Generating Station, OPG, FP3–10101–8, V. 1, Item 114.

14 Assistant Solicitor [illegible, presumably W.S. Campbell] to E.T. Ireson, re. Winnipeg River—White Dog Power Site, 6 May 1955, Whitedog Falls Generating Station, OPG, FP3–10101–8, V. 1, Item 114.

15 Ontario Hydro, *Ontario Hydro: A Proud Tradition 1906–1999* (Toronto: Ontario Hydro, 1999), 26.

16 Assistant Solicitor [illegible, presumably W.S. Campbell] to E.T. Ireson, re. Winnipeg River—White Dog Power Site, 6 May 1955, Whitedog Falls Generating Station, OPG, FP3–10101–8, V. 1, Item 114.

17 Ibid.

18 Ibid.

19 Whitedog Falls Generating Station: General Description and Design Requirements, 13 September 1955, memorandum, Whitedog Falls Generating Station, OPG, FP3–10-1-228, V. 1, Item 1042.

20 Ibid.

21 N.E. Tregaskes, Generation Engineer, to W.S. Campbell, re. Whitedog Falls Generating Station: Property, 25 August 1955, Whitedog Falls Generating Station, OPG, FP3–10101–8, V. 1, Item 114.

22 Ibid. In 1957, O.E. Johnston, a generating engineer, confirmed that "the water level upstream from The [*sic*] Dalles to Kenora will . . . be about one foot [0.30 metres] higher than the natural high water." O.E. Johnston, Generation Engineer, to Mr. A.E. Huddleston, re: Whitedog Falls G.S. Property Damages, 9 May 1957, Whitedog Falls Generating Station, OPG, FP3–10101–8, V. 1, Item 114.

23 Whitedog Falls Generating Station: General Description and Design Requirements, 13
   September 1955, memorandum, Whitedog Falls Generating Station, OPG, FP3–10-1-228,
   V. 1, Item 1042.

24 U.S. Geological Survey, "Hydroelectric Power: How It Works," USGS Water Science
   School, http://water.usgs.gov/edu/hyhowworks.html.

25 "Hydro Power Turned to Monday—Customers Served," *Kenora Miner and News,* 7
   February 1950, 1. See also "Council Will Sign 2-Year Power Agreement with MANDO,"
   Kenora Miner and News, 11 January 1955, 1.

26 M. Ward, System Planning Engineer, to H.P. Cadario and F. Grosvenor, re: Facilities
   at Kenora SS and for the Incorporation of Whitedog Falls GS into the Northwestern
   Division, 4 November 1955, Whitedog Falls Generating Station, OPG, FP3–10-1-228, V.
   1, Item 1042.

27 The *Kenora Daily Miner and News* reported on energy purchases, confirming that
   HEPCO had taken over some of the load by December 1958. The focus of the article
   was price inflation. An unidentified reporter feared that "the Paper Company buys
   power from Hydro, and re-sells it to the Town at a profit." There was no indication that
   the Ontario-Minnesota Pulp and Paper Company had lost the ability to produce sufficient hydroelectricity at the Norman Dam to service Kenora and mill operations. "Why
   You Should Vote 'Yes' for Power Changeover," *Kenora Daily Miner and News,* 3 December
   1958, n. pag. In 1960, F.C. Lawson, the assistant director of operations, confirmed that the
   company was an active energy consumer; F.C. Lawson, Assistant Director of Operations,
   to L.R. McDonald, General Counsel, re: Preparation of Agreement with the Ontario-
   Minnesota Pulp and Paper Company, 26 September 1960, Whitedog Falls Generating
   Station, OPG, FP3E, V. 1, Item 108.

28 J.B. Bryce, Hydraulic Engineer, to J.S. Crerar, Senior Design Engineer, re: Effects of
   Regulated Water Levels at Minaki on Power Output at Whitedog Falls Generating Station
   and on Power Plants at Kenora, 8 March 1957, Whitedog Falls Generating Station, OPG,
   FP3–10901, Item [65].

29 Ibid.

30 H.M. McFarlane, Hydraulic Design Engineer, to J.B. Bryce, Hydraulic Engineer, re:
   Winnipeg River: Effect of Operation of Whitedog Falls Headpond on Tailwater Elevations
   at the Lake of the Woods Outlets, 15 January 1960, Whitedog Falls Generating Station
   OPG, FP3E, V. 1, Item 108.

31 A.E. Aeberli, Turbine and Governor Engineer, Keewatin Mills "C" and "C": Kenora
   and Norman Dam Generating Stations, 4 April 1960, memorandum, Whitedog Falls
   Generating Station, OPG, FP3E, V. 1, Item 108.

32 H.M. McFarlane, Hydraulic Design Engineer, to J.B. Bryce, Hydraulic Engineer, Internal
   Record, re: Winnipeg River: Effect of Operation of Whitedog Falls Headpond on
   Tailwater Elevations at the Lake of the Woods Outlets, 15 January 1960, Whitedog Falls
   Generating Station, OPG, FP3E, V. 1, Item 108.

33 Ibid.

34 O.E. Johnston, Hydraulic Generation Engineer, The Effect of Regulation of Whitedog
   Falls Generating Station Forebay on Operation of Lake of the Woods Outlet Plants,
   26 April 1960, memorandum, Whitedog Falls Generating Station, OPG, FP3E, V. 1,
   Item 108.

35 H.P. Cadario, Director of Engineering, to H.A. Smith, Assistant General Engineer, re: Negotiations with Ontario and Minnesota Pulp and Paper Company and with Lake of the Woods Milling Company Regarding Loss of Generating Capacity at their Lake of the Woods Plants, 20 June 1960, Whitedog Falls Generating Station, OPG, FP3E, V. 1, Item 108.

36 M. Ward, System Planning Engineer, to H.P. Cadario and F. Grosvenor, re: Facilities at Kenora SS and for the Incorporation of Whitedog Falls GS into the Northwestern Division, 4 November 1955, Whitedog Falls Generating Station, OPG, FP3–10-1-228, V. 1, Item 1042.

37 F.C. Lawson, Assistant Director of Operations, to L.R. McDonald, General Counsel, re: Preparation of Agreement with the Ontario-Minnesota Pulp and Paper Company, 20 June 1960, Whitedog Falls Generating Station OPG, FP3E, V. 1, Item 108.

38 At the time of these estimates, HEPCO had permission to operate at 1,036 feet (315.77 metres) above sea level at Minaki.

39 H.P. Cadario, Director of Engineering, to H.A. Smith, Assistant General Engineer, re: Negotiations with Ontario and Minnesota Pulp and Paper Company and with Lake of the Woods Milling Company Regarding Loss of Generating Capacity at their Lake of the Woods Plants, 20 June 1960, Whitedog Falls Generating Station, OPG, FP3E, V. 1, Item 108

40 Hydraulic Generation Department, *Report on Loss of Power Output at Lake of the Woods Outlet Plants Due to Regulation of the Whitedog Falls Generating Station Headpond and Suggested Method for Replacement of Power* (Toronto: HEPCO, 13 June 1960), Whitedog Falls Generating Station, OPG, FP3E, V. 1, Item 108.

41 The logic behind HEPCO's calculation was explained by mathematician David Kohler de Felice, message to author, 2 August 2014.

42 F.C. Lawson to L.R. McDonald re: Preparation of Agreement with the Ontario-Minnesota Pulp and Paper Company, 26 September 1960, Whitedog Falls Generating Station, OPG, FP3E, V. 1, Item 108.

43 Robertson, *Reservations Are for Indians*, 120.

44 Former Chief Allan Luby (Ogemah), "Regulating Capital, Creating Christians: Banning Indigenous Ceremonies, 1895–1951," e-lecture, Laurentian University, Sudbury, ON, 29 September 2015. In *A Concise History of Canada's First Nations*, 2nd ed. (Don Mills, ON: Oxford University Press, 2010), 248–49, Olive Patricia Dickason similarly notes that "the revised [Indian] Act of 1951 can hardly be called revolutionary," explaining that a "band could now spend its monies as it wished, unless the Governor-in-Council expressed reservation." Although theoretically bands could fund lawsuits against Canada or Ontario after 1951, they would not gain "complete control over their funds" until 1958. Dickason's findings suggest that material hardship might have prevented immediate action against settler-colonists.

45 In Manuel and Derrickson, *The Reconciliation Manifesto: Recovering the Land, Rebuilding the Economy*, 216, Arthur Manuel suggests that industry and government now use court injunctions to facilitate resource exploitation and to limit meaningful engagement with First Nations (216). Attempts legally to curtail dialogue with Indigenous populations remain a colonial tactic to suppress and dispossess them.

46 It is unclear why Gordon Cooper from the Indian Affairs Branch at Fort Frances presided
    over this meeting. Eric Law was the active agent at Kenora circa 1960. Band Council
    Resolution, Islington Band of Indians, Department of Citizenship and Immigration, Indian
    Affairs Branch, 27 June 1956, Whitedog Falls Generating Station, OPG, FP3–10726,
    Item 153. Newspaper reports also limited HEPCO's permissions to road clearing. The
    Kenora Daily Miner and News noted that "slashers are working on the portion of the
    road through the Oslington [*sic*] Indian Reserve where clearance had to be obtained
    from the Indian Council Tribe leaders and the Dept. of Indian Affairs before work could
    proceed." "The Caribou Pushing North From Whitedog," *Kenora Daily Miner and News*, 15
    August 1956, 1.

47 Robertson, *Reservations Are for Indians*, 112.

48 Ibid., 120.

49 Elder Charlie Fisher, interview with Andrew Chapeskie, Kenora, ON, 22 March 1995.

50 Ibid.

51 Ibid.

52 E.T. Ireson, Generation Engineer, to Mr. H. Hustler, re: Whitedog Falls Generating
    Station: Property Damages, 12 September 1955, Whitedog Falls Generating Station, OPG,
    FP3–10101–8, V. 1, Item 114. Today, Canada claims that "reserves are held by Her Majesty
    for the use and benefit of the respective bands for which they were set apart, and subject
    to this Act and to the terms of any treaty or surrender, the Governor in Council may deter-
    mine whether any purpose for which lands in a reserve are used or are to be used is for the
    use and benefit of the band." Canada, "Reserves," *Indian Act* (R.S.C., 1985, c. I-5), https://
    laws-lois.justice.gc.ca/eng/acts/i-5/ (https://perma.cc/U9HC-HVQQ).

53 O.E. Johnston, Hydraulic Development Engineer, to W.G. Wigle, Department of
    Highways, re: Caribou Falls Generating Station, Whitedog Falls Generating Station
    Access Road from Minaki, 9 February 1967, Whitedog Falls Generating Station, OPG,
    FP3–10726, Item 153.

54 Robertson, *Reservations Are for Indians*, 112.

55 Canada, *Treaty 3 between Her Majesty the Queen and the Saulteaux Tribe of the Ojibbeway
    Indians at Northwest Angle on the Lake of the Woods with Adhesions*, https://www.aadnc-
    aandc.gc.ca/eng/1100100028675/1100100028679 (https://perma.cc/G52X-WT8B).

56 E.T. Ireson, Generation Engineer, to Province of Ontario, Department of Lands and
    Forests, Application for Land Permit Use, 28 September 1955, Whitedog Falls Generating
    Station, OPG, FP3-B, Item 106.

57 Clare E. Mapledoram, Minister of Lands and Forests, Province of Ontario, to the Hydro-
    Electric Power Commission of Ontario, Licence of Occupation, No. 7194, 25 January
    1956, Whitedog Falls Generating Station, OPG, FP3-B, Item 106. As early as December
    1955, A.S. Bray agreed to license "the area adjacent to the White Dog [*sic*] Falls Generating
    Station, containing 27 miles, . . . to the Commission for policing purposes." He requested
    that E.T. Ireson "favour the Department [of Lands and Forests] with a cheque for $150.00"
    so that a licence of occupation could be prepared. A.S. Bray, Chief, Division of Lands,
    Department of Lands and Forests, to E.T. Ireson, 9 December 1955, Whitedog Falls
    Generating Station, OPG, FP3-B, Item 106.

58 Clare E. Mapledoram, Minister of Lands and Forests, Province of Ontario, to the Hydro-Electric Power Commission of Ontario, Licence of Occupation, No. 7194, 25 January 1956, Whitedog Falls Generating Station, OPG, FP3-B, Item 106.

59 O.E. Johnston, Hydraulic Generation Engineer, to J.L. Alexander, Operations Division, re: Whitedog Falls Generating Station—Public Use of Pistol Lake Road, 12 March 1959, Whitedog Falls Generating Station, OPG, FP3–10726, Item 153.

60 E.B. Easson, Secretary, to C.E. Mapledoram, Minister of Lands and Forests, 12 September 1955, Whitedog Falls Generating Station, OPG, F010, Box 91.119.

61 Ibid.

62 W.S. Campbell, Assistant Solicitor, to J. Stark, re: Whitedog Falls – Caribou Falls G.S.: Use of Access Road by the Public with Hydro-Electric Power Commission of Ontario Application Whitedog Falls Generating Station, OPG, FP3–10726, Item 153.

63 O.E. Johnston, Hydraulic Generation Engineer, to J.L. Alexander, Operations Division, re: Whitedog Falls Generating Station—Public Use of Pistol Lake Road, 12 March 1959, Whitedog Falls Generating Station, OPG, FP3–10726, Item 15.

64 Elder Lindsay, interview with Cotton, 2 October 1992. The transcriptionist appears to have paraphrased interview text.

65 Elder Clarence Henry, interview with Cuyler Cotton, transcript, Dovetail Resources, Kenora, ON, 19 October 1992. The transcriptionist appears to have paraphrased interview text.

66 Elder Fisher, interview with Chapeskie, 22 March 1995.

67 Ibid.

68 Ibid.

69 Whitedog Falls Generating Station: General Description and Design Requirements, 13 September 1955, memorandum, Whitedog Falls Generating Station, OPG, FP3–10-1-228, V. 1, Item 1042.

70 Whitedog Falls Generating Station Operations Access Road from Kenora T.S. to Minaki, 9 March 1956, filing memorandum, Whitedog Falls Generating Station, OPG, FP3-10726, Item 153.

71 Whitedog Falls Generating Station: General Description and Design Requirements, 13 September 1955, memorandum, Whitedog Falls Generating Station, OPG, FP3–10-1-228, V. 1, Item 1042.

72 Elder Fisher, interview with Chapeskie, 22 March 1995.

73 Minutes of Meeting, re: Whitedog Falls G.S. and Deer Falls G.S. Methods of Operation, 7 September 1955, Whitedog Falls Generating Station, OPG, FP3–10-1-228, V. 1, Item 1042.

74 Indian Affairs Branch, quoted in Deputy Director of Property to H.A. Smith, Assistant General Manager, Engineering Division, re: Caribou Falls Development and Flooding of Lands, 19 June 1963, Whitedog Falls Generating Station, OPG, FP3–109311.

75 In 1959, Whitedog and One Man Lake Indian Reserves anticipated ten years of economic decline. Indeed, the annual report of the Indian Affairs Branch for 1965, six years after the initial damage claim, reiterated a loss of trapping income: "[Musk]rat trapping will not provide a livelihood for many families. Muskrats are not particularly plentiful and prices

have been low for the past several years." Eric Law, Superintendent, Kenora Agency, to Regional Supervisor, Northern Ontario, re: Superintendent's Report, 31 March 1965, LAC, RG 10, V. 8441, File 487/23-4, pt. 3.

76 Captain Frank Edwards, Records, c. 1926, LOWM, Folder: Anishinaabe—Lake of the Woods.

77 Captain Frank Edwards, Indians in the Kenora District and Savanne, 31 March 1938, memorandum, LOWM, Folder: Anishinaabe—Lake of the Woods.

78 Deputy Director of Property to H.A. Smith, Assistant General Manager, Engineering Division, re: Caribou Falls Development and Flooding of Lands, 19 June 1963, Whitedog Falls Generating Station, OPG, FP3–109311.

79 Ibid.

80 Ibid.

81 Ibid.

82 Ibid.

83 Lorne McDonald, General Counsel, to C.F.S. Tidy, Special Negotiator, re: Caribou Falls Development—Flooding—Islington Indian Reserve No. 28 and One Man Lake Indian Reserve No. 29, 6 June 1961, Whitedog Falls Generating Station, OPG, FP3–10-1-228, V. 1, Item 1042.

84 The counterargument of the Indian Affairs Branch mimicked the language of Treaty 3: "Her Majesty further agrees with Her said Indians that they, the said Indians, shall have right to pursue their avocations of hunting and fishing throughout the tract surrendered." Canada, *Treaty 3 between Her Majesty the Queen and the Saulteaux Tribe of the Ojibbeway Indians at Northwest Angle on the Lake of the Woods with Adhesions*, https://www.aadnc-aandc.gc.ca/eng/1100100028675/1100100028679 (https://perma.cc/G52X-WT8B).

85 Elder Terry Greene, interview with Samantha Mehltretter, Dalles 38C Indian Reserve, ON, 15 September 2019.

Chapter 4: Labouring to Keep the Reserve Alive

1 "Grassy Narrows Highway Number One 'Must' for District," *Kenora Miner and News*, 1 April 1950, 1.

2 "Editorially Speaking: Hydro Extensions," *Kenora Miner and News*, 25 April 1950, 4.

3 "What New Industrial Jobs Mean to a Community," *Kenora-Keewatin Daily Miner and News*, 25 January 1955, 4.

4 "1950 Proved Eventful Year for Twin Communities," *Kenora Miner and News*, 29 December 1950, 1.

5 Employment with HEPCO was not universally desired by band members. Elder May Greene (nee Henry) from Dalles 38C testified that her father preferred an isolationist rather than a pro-industry approach: "Dad used to keep an eye on the reserve as he did not want any whitemen to come." Interview synopses by Cuyler Cotton, Dovetail Resources, Kenora, ON, 1993, Dalles 38C, Elder Interview Collection. The transcriptionist appears to have paraphrased interview text.

6   HEPCO had no legal obligation at the time to hire Anishinaabe labourers. The term
     "employment equity" did not come into use in Canada until the 1980s when the Royal
     Commission on Equality in Employment coined the term to describe the elimination of
     discriminatory hiring practices. In 1986, the commission's report led to the Employment
     Equity Act. See Rosalie Silberman Abella, *Report of the Commission on Equality in
     Employment* (Ottawa: Government of Canada, 1984).

7   Captain Frank Edwards, "Indians in the Kenora District and Savanne," 31 March 1938,
     memorandum, LOWM, Folder: Anishinaabe—Lake of the Woods.

8   Ibid. Claire Elizabeth Campbell, in *Shaped by the West Wind: Nature and History in
     Georgian Bay* (Vancouver: UBC Press, 2005), found that Indigenous employment
     stemmed, in part, from a lack of navigational charts at the turn of the twentieth century.
     The paucity of resources "elevated the importance of experiential mapping, or navigat-
     ing by memory," stimulating campers' demand for local (i.e., Indigenous) guides (55).
     During the interwar era, tourists were drawn to Georgian Bay by the perceived "wildness"
     of the landscape and its Indigenous inhabitants (101-02). Tourists' desire to access "*terre
     sauvage*" likely maintained demand for Indigenous guides. Sharon Wall, in *The Nurture of
     Nature: Childhood, Antimodernism, and Ontario Summer Camps, 1920-1955* (Vancouver:
     UBC Press, 2009), supports this claim. She finds that Ontario summer camps hoped
     to create an "Indian atmosphere" and hired Indigenous guides and canoeing instructors
     (235). As in the upper Winnipeg River drainage basin, Indigenous men took advantage of
     American and Canadian stereotypes, securing "relatively good pay" before fall and winter
     trapping and hunting began (236).

9   Edwards, "Indians in the Kenora District and Savanne."

10   For example, *Field and Stream* (one of Canada's most popular sport magazines in the
     1950s) awarded multiple "Biggest Fish" prizes to the Kenora District. The biggest reported
     muskellunge in 1955 was pulled from the English River. The fifth-biggest muskellunge
     was pulled from Lake of the Woods. "*Field and Stream* Stories Tell of Success in District
     Waters," *Kenora-Keewatin Daily Miner and News*, 25 February 1955, 1. A similar obser-
     vation is made by Rick Brignal, "Lodged in the Past," Lake of the Woods Vacation Area,
     http://lakeofthewoods.com/stories-from-the-lake/lodged-in-the-past/.

11   In his analysis of "Resource Ontario," historian Rolf Knight suggested that "ingrained
     ethnic stereotypes" might have limited employment options for Indigenous workers in
     other industries, particularly at the railway camps of northern Ontario. Knight, *Indians
     at Work*, 283. Yet some record of employment exists. In 1882, G. McPherson claimed
     that "the employment of the Indians by railway contractors and lumbering firms secured
     them subsistence through the severest part of winter"; quoted in Michelle Chochla et al.,
     "Tracks/Chemin de fer," 1972, Tracks: An Opportunities for Youth Project, Kenora Public
     Library, 9. Other interviews in the Tracks series also indicate that at least some Indigenous
     men had employment with the CPR.

12   Lutz, *Makúk*, 217. See also McCallum, *Indigenous Women, Work, and History*, 23-24.

13   Everson, *May Whin Shah Ti Pah Chi Mo Win*, 12. Everson was born at Shoal Lake Indian
     Reserve in 1908 but does not specify whether her natal home was Shoal Lake #39 or
     Shoal Lake #40. She was removed from her community and registered at Cecilia Jaffray
     Residential School around 1915. Everson would not be released from the school until
     approximately 1926. Although employment opportunities peaked during the summer
     months, some Anishinaabe women such as Everson managed to secure full-time

employment. She worked as a housekeeper for Eric Holmstrom for two continuous years sometime between 1926 and 1932 (13–14).

14   Martin-McKeever, *The Chief's Granddaughter*, 72.

15   Edwards, "Indians in the Kenora District and Savanne."

16   Everson, *May Whin Shah Ti Pah Chi Mo Win*, 20.

17   Families who did not garden were considered exceptional. Indeed, Elder Charlie Fisher could remember by name families who did not garden. Elder Fisher, interview with Chapeskie, 22 March 1995.

18   Redsky, *Great Leader of the Ojibway*, 118.

19   Redsky, ibid., suggested that "all the people, even the children, used to help plant. They planted potatoes, corn, pumpkins, carrots, turnips and things like that. When they were ripe in the fall and ready to be put away, they came together again to pick them."

20   Elder Larry Kabestra, interview with the author, Dalles 38C Indian Reserve, ON, 6 July 2012; Elder David Wagamese, interview with the author, Dalles 38C Indian Reserve, 8 August 2012.

21   Edwards, "Indians in the Kenora District and Savanne." In *The Industrial Transformation of Subarctic Canada*, Liza Piper presents evidence of Indigenous participation in the mining industry elsewhere in the Subarctic zone. She notes that "Native and Métis men . . . worked staking ground for others, bringing in samples, cutting lines, and geigering" (121). She further notes that settler stereotypes about Indigenous (in)ability prevented settlers from classifying this labour as "prospecting." Instead, Indigenous labourers were commonly understood to support settler prospectors. It is unclear whether Edwards's reference to "cutting wood" for mining companies in Treaty 3 territory is a reference to line cutting, a form of exploratory labour required to establish a claim, and therefore Anishinaabe prospecting.

22   Knight, *Indians at Work*, 283.

23   Edwards, "Indians in the Kenora District and Savanne."

24   Quoted in Waisberg and Holzkamm, "A Tendency to Discourage Them from Cultivating," 180.

25   Quoted in Kinew, "Manito Gitigaan," 217. In 1892, ten Chiefs from Lake of the Woods alerted the superintendent of Indian Affairs to the "fear of starvation" as a direct result of flooding (217).

26   International Joint Commission, *Final Report,* 27.

27   Kathi Avery [Kinew] and Thomas Pawlick, "Last Stand in Wild Rice Country," *Harrowsmith* 3 (1979): 44.

28   Ibid.

29   "Lake of the Woods 1941–1945," Lake of the Woods Control Board, 18 June 2009, http://www.rlwwb-temp.lwcb.ca/permpdf/LW/5-Yr_LW-1941–1945.pdf; "Lake of the Woods 1951–1955," Lake of the Woods Control Board, 18 June 2009, http://www.rlwwb-temp.lwcb.ca/permpdf/LW/5-Yr_LW-1951–1955.pdf.

30   Edwards, "Indians in the Kenora District and Savanne."

31 According to Kinew, Anishinaabe harvesters had a market advantage in and around Kenora in the 1930s since non-Indigenous entrepreneurs purchased traditionally processed manomin. Anishinaabe families could thus afford to negotiate price points: their product would not spoil. Negotiating power decreased in the 1950s, however, as non-Indienous entrepreneurs began buying "green rice" and processing it independently. As yields declined on the Winnipeg River, Anishinaabe harvesters faced increasing presure to secure a quick sale: "Unprocessed rice has to be sold within a short while of being harvested or it will spoil and mould." Kinew, "Manito Gitigaan," 166.

32 Edwards, "Indians in the Kenora District and Savanne."

33 Ibid.

34 Benidickson, *Levelling the Lake*, 151–52.

35 Tough, *"As Their Natural Resources Fail,"* 291.

36 Frank Belmore, "The Tikinagun," n.d., LOWM, Folder: Anishinaabe—Essays and Papers.

37 Ibid.

38 Edwards, "Indians in the Kenora District and Savanne." Barriers to Indigenous participation in commercial fishing were not unique to Treaty 3 territory but occurred elsewhere in the Subarctic. In *The Industrial Transformation of Subarctic Canada*, Piper notes that "government officials used conservation and economic development to restrict Native fisheries on large lakes," such as Lake Winnipeg and Great Slave Lake (211). It seems that state restrictions allowed settlers to dominate the industry (210, 213).

39 Edwards, "Indians in the Kenora District and Savanne."

40 Ibid.

41 Max Foster letter to the Lake of the Woods Museum, undated, LOWM, Folder: Fish Hatchery Papers, file 2011.10.6.

42 Elder Matilda Martin (Ogimaamaashiik), interview with the *Kenora Daily Miner and News*, 30 June 1972, n. pag., LOWM.

43 Edwards, "Indians in the Kenora District and Savanne."

44 Ibid.

45 "Minutes of the Mayor's Indian Committee Meeting Held on Friday, April 26th, 1968," Archives of Ontario (hereafter AO), RG 29–01–1474, B334469, file "Indians-Kenora."

46 W. Welldon, Director, Ministry of Communication and Social Services, "Action on Kenora, 6 August 1975," memorandum, AO, RG 47–138, B212821, file "Kenora Action Recommendations." Hiring bars in Kenora ran counter to federal assimilation initiatives after the Second World War. In 1957, Canada launched the Indian Placement and Relocation Program to "facilitate Indian integration" by "plac[ing] First Nations people in permanent positions in urban areas." McCallum, *Indigenous Women, Work and History*, 66–67.

47 "Minutes of the Mayor's Indian Committee Meeting Held on Friday, April 26th, 1968," AO, RG 29–01–1474, B334469, file "Indians-Kenora."

48 Cardinal, *The Unjust Society*, 5. Piper found evidence of hiring bars elsewhere in the Subarctic, particularly in the mining industry: "Native and Métis workers were excluded from [mining] work underground"; rather than hire Indigenous workers, "Eldorado,

Cominco, Giant, and the many smaller companies imported men to the Northwest" until 1958. Piper, *The Industrial Transformation of Subarctic Canada*, 122.

49 In particular, the report quoted testimony provided by the head of the Welfare Division to the joint parliamentary committee in 1947. Quoted in Shewell, *"Enough to Keep Them Alive,"* 231.

50 More specifically, Shewell claims that "welfare expenditure remained extremely frugal [for] Indians thought capable of work." Relief was often denied to them immediately after the war. It is my assumption—given Shewell's earlier emphasis on "able-bodied" applicants—that "capable" is associated with "able-bodied." Ibid., 237.

51 Tough, *"As Their Natural Resources Fail,"* 296.

52 Elder Larry Kabestra, interview with the author, 6 July 2012.

53 Elder Kelly, interview with the author, 30 July 2012.

54 Quoted in Shewell, *"Enough to Keep Them Alive,"* 239.

55 Ibid., 242.

56 Elder Larry Kabestra, interview with the author, 6 July 2012.

57 Peter Holdsworth, "Social Network Analysis of Church Vital Records Related to Dalles 38C Indian Reserve Near Kenora, Ontario in the Lake of the Woods District," report, Dalles 38C Indian Reserve, 2014, 8–10.

58 Elder Fisher, interview with Chapeskie, 22 March 1995.

59 Ibid.

60 "Work Commences at Caribou Falls," *Kenora Daily Miner and News*, 8 June 1956, 8.

61 Elder Bert Fontaine, telephone interview with the author, 16 July 2012.

62 "St. Mary's, Marriage Certificate No. 11 (1940), Robert Kabestran [*sic*]—Flora McLeod," Notre Dame Parish, Kenora, ON, Indian Family Records.

63 Elder Larry Kabestra, interview with the author, 6 July 2012.

64 Meg Stanley, *Voices from Two Rivers: Harnessing the Power of the Peace and Columbia* (Vancouver: BC Hydro Power Pioneers Association with Douglas and McIntyre, 2010), 90.

65 Elder Fontaine, telephone interview with the author, 16 July 2012.

66 For example, John Grieve, a non-Indigenous employee interviewed in England, claimed that "the only words I spoke were to introduce myself and to thank him [the interviewer] for the job offer." There is no indication that Grieve worked in the Northwestern Division between 1950 and 1958. Yet his testimony reflects HEPCO's casual hiring process in the postwar era. *Ontario Hydro*, 45.

67 "Young Hydro Worker Is Pronounced Dead," *Kenora Daily Miner and News*, 16 June 1956, 1.

68 "310 Men Now Working on Whitedog Project," *Kenora Daily Miner and News*, 16 February 1956, 1.

69 "Caribou Falls Generating Station Adds More Power for Growing North," *Kenora Daily Miner and News*, 28 October 1958, 4.

70 Elder Fisher, interview with Chapeskie, 22 March 1995.

71 "310 Men Now Working on Whitedog Project," *Kenora Daily Miner and News*, 16 February 1956, 1.

72 J.A. Sherrett, "Impression of a Visit to Whitedog," *Kenora Daily Miner and News*, 26 October 1956, 1.

73 "Progress Scenes at Whitedog-Caribou Falls," *Kenora Daily Miner and News*, 4 September 1957, 4.

74 Elder Larry Kabestra, interview with the author, 6 July 2012.

75 Elder Fontaine, telephone interview with the author, 16 July 2012.

76 "Whitedog's Machine Shop Carries Big Load," *Kenora Daily Miner and News*, 26 November 1956, 4.

77 "The Caribou Pushing North from Whitedog," *Kenora Daily Miner and News*, 15 August 1956, 1.

78 Sherrett, "Impression of a Visit to Whitedog," 1.

79 Elder Fontaine, telephone interview with the author, 16 July 2012.

80 "The Caribou Pushing North from Whitedog," *Kenora Daily Miner and News*, 15 August 1956, 1.

81 "Whitedog Station Now in Production—Electricity Now Flowing into Hydro's N.W. Ontario System," *Kenora Daily Miner and News*, 5 March 1958, 1.

82 Elder Fontaine, telephone interview with the author, 16 July 2012.

83 Ibid.

84 Ontario Hydro, *Ontario Hydro*, 29.

85 Programming and Control Department: Conference Report, 16 November 1955, OPG, Whitedog Falls Generating Station, FP3–10901, Item 155.

86 William Noden, "Ontario Hydro Activities," *Kenora Daily Miner and News*, 25 February 1957, n. pag.

87 "Whitedog Falls GS Project Schedule," 4 February 1957, OPG, Whitedog Falls Generating Station, F010, Box 91.119.

88 R.G. Wykes, Construction Engineer—Generation, to A. Gusen, Program Planning and Control Engineer, re: Whitedog Schedule, 18 June 1957, OPG, Whitedog Falls Generating Station, Box 91.119.

89 Program Planning and Control Department Conference Report, 4 December 1956, OPG, Whitedog Falls Generating Station, FP3–10901, Item 155. F. Grosvenor, Estimate and Cost Control Engineer, suggested that "the project . . . resorted to overtime and double shifting" in 1956 to make up for delays resulting from "a chain of circumstances starting with the six weeks delay in providing access to the site by road." F. Grosvenor, Estimate and Cost Engineer, to G.D. Floyd, Assistant Manual Manager—Engineering, re: Forecast of Final Cost, 6 December 1956, OPG, Whitedog Falls Generating Station F010, Box 91.119.

90 R.G. Wykes, Construction Engineer—Generation, to A. Gusen, Program Planning and Control Engineer, re: Whitedog Schedule, 18 June 1957, OPG, Whitedog Falls Generating Station, Box 91.119.

91 Elder Fontaine, telephone interview with the author, 16 July 2012; also Elder Larry Kabestra, interview with the author, 6 July 2012.

92 G.V.D. Crombie, "Program Planning and Control Department Conference Report," 22 February 1956, OPG, Whitedog Falls Generating Station, FP3-L, Item 112.

93 "Cofferdam Construction Proceeds in Spite of Difficult Conditions," *Kenora Daily Miner and News*, 17 May 1956, 1.

94 Ibid.

95 Elder Fontaine, telephone interview with the author, 16 July 2012.

96 Ibid.

97 "Hydro Worker Drowns at Caribou Falls," *Kenora Daily Miner and News*, 12 July 1958, 1.

98 "Man Drowned at Whitedog," *Kenora Daily Miner and News*, 20 October 1958, 1.

99 W.I. Clifton, Technical Assistant, Accident Prevention Division, to J. MacLellan, re: Safety Inspection of New Powerhouses at Whitedog Falls, Caribou Falls, and Manitou Falls, and Inspection of New Units at Alexander GS and Cameron GS, 22 September 1958, OPG, Whitedog Falls Generating Station, FP3–10-1-228, V. 1, Item 1042.

100 Quoted in "Presentation of Safety Awards Made to Hydro Men," *Kenora Daily Miner and News*, 3 August 1956, 1, 6.

101 Elder Larry Kabestra, interview with the author, 6 July 2012.

102 Elder Fontaine, telephone interview with the author, 16 July 2012.

103 Elder Larry Kabestra, interview with the author, 6 July 2012.

104 Elder Fontaine, telephone interview with the author, 16 July 2012.

105 G.V.D. Crombie, "Program Planning and Control Department Conference Report," 22 February 1956," OPG, Whitedog Falls Generating Station, FP3-L, Item 112.

106 Stanley, *Voices from Two Rivers*, 90.

107 Elder Fontaine, telephone interview with the author, 16 July 2012.

108 Elder Larry Kabestra, interview with the author, 6 July 2012.

109 Ibid.

110 Elder Fontaine, telephone interview with the author, 16 July 2012.

111 "310 Men Now Working on Whitedog Project," *Kenora Daily Miner and News*, 16 February 1956, 1.

112 Sherrett, "Impression of a Visit to Whitedog," 1, 10.

113 "An Economic Necessity," *Kenora Daily Miner and News*, 20 June 1956, 1.

114 Elder Alice Kelly explained "My grandma [paddled] all the way to Whitedog Falls to do the shopping . . . . that's how far the store was. Big [supply] trucks, two times a week, I think." Elder Kelly, interview with the author, 30 July 2012. See also "13 Year Old Indian Drowned Thursday," *Kenora Daily Miner and News*, 2 May 1958, 1.

115 Sherrett, "Impression of a Visit to Whitedog," 1, 10.

116 Stuart King, "Kenora Chamber Members See Huge Power Development," *Kenora Daily Miner and News*, 26 October 1956, 1, 10. See also Sherrett, "Impression of a Visit to Whitedog," 1, 10.

117 Sherrett, "Impression of a Visit to Whitedog," 1, 10.

118 Director of Construction to G.D. Floyd, Assistant Manual Manager—Engineering, re: Provision of Staff Housing, 1 December 1955, OPG, Whitedog Falls Generating Station, F010, Box 91.119.

119 Elder Larry Kabestra, interview with the author, 6 July 2012.

120 Ibid.

121 Ibid.

122 "Dismantling Operations Almost Complete at Caribou Falls," *Kenora Miner and News*, 27 September 1958, 1.

123 Lorne McDonald, General Counsel, to C.F.S. Tidy, Special Negotiator, Property Division, re: Caribou Falls Development—Flooding—Islington Indian Reserve No. 28 and One Man Indian Reserve No. 29, 6 June 1961," OPG, Whitedog Falls Generating Station, OPG, FP3–10-1-228, V. 1, Item 1042.

124 Elder Kelly, interview with the author, 30 July 2012.

125 Carol Lawson (née Kipling), interview with the author, Kenora, ON, July 2012.

126 McDonald and Isogai, *From Grassy Narrows*, 43.

127 Chief Simon Fobister, interview with the author, Grassy Narrows Indian Reserve, ON, 5 August 2008.

128 Shkilnyk, *A Poison Stronger than Love*, 137.

129 Ibid., 138.

130 Lutz, *Makúk*, 8.

131 Interview synopses by Cuyler Cotton, Dovetail Resources, Kenora, ON, 1993, Dalles 38C, Elder Interview Collection.

132 Elder Larry Kabestra, interview with the author, 6 July 2012.

Chapter 5: Waste Accumulation in a Changed river

1 According to the records of Notre Dame Parish in Kenora, ON, Clarence Henry was born to Catherine Hunter and Guy Henry on 6 July 1929. "Bird, Sa Baptiste," Notre Dame Parish, Whitefish Record of Families.

2 Elder Henry's childhood experience has been extrapolated using anonymous Elder testimony from Dalles 38C. Elder #5, interviewed by Sheldon Ratuski, Dalles 38C Indian Reserve, ON, 17 February 2010, referenced in Sheldon Ratuski, "Gathering Traditional Knowledge and Perspectives of Sturgeon on the Winnipeg River from Dalles Community Members," unpublished report, 2005, LOWM, 5.

3 "Escape Channel at Dalles Rapids Is Blown Open," *Kenora Miner and News*, 12 May 1950, 1.

4 In 1971, the *Fort Frances Times and Rainy Lake Herald* noted that "the Kenora mill ... produced its own chemical pulp by the sulfite process"; "O-M Kraft Mill Now in Production: Why Fort Frances? Much Study Preceded Actual Construction," *Fort Frances*

Times and Rainy Lake Herald, November 1971, http://www.fftimes.com/100-years-100-stories/whyFF.html. Jamie Benidickson found evidence that "no attempt was made to recover sulphite liquor, which entered the river 'without treatment'" in the early 1960s; Benidickson, *Levelling the Lake*, 177.

5   National Electric Week ran from 9 to 15 February 1958. The *Kenora Daily Miner and News* published National Electric Week advertisements on 10 February 1958, 4, and 11 February 1958, 5. See also "Festival Public Speaking Entrants to Choose Electricity as Topics," *Kenora Daily Miner and News*, 25 November 1958, 1.

6   "E. Hutchinson, Letter to Editor," *Kenora Daily Miner and News*, 24 November 1955, 15.

7   A.E. Berry, "Sewage Disposal Practice in Canada," *Sewage Wastes Journal* 8, no. 1 (1936): 110.

8   The *Diamond Jubilee Guide* helps to define "community" as perceived by settlers at the north shore of Lake of the Woods. Author Hugh Hughes largely describes Rat Portage (now known as Kenora) by its retailers and service providers; his introduction, however, does not include Anishinaabe communities. Hugh Hughes, *Souvenir, Diamond Jubilee Guide: Rat Portage and Lake of the Woods* ([Toronto?]: Martel and Tilley, 1897), 4–12.

9   Quoted in D'Arcy Jenish, *Epic Wanderer: David Thompson and the Opening of the West* (Toronto: Anchor Canada, 2004), 58.

10 Stephen H. Long, *Narrative of an Expedition to the Source of St. Peter's River, Lake Winnepeek, Lake of the Woods, &c., &c.* (Philadelphia: H.C. Carey and I. Lea, 1824), 105.

11 Mike Aiken, "Winnipeg River/Dalles Tour: A Journey Back in Time," *Kenora Daily Miner and News*, 21 July 2008, n. pag.

12 "Water Powers in Ontario and Manitoba, c. 1930," LOWM, Folder: Powerhouse and Dams.

13 T.D. Green, "Diary of survey of Pistol Lake, Winnipeg River and Summer Resort Locations, November 1911," AO, microfilm MS 924, reel 28.

14 Elder Henry, interview with Cotton, 14 June 1993.

15 "Escape Channel at Dalles Rapids Is Blown Open," *Kenora Miner and News*, 12 May 1950, 1.

16 Aiken, "Winnipeg River/Dalles Tour," n. pag.

17 "Development Planned: Hydro Starts Road from Minaki to White Dog and Deer Falls," *Keewatin Daily Miner and News*, 16 September 1955, 1.

18 "Whitedog Falls Generating Station," Ontario Power Generation, 15 December 2015, http://www.opg.com/generating-power/hydro/northwest-ontario/Pages/white-dog-falls-station.aspx.

19 Chongrak Polprasert, *Organic Waste Recycling: Technology and Management*, 3rd ed. (London: IWA Publishing, 2007), 57.

20 Raymond Coppinger and Will Ryan, "James Bay: Environmental Considerations for Building Large Hydroelectric Dams and Reservoirs in Quebec," in *The Social and Environmental Impacts of the James Bay Hydroelectric Project*, ed. James F. Hornig (Montreal and Kingston: McGill-Queen's University Press, 1999), 42.

21 Cyclical flooding during the early 1900s is described in "Lake of the Woods Now Approaching 1062 Level," *Kenora Miner and News*, 16 May 1950, 1.

22 See, for example, Don E. Bloodgood, "Water Dilution Factors for Industrial Wastes,"
    Sewage and Industrial Wastes 26, no. 5 (1954): 644.

23 Elder Robert Kabestra, interview with Cuyler Cotton, transcript, Dovetail Resources,
    Kenora, ON, 29 September 1992. The transcriptionist appears to have paraphrased
    interview text.

24 Polprasert, *Organic Waste Recycling*, 94.

25 "What New Industrial Jobs Mean to a Community," *Kenora-Keewatin Daily Miner and
    News*, 25 January 1955, 4.

26 "Our Growing Population," *Kenora Miner and News*, 3 January 1950, 4.

27 In March 1955, the *Kenora-Keewatin Miner and News* commented on the installation of a
    new paper machine by the Ontario-Minnesota Pulp and Paper Company. Construction
    was associated with "subsequent addition to staff" at the mill; "Industrial Prospects
    Considered Excellent," *Kenora-Keewatin Miner and News*, 25 March 1955, 1. In September
    1955, the *Kenora Miner and News* noted that "preliminary work on the required access
    road" to the Whitedog Falls Generating Station was under way; "Road to Whitedog Starts,"
    Kenora Daily Miner and News, 30 September 1955, 1. By February 1956, HEPCO had 310
    men on payroll for the Whitedog Falls project; "310 Men Now Working on Whitedog
    Project," *Kenora Daily Miner and News*, 16 February 1956, 1.

28 "New MANDO Machine Adds 150 to Local Payroll—250 to Timber Department,"
    Kenora Daily Miner and News, 11 February 1957, 1.

29 "Building Permits Total $747,700: Ahead of 1955 Record Year by $1/4 Million; 61 Houses
    Started," *Kenora Daily Miner and News*, 10 August 1956, 1.

30 "Ratepayers to Be Asked to Vote on Sewage Question Again," *Kenora-Keewatin Daily Miner
    and News*, 25 October 1955, 1.

31 Lake of the Woods Writers' Group and Kenora Centennial Committee, *Through the Kenora
    Gateway*, 129. Direct references to privies and/or private disposal can also be found in
    "Letter to the Editor," *Kenora Daily Miner and News*, 8 November 1955, 9, and in "District
    Health Good Says December Report," *Kenora-Keewatin Daily Miner and News*, 12 January
    1955, 10.

32 "Creek Clean-Up Permits Use Now by Small Boats," *Kenora Daily Miner and News*, 11
    July 1958, 1.

33 "Creek Yields Varied Materials to Dragging Crew," *Kenora Daily Miner and News*, 10
    July 1956, 1.

34 "Keewatin," *Rat Portage Weekly Record*, 21 April 1893, 2.

35 "Town of Kenora Police Department Records of Sanitary Inspector H. King, August
    1910," LOWM, Folder: Waterworks and Public Utilities.

36 "Council Gives 'Go-Ahead' Signal to Sewer and Water Projects," *Kenora-Keewatin Daily
    Miner and News*, 4 May 1955, 1.

37 The *Kenora-Keewatin Daily Miner and News* suggested that delays resulted in part from
    "difficulties in providing services in the new housing development." Indeed, "it is known
    that sewer and water problems are the main stumbling block to final approval of plans."
    "With Time of the Essence Engineer Flies to Housing Conference," *Kenora-Keewatin Daily
    Miner and News*, 18 April 1955, 1. The proposed three-stage sewage disposal program was

detailed in "Ratepayers to Be Asked to Vote on Sewage Question Again," *Kenora Daily Miner and News*, 25 October 1955, 1.

38 "Ratepayers to Be Asked to Vote on Sewage Question Again," *Kenora Daily Miner and News*, 25 October 1955, 1.

39 E. Hutchinson, "Letter to Editor," *Kenora Daily Miner and News*, 24 November 1955, 15.

40 "Town's Brief to Water Resources Commission Is Well Received," *Kenora Daily Miner and News*, 26 September 1956, 1.

41 "Our Editorial Viewpoint: Housing Break-Through," *Kenora Daily Miner and News*, 10 September 1956, 1.

42 Madlen Davies, "What will your body do this year?" *Daily Mail* [United Kingdom], 28 January 2015, https://www.dailymail.co.uk/health/article-2929972/What-body-year-Graphic-reveals-ll-produce-urine-two-bathtubs-shed-half-stone-skin.html; Lisa Bowman, "Here's how much poo you'll produce in your life," *Metro* [United Kingdom], 23 March 2018, https://metro.co.uk/2018/03/23/much-poo-produce-life-7410405/.

43 Elder Henry, interview with Cotton, 14 June 1993.

44 Elder Lindsay, interview with Cotton, 2 October 1992.

45 H.W. Clark, "Past and Present Developments in Sewage Disposal and Purification," *Sewage Works Journal* 24, no. 4 (1930): 561–71.

46 Ibid., 561; see also Berry, "Sewage Disposal Practice in Canada," 110.

47 E.K. Day, "Sewage and Waste Disposal Problems," *Public Health Reports* 66, no. 29 (1951): 923.

48 J.R. Menzies, "Sewage Disposal and Waste Treatment in Canada," *Sewage and Industrial Wastes* 28, no. 3 (1956): 276.

49 Day, "Sewage and Waste Disposal Problems," 927.

50 Menzies, "Sewage Disposal and Waste Treatment in Canada," 278.

51 "Portion of Mill Site Allotted for Sewage Disposal Plant," *Kenora Daily Miner and News*, 15 July 1958, 1.

52 "Chamber of Commerce Seek Alternate Site for Sewage Plant," *Kenora Daily Miner and News*, 6 November 1958, 1.

53 Ibid. For an example of a mill tour advertisement, see "You Are Invited to Visit MANDO's Kenora Mill, June 19–20," *Kenora Daily Miner and News*, 11 June 1957, 4.

54 "Chamber of Commerce Seek Alternate Site for Sewage Plant," *Kenora Daily Miner and News*, 6 November 1958, 1.

55 Joseph W. Ellms, "Water Purification and Sewage Disposal on the Great Lakes," *The Scientific Monthly* 33, no. 5 (1931): 424.

56 Ibid., 425.

57 For a summary of works dealing with the possible transmission of tuberculosis through sewage, see Arnold E. Greenberg and Edward Kupka, "Tuberculosis Transmission by Waste Waters: A Review," *Sewage and Industrial Wastes* 29, no. 5 (1957): 524–37. For references to tuberculosis at Kenora District residential schools, see "*Bakaan nake'ii*

ngii-izhi-gakinoo'amaagoomin: We Were Taught Differently: The Indian Residential School Experience," 2008, 20, LOWM.

58 Albert E. Berry, interview with Norman Ball and Robert Ferguson, 1983, transcript, Public Works Oral History, Public Works Historical Society, Chicago 1988, 9.

59 "District Health Good Says December Report," *Kenora-Keewatin Daily Miner and News*, 12 January 1955, 10.

60 "Residents of N.E. Area Seek Water Service," *Kenora Daily Miner and News*, c. spring 1957, 1.

61 Sheila McRae, interview with the author, Kenora, ON, 18 May 2012; M.J.W. German, "A Study of the Pollution Status of Rat Portage Bay and the Winnipeg River," Ontario Water Resources Commission, October 1968, 2, TARR, Winnipeg River Watershed— Water Pollution, 1965–95—Reports.

62 "Redditt's Water Supply," *Kenora Miner and News*, 16 May 1950, 4.

63 Elder Lindsay, interview with Cotton, 2 October 1992.

64 D.T. Wigle, *Child Health and the Environment* (New York: Oxford University Press, 2003), 357.

65 Ibid., 358.

66 T. Kue Young, *The Health of Native Americans: Towards a Biocultural Epidemiology* (Toronto: Oxford University Press, 1994), 92.

67 Linda Wasakkejick, telephone interview with the author, 7 August 2008.

68 Polprasert, *Organic Waste Recycling*, 60.

69 A.E. Kelen and N.A. Labzoffsky, "Variations in the Prevalence of Enterovirus Infections in Ontario, 1956–1965," *Canadian Medical Association Journal* 97, no. 13 (1967): 797.

70 "Ratepayers to Be Asked to Vote on Sewage Question Again," *Kenora-Keewatin Daily Miner and News*, 25 October 1955, 1.

71 "Letter to the Editor," *Kenora-Keewatin Daily Miner and News*, 8 November 1955, 9.

72 Ibid., 8.

73 "Answers to Sewage Questions Given," *Kenora Daily Miner and News*, 23 November 1955, 1.

74 "For Norman: To Vote on $276,000 Sewer-Water Project," *Kenora Daily Miner and News*, 13 November 1956, 1.

75 "Overflow Crowd at Meeting: Water Project Endorsed by Norman—10 Man Committee Named to Promote Issue before Balloting," *Kenora Daily Miner and News*, 14 November 1956, 1.

76 Ibid.

77 "No. 10 Machine at Work—New Paper Machine in Operation," *Kenora Daily Miner and News*, 30 January 1957, 1. The article also referenced "expansion of the electric power system," which implies a connection to HEPCO given the limited electrical capacity of the Norman Dam.

78 "O & M Production Will Increase," *Kenora-Keewatin Daily Miner and News*, 11 March 1955, 7; "Industrial Prospects Considered Excellent," *Kenora-Keewatin Daily Miner and News*, 25 March 1955, 1.

79   "Industrial Prospects Considered Excellent," *Kenora-Keewatin Daily Miner and News*, 25 March 1955, 1; "Predict Completion of MANDO's Kenora Mill in Record Time," *Kenora Daily Miner and News*, 1 October 1955, 1.

80   "New MANDO Machine Adds 150 to Local Payroll—250 to Timber Department," *Kenora Daily Miner and News*, 11 February 1957, 7.

81   See "Norman Generating Station (10MW)—Kenora: Winnipeg River," Ontario Power Authority, http://www.powerauthority.on.ca/hydroelectric/norman-generating-station-10-mw-kenora-winnipeg-river.

82   "During 1955 . . . Mandonians," *Kenora Daily Miner and News*, 22 March 1956, 4.

83   Golder Associates, "Report on Phase II Environmental Site Assessment, Kenora Pulp and Paper Mill," March 2008, Mississauga, ON, i, ii, viii.

84   D.S. Calvary, General Manager of Pulp and Paper Mills at Kenora, Fort Frances, and Dryden, memorandum to the Honorable G.A. Kerr, Minister of Department of Energy and Resources Management, 21 May 1970, Ontario Water Resources Commission: Pulp and Paper Mills, Kenora, Fort Frances, Dryden, box 237549, AO, Toronto, Ontario.

85   "Predict Completion MANDO's Kenora Mill in Record Time," *Kenora Daily Miner and News*, 1 October 1955, 1.

86   P.F. Playfair, Medical Officer of Health and Director of the Northwestern Health Unit, to Sanitary Engineering Division of the Ontario Water Resources Commission, 17 September 1963, AO, RG 84-22, b125018.

87   "During 1955 . . . Mandonians," *Kenora Daily Miner and News*, 22 March 1956, 4.

88   Jon Thompson, "Dalles Team Looks at River Bed to Sustain Reintroduction of Sturgeon," *Kenora Daily Miner and News*, 18 October 2011, http://www.kenoradailyminerandnews.com/ArticleDisplay.aspx?archive=true&e=3337684.

89   Bruce Fairbairn, "Sawlog Pollution in the Lower Fraser River" (MA thesis, Vancouver, University of British Columbia, 1974), 40.

90   Elder Lindsay, interview with Cotton, 2 October 1992.

91   Elder Robert Kabestra, interview with Cotton, 29 September 1992.

92   Elder Henry, interview with Cotton, 14 June 1993.

93   R.A. McKenzie, "The Reported Decrease in Fish Life and the Pollution of the Winnipeg River, Kenora, Ontario," *Transactions of the American Fisheries* 60, no. 1 (1930): 320. Although the relationship between mill inputs and reduced oxygen levels was noted in Rideout Bay, McKenzie suggested that clean water conditions were re-established farther from the bay. Oxygen content was attributed to the "various swift stretches in the river" and the oxygenation of the water (315).

94   Melvin L. Warren and Brooks M. Burr, eds., *Freshwater Fishes of North America: Petromyzontidae to Catosomidae, Volume 1* (Baltimore: Johns Hopkins University Press, 2014), 177. Low oxygen environments have been shown to "impair . . . respiratory metabolism, foraging activity, and growth rates" in many sturgeon species; V.W. Blevins, "Water-Quality Requirements, Tolerances, and Preferences of Pallid Sturgeon (*Scaphirhynchus albus*) in the Lower Missouri River," U.S. Geological Survey Scientific Investigation Report 2011–5186, 2011, 8. Christine Kemker suggests that other fish are more tolerant of low oxygen environments. Walleye, a popular fish

for year-round consumption in the upper Winnipeg River drainage basin, "prefer levels over 5mg/L, though they can survive at 2 mg/L DO for a short time"; northern pike, a fish preferred seasonally, can survive "for an infinite amount of time" at 1.5mg/L." Christine Kemker, "Dissolved Oxygen," in *Fundamentals of Environmental Measurements*, Fondriest Environmental, 19 November 2013, http://www.fondriest.com/environmental-measurements/parameters/water-quality/dissolved-oxygen/#9.

95 Elder Janet Green, interview with Cuyler Cotton, transcript, Dovetail Resources, Kenora, ON, 1993. The transcriptionist appears to have paraphrased interview text.

96 Long, *Narrative of an Expedition to the Source*, 106.

97 Holzkamm and Waisberg, "Native American Utilization of Sturgeon," 28.

98 Elder Lindsay, interview with Cotton, 2 October 1992.

99 Elder Henry, interview with Cotton, 14 June 1993.

100 "George A. Kerr, Memorandum, to Stanley Randall, Minister of the Department of Trade and Development, 16 September 1969, re: Ontario-Minnesota Pulp and Paper Company Limited," TARR, Winnipeg River Watershed—Water Pollution, 1965–95—Correspondence.

101 D.J. Collins, Ontario Water Resources Commission, to Stanley Randall, Minister of the Department of Trade and Development, 24 September 1969, re: Memorandum of August 29 Concerning Ontario-Minnesota Pulp and Paper Company, AO.

102 "George A. Kerr, Memorandum."

103 Quoted in Bloodgood, "Water Dilution Factors for Industrial Wastes," 645.

104 Quoted in ibid., 646.

105 Ibid.

106 "Biggest Industry: Pulp and Paper," *Kenora Miner and News*, 2 April 1955, 6; "During 1955 . . . Mandonians," *Kenora Daily Miner and News*, 22 March 1956, 4.

107 Minister René Brunelle to Stanley Randall, Minister of the Department of Trade and Development, 9 October 1969, re: Ontario-Minnesota Pulp and Paper Co., TARR, Winnipeg River Watershed—Water Pollution, 1965–95—Correspondence.

108 Dan Gauthier, "Restocking Program Attempts to Restore Winnipeg River Sturgeon Fishery," Lake of the Woods Enterprise, 3 June 2005, http://www.kenoradailyminerand-news.com/ArticleDisplay.aspx?archive=true&e=1856585.

109 Jon Thompson, "Elders, Biologists Confer on Winnipeg River Sturgeon," *Kenora Daily Miner and News*, 8 October 2010, http://www.kenoradailyminerandnews.com/2010/10/08/elders-biologists-confer-on-winnipeg-river-sturgeon.

110 Scott Brennan and Jay Withgott, *Essential Environment: The Science behind the Stories* (San Francisco: Pearson Education, 2005), 244.

111 Thompson, "Elders, Biologists Confer on Winnipeg River Sturgeon."

112 "Article V," in Treaty between the United States and Great Britain in Relation to Boundary Waters, and Questions Arising between the United States and Canada (1910), International Joint Commission, http://www.ijc.org/rel/agree/water.html#text.

Chapter 6: Mother Work and Managing Environmental Change

1   This chapter is dedicated to Elder Alice Kelly, who passed away on 18 July 2019. Alice, you taught me about the challenges faced by Anishinaabe women. You showcased their strength and creativity in your stories. I hope to walk honourably along the path that you cleared for me to return to my ancestral community as a learner and a history keeper.

2   Martin-McKeever, *The Chief's Granddaughter*, 9–11.

3   Lawson, interview with the author, 12 July 2012.

4   Between 1962 and 1975, Dryden Chemicals "flushed its waste products into the Wabigoon River. The mill effluent contained a relatively high level of mercury, which worked its way into the aquatic food chain of the river system. In 1970, the Ontario government discovered that the level of mercury found in fish in a 500-km stretch downstream from the pulp and paper mill was dangerous to health, and advised the Ojibway communities at Grassy Narrows and Whitedog reserves not to eat fish from these rivers" (Robert M. Bone, *The Geography of the Canadian North: Issues and Challenges*, 3rd ed. (Don Mills, ON: Oxford University Press, 2009), 199.). See also Len Manko, "The Grassy Narrows and Islington Bands Mercury Disability Board: A Historical Report, 1986–2001," Grassy Narrows and Islington Bands Mercury Disability Board, September 2006, http://www.mercurydisabilityboard.com/booklet.pdf.

5   Dan Pine, "*Anishinaabe miikan*/The Anishinaabe Road," in *Gechi-piitzijig dbaajmowag/ The Stories of Our Elders*, ed. Alan Corbiere (West Bay, ON: Ojibwe Cultural Foundation, 2011), 14–15. Henry Rowe Schoolcraft, commenting almost a century earlier on Anishinaabe household relations near Sault Ste. Marie, Michigan, similarly noted that "the lodge itself, with all its arrangements, is the precinct of the rule and government of the wife." Quoted in Priscilla Buffalohead, "Farmers, Warriors, Traders: A Fresh Look at Ojibway Women," *Minnesota History* 48, no. 6 (1983): 241.

6   Elder Kelly, interview with the author, 30 July 2012.

7   Ibid. See also Anderson, *Life Stages and Native Women*, 44. Child, *Holding Our World Together*, 16, notes that plants could be used to "treat menstrual discomforts, pregnancy and childbirth issues, and menopause."

8   Densmore, *Chippewa Customs*, 6.

9   "An Older Woman," quoted in Jennifer Leyson, "Looking Forward, Looking Back: Chronic Disaster, Collective Trauma, and Community Restoration in the Ochiichagwe'Babigo'Ining First Nation [Dalles 38C Indian Reserve]" (MA thesis, George Mason University, 2002), 117.

10 Elder Kelly, interview with the author, 30 July 2012.

11 Peter Bakker, in *A Language of Our Own: The Genesis of Michif, the Mixed Cree-French Language of the Canadian Métis* (New York: Oxford University Press, 1997), identified a number of historical sources that demonstrated land sharing between Anishinaabe and Cree communities around Lake of the Woods (now part of Treaty 3 territory) in the eighteenth century (256). As early as 1790, for example, Edward Umfreville observed that "these two nations have always been in strict alliance with each other, and many of the Ochipawas [Anishinabeg] live in a promiscuous manner among the Ne-heth-aw-as [Crees]" (266).

12 The seclusion of Anishinaabe women during their menses further speaks to the perceived medicinal power of female bodies. However, a full description of menstrual seclusion is outside the scope of this chapter. Hilger, *Chippewa Child Life*, 50–55.

13 At the time of publication, Robinson and Quinney identified publicly as "Cree." There is no known public record to help me determine whether they also identified as Nehiyawak, Mushkego, or Omushkego. Eric Robinson and Henry Bird Quinney, *The Infested Blanket: Canada's Constitution–Genocide of Indian Nations* (Winnipeg: Queenston House, 1985), 11–12.

14 Ibid. Child, *Holding Our World Together*, similarly notes that "women were thought to hold an innate strength because of their life-giving ability" (5). Indeed, the Anishinabeg associated the development of a woman's spiritual power with her first menstruation (6).

15 Unidentified traditional educator, quoted in Joan Dodgson and Roxanne Struthers, "Traditional Breastfeeding Practices of the Ojibwe of Northern Minnesota," *Health Care for Women International* 24, no. 1 (2003): 57.

16 Written records of breast milk's socio-cultural significance to Anishinaabe families date back to 1826. *Totoashaúbo*, translated as "milk" or "breast liquor," featured in Thomas L. McKenney's "Vocabulary of the Algic, or Chippeway Language," copies of which the Department of War gave to American missionaries. McKenney deemed *totoashaúbo* as important to learn as *waydokaugadgig* (allies), *puckway'zhegun* (bread), *shominau'bo* (wine), and *mey'im* (victuals). Thomas L. McKenney, "Vocabulary of the Algic, or Chippeway Language," in *Sketches of a Tour to the Lakes, of the Character and Customs of the Chippeway Indians, and of Incidents Connected with the Treaty of Fond du Lac* (Barre, MA: Imprint Society, 1972), 407–13.

17 Elder Matilda Martin (Ogimaamaashiik), interview with the *Kenora Daily Miner and News*, 27 July 1972, n. pag., LOWM. Kim Anderson, who researches Algonquian peoples in northwestern Ontario, focuses on the use of herbal mixtures to limit family size, citing no examples of breastfeeding to space out pregnancies. Anderson, *Life Stages and Native Women*, 40–41. Oral informants from Dalles 38C Indian Reserve made no reference to herbal mixtures as a form of birth control. However, Mary Inez Hilger found that Anishinaabe women used tea decoctions to induce abortion on some American reservations; Hilger, *Chippewa Child Life*, 10–11.

18 M. Vekemans, "Postpartum Contraception: The Lactational Amenorrhea Method," *European Journal of Contraception and Reproductive Health* 2, no. 2 (1997): 105–11.

19 "Breastfeeding as Birth Control," Planned Parenthood Federation of America, https://www.plannedparenthood.org/learn/birth-control/breastfeeding.

20 Hilger, *Chippewa Child Life*, 28.

21 Elder Kelly, interview with the author, 30 July 2012.

22 Martin-McKeever, *The Chief's Granddaughter*, 18; Hilger, *Chippewa Child Life*, 11.

23 Wendy Dasler Johnson, "Cultural Rhetorics of Women's Corsets," *Rhetoric Review* 20, nos. 3–4 (2001): 204.

24 Elizabeth Matelski, "The Color(s) of Perfection: The Feminine Body, Beauty Ideals, and Identity in Postwar America, 1945–1970" (PhD diss., Loyola University, 2011), 51. Writing in the Canadian context specifically, Cynthia R. Comacchio, *The Infinite Bonds of Family: Domesticity in Canada, 1850–1940* (Toronto: University of Toronto Press,

1999), 73, confirms that "the large-breasted, wide-hipped, maternal feminine ideal" remained desirable until after the First World War, when "a slender boyish frame" became more popular.

25 Johnson, "Cultural Rhetorics of Women's Corsets," 211.

26 Johnston, *Ojibway Ceremonies*, 79.

27 Ibid., 79, 84.

28 Ibid., 84.

29 In *History of the Ojibway People*, 98, William Warren noted that "their shirts and leggins [*sic*] were made of finely dressed deer and elk skins sewn together with the sinews of these animals." He associated this style of dress with the early eighteenth century. Hilger suggests in *Chippewa Child Life*, 129, that "in the early days adults wore clothing made of finely tanned hides of deer, moose, bear, and elk; and of dressed skins of rabbit, beaver, and other small fur-bearing animals." Her temporal framework is unclear.

30 Densmore, *Chippewa Customs*, 31.

31 Katherine Krohn, *Calico Dresses and Buffalo Robes: American West Fashions from the 1840s to the 1890s* (Minneapolis: Twenty-First Century Books, 2012), 11.

32 Densmore, *Chippewa Customs*, 33.

33 Ibid., 32.

34 Ibid., 31.

35 Ibid., 32.

36 Elder Martin, interview with the *Kenora Daily Miner and News*, 11 July 1972, n. pag., LOWM.

37 Frank Belmore, "The Tikinagun," n.d., LOWM, Folder: Anishinaabe—Essays and Papers.

38 Bruce White, *We Are at Home: Pictures of the Ojibwe People* (St. Paul: Minnesota Historical Society Press, 2007), 21.

39 Belmore, "The Tikinagun."

40 "Uncivilized Man," *Eclectic Magazine of Foreign Literature, Science, and Art* 51, no. 4 (1861): 471.

41 Belmore, "The Tikinagun."

42 Elder Martin, interview with the *Kenora Daily Miner and News*, 11 July 1972.

43 "Uncivilized Man," *Eclectic Magazine*, 471.

44 Elder Martin, interview with the *Kenora Daily Miner and News*, summer 1972, n. pag., LOWM.

45 Kathleen Morgan Drowne and Patrick Huber, "Fashion," *American Popular Culture through History: The 1920s*, ed. Ray B. Browne (Westport, CT: Greenwood Press, 2004), note that "during the 1920s women's underwear . . . became lighter and less constricting" than the corset (105). Older women, however, continued to purchase corsets despite the rising popularity of the brassiere. Drowne and Huber explain that most undergarments "manufactured during the 1920s were intended to flatten rather than accentuate women's breasts" (106).

46 Maysa Rawi, "The First Ever Push-Up Bra: So, Bust-Boosting Dates Back to the 1800s," *Daily Mail* [United Kingdom], 23 April 2010, http://www.dailymail.co.uk/femail/article-1268276/The-push-bra-Bust-booster-dates-1800s.html#ixzz2omt0AAR9; Jane Farrell-Beck and Colleen Gau, *Uplift: The Bra in America* (Philadelphia: University of Pennsylvania Press, 2002), 121.

47 Rawi, "The First Ever Push-Up Bra."

48 Matelski, *The Color(s) of Perfection*, 99, 62.

49 Ibid., 65–69.

50 Elder Kelly, interview with the author, 30 July 2012.

51 Johnston, *Ojibway Ceremonies*, 79.

52 Ibid., 91, 92.

53 Ibid., 90.

54 Elder Kelly, interview with the author, 30 July 2012.

55 Anderson, *Life Stages and Native Women*, 44.

56 Elder Kelly, interview with the author, 30 July 2012.

57 Dodgson and Struthers, "Traditional Breastfeeding Practices," 58.

58 Quoted in Anderson, *Life Stages and Native Women*, 44. Hilger, *Chippewa Child Life*, 29, also found that many Anishinaabe women believed that porridge boiled in fish broth could increase milk secretion.

59 Elder Kelly, interview with the author, 30 July 2012.

60 Ibid.

61 Hilger, *Chippewa Child Life*, 6–7.

62 Johnston, *Ojibway Heritage*, 53, identifies the turtle as a symbol of "communication, [an] emissary."

63 Anderson, *Life Stages and Native Women*, 57.

64 Robinson and Quinney, *The Infested Blanket*, 9.

65 Anderson, *Life Stages and Native Women*, 57. Although Anderson suggested that the fontanelle was associated with an openness to the spirit world, Hilger, *Chippewa Child Life*, 18, found that Anishinaabe women attached no meaning to it (c. 1930). According to Hilger, the fontanelle was only recognized as a sensitive area. She found that the fear of injury encouraged many Anishinabeg to refrain from washing the top of an infant's head.

66 Elder Kelly, interview with the author, 30 July 2012.

67 Elder Martin, interview with the *Kenora Daily Miner and News*, 27 July 1972.

68 Harvey Levenstein, "'Best for Babies' or 'Preventable Infanticide'? The Controversy over Artificial Feeding of Infants in America, 1880–1920," *Journal of American History* 70, no. 1 (1983): 75–94. See also Samuel X. Radbill, "Infant Feeding through the Ages," *Clinical Pediatrics* 20, no. 10 (1981): 613–21.

69 E.L. Drewry, located in Winnipeg, supplied Maltum Stout to businesses in the Kenora District and regularly advertised the product in the *Kenora Miner and News* in the fall

of 1918. See, for example, "Maltum Stout" [advertisement], *Kenora Miner and News*, 7 September 1918, 3.

70 Levenstein, "'Best for Babies,'" 83. See also "Klim Powdered Whole Milk" in *Kenora Miner and News*, 15 September 1923, 3; 1 December 1923, 3; 2 February 1924, 4.

71 Quoted in "Have Goats a Place in Ontario?" *Kenora Miner and News*, 4 November 1916, 2.

72 "The Fair Decided Success," *Kenora Miner and News*, 28 August 1915, 1.

73 "Old Time Resident Fondly Recalls Walk from Dalles," *Kenora Daily Miner and News*, n.d., n. pag. This document can also be found in "Memoirs of Matilda Josephine Lavergne Kipling Martin," 1987, LOWM.

74 "He Kept the Goat," *Kenora Miner and News*, 27 October 1915, 3.

75 "Goats for Hospital," *Kenora Miner and News*, 20 August 1919, 3.

76 Elder Martin, interview with the *Kenora Daily Miner and News*, 27 July 1972.

77 Elder Fisher, interview with Chapeskie, 22 March 1995.

78 Lawson, interview with the author, 12 July 2012.

79 Ibid.

80 Elder Robert Kabestra, interview with Cotton, 29 September 1992.

81 Elder Henry, interview with Cotton, transcript, 14 June 1993.

82 Elder Robert Kabestra and Joe Wagamese, interview with Cotton, 26 October 1992. It is unclear in the interview transcript whether Kabestra or Wagamese uttered these words. Speech appears to have been paraphrased.

83 Elder Henry, interview with Cotton, 14 June 1993.

84 Elder Robert Kabestra, interview with Cotton, 29 September 1992.

85 Paula Spencer, Ministry of the Environment, email to the author, 14 November 2011.

86 Benidickson, *Levelling the Lake*, 211.

87 Shkilnyk, *Poison Stronger than Love*, 185.

88 H.B. Cotnam, Supervising Coroner, to T.M. Eberlee, Deputy Minister of the Ministry of Community and Social Services, 6 February 1973, "Re: Inquest into the Death of Thomas Strong Deceased—16 August 1972," AO, Indian Community Branch General 1973, RG 47–138, b212821.

89 Ross C. Bennett, Deputy Chief Coroner, to T.M. Eberlee, Deputy Minister of the Ministry of Community and Social Services, 8 March 1973, "Re: Inquest into the Death of Thomas Strong," AO, Indian Community Branch General 1973, RG 47–138, b212821.

90 These fears remain. During a community meeting in 2008, band members expressed a desire to take hair samples to determine whether perceived health risks are scientifically verifiable. The stress caused by living with a potential illness has been amplified by Health Canada's historical lack of interest in monitoring water quality at Dalles 38C. As Cuyler Cotton explained, "right now there's not data on the extent of mercury levels, historic or otherwise, in this community." Ochiichagwe'Babigo'Ining Ojibway Nation Band Meeting, Ochiichagwe'Babigo'Ining Ojibway Nation, ON, 19 November 2011. Unfortunately, the cost of knowing whether country foods were poisoned is beyond the means of Dalles 38C. So questions about whether to eat from local lands and waters remain unanswered.

91 In the Winnipeg River drainage basin, this trend is demonstrated by Shkilnyk, *Poison Stronger than Love*, 200–06, 217–19.

92 Unidentified Elder quoted in Leyson, "Looking Forward, Looking Back," 96.

93 "Women's Mini Conference, Grassy Narrows," *Treaty #3 Council Fire* 2, no. 5 (1973): 1. Anishinaabe women's fears about obscured evidence might have been tied to parliamentary debates about the existence of methyl mercury in Treaty 3 territory. For further information, see Len Manko, "The Grassy Narrows and Islington Band Mercury Disability Board: A Historical Report, 1986–2001," funded by The Grassy Narrows First Nation and Wabaseemoong Independent Nations Mercury Disability Board, Kenora, ON, September 2006.

94 Quoted in "Women's Mini Conference, Grassy Narrows," 3.

95 Tony Ashopenase, "Cleaning Up Grassy," *Treaty #3 Council Fire* 2, no. 5 (1973): 5.

96 Unidentified Artist, "Gov't Stops Mercury Pollution?!!!," *Treaty #3 Council Fire* 2, no. 5 (1973): 3.

97 Elder Roberta Jameson, interview with the author, Dalles 38C Indian Reserve, ON, 27 August 2012.

98 Elder Kelly, interview with the author, 30 July 2012.

99 Lawson, interview with the author, 12 July 2012.

100 Roger Spielmann, *"You're So Fat!" Exploring Ojibwe Discourse* (Toronto: University of Toronto Press, 1998), 30.

101 Nancy MacDonald and Judy MacDonald, "Reflections of a Mi'kmaq Social Worker on a Quarter of a Century Work in First Nations Child Welfare," *First Peoples Child and Family Review* 3, no. 1 (2007): 38.

102 Patrick Johnston, *Native Children and the Welfare System* (Toronto: Canadian Council on Social Development in association with James Lorimer, 1983).

103 MacDonald and MacDonald, "Reflections of a Mi'kmaq Social Worker," 39.

104 Unidentified Elder quoted in Leyson, "Looking Forward, Looking Back," 88. In a summary of Elder Harriet McDonald's interview, the transcriptionist noted that "children were lost to agencies." Interview synopses by Cuyler Cotton, Dovetail Resources, Kenora, ON, 1993, Dalles 38C, Elder Interview Collection.

105 As of January 2016, families at Dalles 38C were still trying to locate victims of the Sixties Scoop believed to have been placed with other status Indians. To learn more about the challenges faced by birth families, contact the band office at Ochiichagwe'Babigo'Ining Ojibway Nation. Administration can be reached at ph. 807-548-5876.

106 I have yet to find documents corroborating these stories of in-kind Carnation Milk rations, and to a certain extent the suggestion of in-kind welfare runs counter to trending bureaucratic practices in the Kenora District in the 1960s. For instance, cash began to replace government benefits "in the form of goods and services" by 1965 at Fort Hope Indian Reserve (approximately 800 kilometres east of Dalles 38C). Paul Driben and Robert Sanderson Trudeau, *When Freedom Is Lost: The Dark Side of the Relationship between Government and the Fort Hope Band* (Toronto: University of Toronto Press, 1983), 29. However, given historian Ian Mosby's recent exposé of collusion between Indian Affairs (e.g., Dr. Percy Moore, Indian Affairs Branch superintendent of medical services) and

the Canadian food industry (e.g., Dr. Frederick Tisdall, co-inventor of the infant food Pablum) in the postwar era, it is too early to dismiss whispers of product distribution. Ian Mosby, "Administering Colonial Science: Nutrition Research and Human Biomedical Experimentation in Aboriginal Communities and Residential Schools, 1942–1952," *Histoire sociale/Social History* 46, no. 91 (2013): 145–72.

107 Child, *Holding Our World Together*, 95.

108 According to research compiled by the Council of Ontario Drama and Dance Educators, tin cones are frequently made with the lids of chewing tobacco cans. "Student/Teacher Resource: ATC 30—Jingle Dress Dance," Council of Ontario Drama and Dance Educators, http://code.on.ca/sites/default/files/assets/resources/282-aboriginal-dance/documents/atc3o-aboriginaldance-blm1jingledressdance.pdf.

109 For further information, see ibid. Child, *Holding Our World Together*, 94, notes that the jingle dress might also have originated in Mille Lacs, Minnesota. Both American and Canadian origin stories identify this healing tradition as a response to Spanish influenza in the 1910s.

Conclusion

1   Lloyd Mack, "Utility Chairman Apologizes to Dalles Members," *Kenora Daily Miner and News*, 4 July 2008, http://www.kenoradailyminerandnews.com/2008/07/04/utility-chairman-apologizes-to-dalles-members.

2   Elder Henry, interview with Cotton, 14 June 1993.

3   Elder Kelly, interview with the author, 30 July 2012. Journalist Mike Aiken has similarly reported that Dalles 38C was "eventually deserted, as inhabitants could no longer live their traditional lifestyle." He attributes socio-economic challenges to environmental modifications, particularly the damming of the Winnipeg River by HEPCO and notes that Dalles 38C was not repopulated until about 1980. Mike Aiken, "Flood Memorial at Dalles," *Kenora Daily Miner and News*, 19 October 2010, http://www.kenoradailyminerandnews.com/2010/10/19/flood-memorial-at-dalles.

4   Bryan D. Palmer, *Canada's 1960s: The Ironies of Identity in a Rebellious Era* (Toronto: University of Toronto Press, 2009), 386.

5   Bumsted, *A History of the Canadian Peoples*, 358.

6   Ibid.; Owram, *Born at the Right Time*, preface.

7   It is difficult to identify the origins of these misconceptions. They have become accepted "historical facts" and circulate in general texts (e.g., Canadian textbooks, encyclopedia entries, and teacher resources). In her textbook, *A Concise History of Canada's First Nations*, 2nd ed. (Don Mills, ON: Oxford University Press, 2010), 248, Olive Patricia Dickason claims that the revised act of 1951 "heralded in the dawn of a new era" but adds that the act "can hardly be called revolutionary." The sense that Canada "removed some of the most egregious political, cultural and religious restrictions" with the 1951 amendment is also identified by William B. Henderson, "Indian Act," 7 February 2006, updated by Zach Parrott, 23 October 2018, in *The Canadian Encyclopedia*, http://www.thecanadianencyclopedia.ca/en/article/indian-act. It is echoed in teacher resources such as Erin Hanson, "The Indian Act," Indigenous Foundations, http://indigenousfoundations.arts.ubc.ca/home/government-policy/the-indian-act.html#amendments.

8   Other historians have emphasized the extent to which the 1951 amendments were
    failed remedies. In her discussion, Dickason, *A Concise History of Canada's First Nations*,
    mentions that Canada prevented status Indians from establishing their own forms of
    government (248). Bands lacked complete control over their funds until 1958 (249).
    Parrott, "Indian Act," centres his argument about failed remedial legislation on gender,
    concluding that "additional restrictions on the transfer of status did harm to First Nations
    women and children." Lynn Gehl, an Anishinaabe scholar and advocate, makes similar
    claims in her public education video *Sex Discrimination and the Indian Act*, http://www.
    lynngehl.com/video-publications.html. Hanson, "The Indian Act," does not explicitly state
    the limits of the 1951 amendments but references the Royal Commission on Aboriginal
    Peoples to claim that amendments were "ultimately unsuccessful." None of these authors
    refers to concurrent federal programming that limited Indigenous opportunities to benefit
    from the 1951 amendments to the Indian Act.

9   For a sustained analysis of the impact of colonization on Indigenous diet and nutrition,
    see Mary-Ellen Kelm, *Colonizing Bodies: Aboriginal Health and Healing in British Columbia,
    1900–1950* (Vancouver: UBC Press, 1998), 19–37.

10 For a sustained analysis of the impact of federal policy on Indigenous land use and terri-
    torial holdings in what we know now as the Canadian prairies, see Sarah Carter, *Lost
    Harvests: Prairie Indian Reserve Farmers and Government Policy* (Montreal-Kingston:
    McGill-Queen's University Press, 1990).

11 Tom Flanagan, *First Nations? Second Thoughts* (Montreal and Kingston: McGill-Queen's
    University Press, 2008), 7.

12 Waldram, *As Long as the Rivers Run*, xv, xvi, 4, 6, 123, 172–74, 179–80, 182.

13 Notable exceptions include White, *The Organic Machine*, and Armstrong, Evenden, and
    Nelles, *The River Returns*. In his analysis of the Columbia River, White found that "[Euro-
    Americans] regarded the space at the Cascades and the Dalles as open, as culturally
    empty. Indians regarded it as full" (15). Armstrong, Evenden, and Nelles similarly found
    that "the Bow River was at once a homeland and a margin [before Euro-Canadian settle-
    ment]. As a homeland, it lay at the centre of an indigenous world. . . . As a margin, the
    Bow existed at the ragged southwestern edge of a continental fur trade" (24). In this story,
    the Bow River became central to Euro-Canadians as they settled the region in the 1880s.
    Although both *The Organic Machine* and *The River Returns* acknowledge Indigenous
    centres, Indigenous Peoples themselves operate in the background. Neither book sustains
    an "Indigenous centre," shifting readers' attention instead to settler activities on the two
    rivers. In *Wilderness and Waterpower*, 10, Christopher Armstrong and Henry Vivian Nelles
    also make a subtle nod to an Indigenous homeland, noting that "Native peoples" and
    their ancestors formed the "first human habitation[s]" on the upper reaches of the Bow
    River. Armstrong and Nelles, however, do not make these habitations central. *Wilderness
    and Waterpower* more accurately begins in 1883 with the identification of the Bow River,
    particularly the hot springs near present-day Banff, as a site of potential development by
    the Canadian Pacific Railway.

14 Child, *Holding Our World Together*, 85.

15 Tough, *"As Their Natural Resources Fail,"* 301.

16 Whitedog Falls Generating Station: General Description and Design Requirements, 13
    September 1955, memorandum, Whitedog Falls Generating Station, OPG, FP3–10-1-228,
    V. 1, Item 1042.

17 Cardinal, *The Unjust Society*, 90; Naithan Lagace and Niigaanwewidam James Sinclair, "The White Paper, 1969," in *The Canadian Encyclopedia*, http://www.thecanadianencyclopedia.ca/en/article/the-white-paper-1969/; Ray, *I Have Lived Here since the World Began*, 335; "The White Paper 1969," Indigenous Foundations, http://indigenousfoundations.arts.ubc.ca/home/government-policy/the-white-paper-1969.html.

18 Palmer, *Canada's.1960s*, 378.

19 Whereas I consider adaptation a form of moderate "resistance," Kahnawá:ke Mohawk scholar Audra Simpson might classify it as "refusal." Resistance requires recognition of an oppressor and self-identification as an oppressed person; refusal, Simpson argues, denies (rather than rejects) colonial authority. Simpson, *Mohawk Interruptus*.

 The Anishinabeg are culturally distinct from the Haudenosaunee. For example, the Anishinabeg are a patrilineal society, whereas the Haudenosaunee are a matrilineal society. I have chosen "resistance" as a description of Anishinaabe activity in Treaty 3 territory because of a long, uninterrupted history of demands for treaty recognition. Anishinaabe leaders have resisted colonial attempts to regulate Anishinaabe affairs. However, they have emphasized equal governing power over their respective nations. The Anishinabeg refuse Canada's right to govern Anishinaabe affairs; they do not refuse Canada's right to govern the settler population. Records of the 1873 treaty negotiations are suggestive of this position; see Morris, *The Treaties of Canada with the Indians of Manitoba and the North-West Territories*, 69, 72, 73.

20 Bill McKinlay, Senior Communications Adviser, Ontario Power Generation, email to the author, 9 July 2008, re OPG Apology to Ochiichagwe'Babigo'Ining Ojibway Nation [Dalles 38C Indian Reserve], 3 July 2008, author's collection.

21 Ibid.

22 Simpson, *Dancing on Our Turtle's Back*, 22.

23 Raibmon, "Unmaking Native Space," 78.

A Note on Sources

1 S. 78(1) of the Indian Act (2018) reads thus: "Subject to this section, the chief and councillors of a band hold office for two years." Canada, "Elections of Chiefs and Band Councils," *Indian Act* (R.S.C., 1985, c. I-5), https://perma.cc/U6WW-ADGZ.

2 The Ontario-Minnesota Pulp and Paper Company owned the Norman Dam. The mill and the Province of Ontario coordinated water levels on Lake of the Woods. The Norman Dam was not under the control of HEPCO. Under contract with the Department of Lands and Forests, Elder Larry Kabestra received experience working on hydroelectric generating stations as a screen cleaner.

3 Elder Larry Kabestra, interview with the author, Dalles 38C Indian Reserve, ON, 6 July 2012.

4 "A Statistical Profile on the Health of First Nations in Canada: Vital Statistics for Atlantic and Western Canada, 2001/2002," Health Canada, last edited 16 February 2011, http://www.hc-sc.gc.ca/fniah-spnia/pubs/aborig-autoch/stats-profil-atlant/index-eng.php#a634.

5 Jean Barman, "Child Labour," in *The Canadian Encyclopedia*, last edited 4 March 2015, http://www.thecanadianencyclopedia.ca/en/article/child-labour/.

6   The Diocese of Keewatin in Kenora permanently closed in 2014. Reverend David
    Ashdown arranged for the transfer of archival records from Kenora to the General Synod
    Archives in Toronto. "Diocese of Keewatin Archives," Anglican Church of Canada,
    https://www.anglican.ca/archives/incanada/keewatin-archives/.

7   Canada, Indian Band Council Procedure Regulations 2018, "Order and Proceedings,"
    https://laws-lois.justice.gc.ca/eng/regulations/C.R.C.,_c._950/FullText.html.

8   Lloyd Mack, "Utility Chairman Apologizes to Dalles Members," *Kenora Daily Miner
    and News*, 4 July 2008, http://www.kenoradailyminerandnews.com/2008/07/04/
    utility-chairman-apologizes-to-dalles-members.

9   Mike Aiken, "Flood Memorial at Dalles," *Kenora Daily Miner and News*, 19 October 2010,
    http://www.kenoradailyminerandnews.com/2010/10/19/flood-memorial-at-dalles.

SELECTED BIBLIOGRAPHY

Alfred, Gerald [Taiaiake]. *Heeding the Voice of Our Ancestors: Kahnawake Mohawk Politics and the Rise of Nationalism*. Toronto: Oxford University Press, 1995.

Anderson, Kim. *Life Stages and Native Women: Memory, Teachings, and Story Medicine*. Winnipeg: University of Manitoba Press, 2011.

Armstrong, Christopher, Matthew Dominic Evenden, and Henry Vivian Nelles. *The River Returns: An Environmental History of the Bow*. Montreal and Kingston: McGill-Queen's University Press, 2009.

Armstrong, Christopher, and Henry Vivian Nelles. *Wilderness and Waterpower: How Banff National Park Became a Hydroelectric Storage Reservoir*. Calgary: University of Calgary Press, 2013.

Bartlett, Richard H. *Aboriginal Water Rights in Canada: A Study of Aboriginal Title to Water and Indian Water Rights*. Calgary: Canadian Institute of Resources Law, 1989.

Benidickson, Jamie. *Levelling the Lake: Transboundary Resource Management in the Lake of the Woods Watershed*. Vancouver: UBC Press, 2019.

Cardinal, Harold. *The Unjust Society*. 2nd ed. Vancouver: Douglas and McIntyre, 1999.

Child, Brenda J. *Holding Our World Together: Ojibwe Women and the Survival of Community*. New York: Penguin Group, 2012.

Denison, Merrill. *The People's Power: The History of Ontario Hydro*. Toronto: McClelland and Stewart, 1960.

Densmore, Frances. *Chippewa Customs*. St. Paul: Minnesota Historical Society Press, 1979.

Doerfler, Jill, Niigaanwewidam James Sinclair, and Heidi Kiiwetinepinesiik Stark, eds. *Centering Anishinaabeg Studies: Understanding the World through Stories*. East Lansing: Michigan State University Press; Winnipeg: University of Manitoba Press, 2013.

Evenden, Matthew Dominic. *Allied Power: Mobilizing Hydro-Electricity during Canada's Second World War*. Toronto: University of Toronto Press, 2015.

Everson, Helen. *May Whin Shah Ti Pah Chi Mo Win: Indian Stories of Long Ago*. Alexandria, MN: Echo Printing Company, c. 1975.

Fleming, Keith Robson. *Power at a Cost: Ontario Hydro and Rural Electrification, 1911–1958.* Montreal and Kingston: McGill-Queen's University Press, 1992.

Hay, Robert H. *Electric Power in Ontario: Hydro, A Municipal Co-operative.* 3rd ed. Toronto: Ontario Municipal Electric Association, 1985.

Hilger, Mary Inez. *Chippewa Child Life and Its Cultural Background.* St. Paul: Minnesota Historical Society Press, 1951.

Hosmer, Brian, and Colleen O'Neill, eds. *Native Pathways: American Indian Culture and Economic Development in the Twentieth Century.* Boulder: University Press of Colorado, 2004.

International Joint Commission (IJC). *Final Report of the International Joint Commission on the Lake of the Woods Reference: Washington-Ottawa.* Washington, DC: Government Printing Office, 1917.

Johnston, Basil. *Ojibway Ceremonies.* Toronto: McClelland and Stewart, 1982.

———. *Ojibway Heritage.* Toronto: McClelland and Stewart, 2003.

Kelly, John. "We Are All in the Ojibway Circle." In *From Ink Lake: Canadian Stories,* edited by Michael Ondaatje, 579–90. Toronto: Lester and Orpen Dennys, 1990.

Kinew, Kathi Avery. "Manito Gitigaan—Governing in the Great Spirit's Garden: Wild Rice in Treaty #3." PhD diss., University of Manitoba, 1995.

King, Thomas. *The Truth about Stories: A Native Narrative.* Toronto: House of Anansi Press, 2003.

Knight, Rolf. *Indians at Work: An Informal History of Native Labour in British Columbia.* Vancouver: New Star Books, 1996.

Loo, Tina. "Disturbing the Peace: Environmental Change and the Scales of Justice on a Northern River." *Environmental History* 12 (2007): 895–919.

———. "People in the Way: Modernity, Environment, and Society on the Arrow Lakes." *BC Studies* 142 (2004): 161–96.

Lutz, John Sutton. *Makúk: A New History of Aboriginal-White Relations.* Vancouver: UBC Press, 2008.

MacFarlane, Daniel. *Negotiating a River: Canada, the U.S., and the Creation of the St. Lawrence Seaway.* Vancouver: UBC Press, 2014.

Manore, Jean L. *Cross-Currents: Hydroelectricity and the Engineering of Northern Ontario.* Waterloo, ON: Wilfrid Laurier University Press, 1999.

———. "Indian Reserves v. Indian Lands: Reserves, Crown Lands, and Natural Resources Use in Northeastern Ontario." In *Ontario since Confederation: A Reader,* edited by Edgar-André Montigny and Lori Chambers, 195–213. Toronto: University of Toronto Press, 2000.

Manuel, Arthur, and Grand Chief Ronald Derrickson. *The Reconciliation Manifesto: Recovering the Land, Rebuilding the Economy.* Toronto: James Lorimer, 2017.

Martin-McKeever, Hazel. *The Chief's Granddaughter.* Charleston, SC: self-published, 2013.

McCallum, Mary Jane Logan. *Indigenous Women, Work, and History 1940–1980.* Winnipeg: University of Manitoba Press, 2014.

McDonald, Anne, and Hiroshi Isogai. *From Grassy Narrows*. Tokyo: Shimizukobundo Shobo, 2001.

McNab, David T. "The Administration of Treaty 3: The Location of the Boundaries of Treaty 3 Indian Reserves in Ontario, 1873–1915." In *As Long as the Sun Shines and Water Flows: A Reader in Canadian Native Studies*, edited by Ian A.L. Getty and Antoine S. Lussier, 145–57. Vancouver: UBC Press, 1983.

Miller, Cary. *Ogimaag: Anishinaabeg Leadership, 1760–1845*. Lincoln: University of Nebraska Press, 2010.

Milloy, John S. "The Early Indian Act: Developmental Strategy and Constitutional Change." In *As Long as the Sun Shines and Water Flows: A Reader in Canadian Native Studies*, edited by Ian A.L. Getty and Antoine S. Lussier, 56–64. Vancouver: UBC Press, 1983.

Morris, Alexander. *The Treaties of Canada with the Indians of Manitoba and the North-West Territories, Including the Negotiations on which They Were Based, and Other Information Relating Thereto*. Toronto: Belfords, Clarke, 1880.

Nelles, H.V. *The Politics of Development: Forests, Mines and Hydro-Electric Power in Ontario, 1849–1941*. 2nd ed. Montreal and Kingston: McGill-Queen's University Press, 2005.

Notzke, Claudia. *Aboriginal Peoples and Natural Resources in Canada*. Concord, ON: Captus Press, 1994.

Piper, Liza. *The Industrial Transformation of Subarctic Canada*. Vancouver: UBC Press, 2009.

Potts, Karen L., and Leslie Brown. "Becoming an Anti-Oppressive Researcher." In *Research as Resistance: Revisiting Critical, Indigenous, and Anti-Oppressive Approaches*, 2nd ed., edited by Leslie Brown and Susan Strega, 255–286. Toronto: Canadian Scholars' Press, 2015.

Raibmon, Paige. "Unmaking Native Space: A Genealogy of Indian Policy, Settler Practice, and the Microtechniques of Dispossession." In *The Power of Promises: Rethinking Indian Treaties in the Pacific Northwest*, edited by John Borrows and Alexandra Harmon, 56–86. Seattle: University of Washington Press, 2008.

Redsky (Esquekesik), James. *Great Leader of the Ojibway: Mis-quona-queb*. Edited by James R. Stevens. Toronto: McClelland and Stewart, 1972.

Rheault, D'Arcy Ishpeming'enzaabid. "Anishinaabe Mino-Bimaadiziwin (The Way of a Good Life)." MA thesis, Trent University, 1998.

Richter, Daniel K. *Facing East from Indian Country: A Native History of Early America*. Cambridge, MA: Harvard University Press, 2001.

Robertson, Heather. *Reservations Are for Indians*. Toronto: James Lorimer, 1970.

"Royal Commission on Aboriginal Peoples: Presentation by Sam Horton, Vice-President, Aboriginal and Northern Affairs Branch, Ontario Hydro." Our Legacy, 3 June 1993. http://digital.scaa.sk.ca/ourlegacy/solr?query=ID:31496&start=0&rows=10&mode=results.

Shewell, Hugh. *"Enough to Keep Them Alive": Indian Welfare in Canada, 1873–1965*. Toronto: University of Toronto Press, 2004.

Shkilnyk, Anastasia M. *A Poison Stronger than Love: The Destruction of an Ojibwa Community*. New Haven, CT: Yale University Press, 1985.

Simpson, Audra. *Mohawk Interruptus: Political Life across the Borders of Settler States*. Durham, NC: Duke University Press, 2014.

Simpson, Leanne Betasamosake. *Dancing on Our Turtle's Back: Stories of Nishnaabeg Re-Creation, Resurgence and a New Emergence.* Winnipeg: Arbeiter Ring Publishing, 2011.

————. *As We Have Always Done: Indigenous Freedom through Radical Resistance.* Minneapolis: University of Minnesota Press, 2017.

Smith, Linda T. *Decolonizing Methodologies: Research and Indigenous Peoples.* London: Zed Books; Dunedin, NZ: University of Otago, 1999.

Struthers, James. *The Limits of Affluence: Welfare in Ontario, 1920–1970.* Toronto: University of Toronto Press, 1994.

Tough, Frank. *"As Their Natural Resources Fail": Native Peoples and the Economic History of Northern Manitoba, 1870–1930.* Vancouver: UBC Press, 1996.

Waisberg, Leo G., and Tim E. Holzkamm. "'A Tendency to Discourage Them from Cultivating': Ojibwa Agriculture and Indian Affairs Administration in Northwestern Ontario." *Ethnohistory* 40, no. 2 (1993): 175–211.

Waldram, James B. *As Long as the Rivers Run: Hydroelectric Development and Native Communities in Western Canada.* Winnipeg: University of Manitoba Press, 1988.

Warren, William. *History of the Ojibway People.* St. Paul: Minnesota Historical Society Press, 1984.

White, Richard. *The Organic Machine: The Remaking of the Columbia River.* New York: Hill and Wang, 1995.

Witgen, Michael. *An Infinity of Nations: How the Native New World Shaped Early North America.* Philadelphia: University of Pennsylvania Press, 2012.

INDEX

claims with HEPCO, 87–89; and racism, 84, 99, 100; relations with HEPCO, 64, 65–66, 67–68, 86–87, 167–68, 202n5; relationship with Creation, 36, 39; and relief/welfare, 99–100; relocation off reserve, 164–65; residential school, 159–60; resistance to 1924 federal-provincial agreement, 35–37, 38–39; seeks right to compensation if treaty broken, 22, 25, 185n24; sense of 'knowing' or 'truth,' 15; and sickness, 43, 59, 129, 131, 142, 155–56; and Sixties Scoop, 160–61; and subsistence gardens, 95, 204n17; tie to Cree, 216n11; and trains, 45–46; and Treaty 3, 8, 18, 20, 22–24, 45, 83; trouble with HEPCO police permits, 83–84; use of ice roads, 41, 43–44, 45–48, 191n23, 191n29; use of manomin by, 6, 64, 116–17, 205n31; use of mitigwakik, 35–39; using fish as substitute for breast milk, 141, 150–51; view of hydroelectric development, 167–68, 170; view of managing natural resources, 20; wage employment of, 91, 92, 93–96, 99; and water rights, 6, 9, 18, 24–25, 29, 31–34; women's clothing and sense of fashion, 146–47, 149; women's medicinal power, 143–45; work on construction of Whitedog Falls Station, 87, 91, 92, 100–106, 169; working conditions on Whitedog Falls Station, 108–11

Ashopenase, Tony, 157

B

Backus, Edward W., 66, 68, 70, 71

Beck, Adam, 31

Benedickson, William M., 88, 89, 169

Berry, A.E., 129–30

berry picking, 45–46, 60–62, 101, 168

Boundary Water Treaty (1909), 50, 140

Bowman, Beniah, 66, 70

breast milk: care in producing quality, 141, 143, 144–45, 150, 161, 217n16; affected by pollution, 142, 156, 159; using fish as substitute for, 141, 150–51

Brenchley, John, 58

Brunelle, René, 138, 139

Burnstein, A., 157

bushing ice roads, 46

C

Campbell, W. S., 68, 70

Canada/Canada, Government of: care of ice roads, 46, 48; criminalization of Indigenous ceremonies, 38; effects of its programs on industrial growth, 166; employment programs for First Nations, 205n46; extent of involvement in economy in 1950s, 5, 65, 67; and flooding compensation for Anishinaabe, 172; inaction on water quality issues, 140; and International Joint Commission, 50–53; and myth of popular affluence after Second World War, 10, 12–13, 165; negotiating Treaty 3, 8, 22–23; and Ontario power needs, 30; passive attitude towards Ontario's taking control, 18; policies which give Ontario-Minnesota Pulp and Paper seat at table, 78; repeal of 1894 Joint Agreement, 32, 34; role in Ontario-Manitoba border dispute, 8–9; settles Indian reserves questions with Ontario, 34–35. *See also* Department of Indian Affairs

Canadian National Railway (CNR), 45, 130

Canadian Pacific Railway (CPR), 45

Cardinal, Harold, 99

Caribou Falls Generating Station, 103–6, 108–15, 114

Carnation Milk, 161, 162, 221n106

Chadwick, C.W., 152

Chapeskie, Andrew, 81, 86

Chasemore v. Richards, 28

Children's Aid Service (CAS), 160–61

Cobiness, Willie, 84

Collins, D.J., 137

G

George, E.D., 193n59, 194n69

Gitchie Manitou, 3–4, 180n3

Grand Trunk Pacific Railway, 45

Grassy Narrows, 156, 216n4

Great Depression, 66

Green, Janet, 135

Green, T.D., 121

Greene, May, 202n5

Greene, Terry, 90

H

Hamer, J., 77

Hansen, Hans, 54

Hanson, Thomas: on ice road use, 43

Hawthorne Report, 99–100, 160

Henry, Clarence: and change in Winnipeg
River, 119, 127; on effect of water
pollution on game, 155; on sturgeon
population, 135, 137; and water
pollution, 134–35; on why people
relocated, 164

Henshaw, George H., 46

herbal medicines, 145

Hoey, R.A., 100

Hogg, Thomas H., 67

Hooper, J.T., 56

Horton, Sam, 67–68, 197n12

Hudson's Bay Company, 6, 7, 56, 185n24

Hunter, Catherine, 164

hydroelectric power: building capacity
for, 9–10; cause of thin ice in winter,
58; consequences of building, 172;
developed by HEPCO, 35; early
years of in Ontario, 28–30; effect on
hunting and trapping, 58–59; effect on
ice roads, 48–50; and flooding effect
on manomin harvest, 96–97; and
International Joint Commission, 51;
pressure to build in 1950s, 65; seen from

Anishinaabe perspective, 167–68, 170.
See also Norman Dam; Whitedog Falls
Generating Station

Hydro-Electric Power Commission of
Ontario (HEPCO): Anishinaabe
attempts for redress due to flooding by,
169–70, 172; Anishinaabe work for in
Whitedog Falls Station construction,
100–106, 169; anti-Indigenous attitude
of, 197n12; benefits to Anishinaabe
working for, 111–16; building a
transmission line on Anishinaabe
land, 82–83; building Whitedog Falls
Station, 9–10, 67; compensates Ontario-
Minnesota Pulp and Paper for lost
energy, 76–80; created, 30, 187n64;
dealing with Anishinaabe damage claims,
87–89; dismantles labour camps for dam
construction, 116; effect of Whitedog
Falls Station on water pollution, 122–23;
electricity development by, 35; and
exercising police permits, 83–84; hiding
effects of new station from Ontario-
Minnesota Pulp and Paper, 65, 71–76;
negative attitudes about working for,
202n5; negotiates with Indian Affairs
rather than Anishinabeg, 80–81;
normalizing its claim for water rights,
70–71; operating plan for Whitedog
Falls Station, 86–87, 119; pressure
on to build capacity, 65; refusal to
hire Anishinaabe workers, 87, 91, 92;
relations with Anishinabeg, 64, 65–66,
67–68, 86–87, 167–68, 202n5; research
into competing claims to Winnipeg
River, 68–71; and road clearance on
Whitedog Reserve, 81–82; working
conditions on dam construction
sites, 108–11. *See also* Ontario Power
Generation (OPG); Whitedog Falls
Generating Station

I

ice roads: Anishinaabe use of, 41, 43–44,
45–47, 48, 191n23, 191n29; danger of
travel on made public, 57–58; effect
of dams on, 48–50, 194n78; and
trapping, 59

CRITICAL STUDIES IN NATIVE HISTORY

ISSN 1925-5888